MW00807812

Dancing for Young Audiences

Dancing for Young Audiences

A Practical Guide to Creating, Managing and Marketing a Performance Company

ELLA H. MAGRUDER

Foreword by Lynnette Y. Overby

McFarland & Company, Inc., Publishers

Jefferson, North Carolina, and London

Illustrations by Claudia Van Koba; photographs by Mary Gearhart,
Andrew Wilds and others (as noted); set drawings by Mark Magruder

ISBN 978-0-7864-7102-7 (softcover : acid free paper)

LIBRARY OF CONGRESS CATALOGING DATA ARE AVAILABLE

British Library cataloguing data are available

© 2013 Ella H. Magruder. All rights reserved

*No part of this book may be reproduced or transmitted in any form
or by any means, electronic or mechanical, including photocopying
or recording, or by any information storage and retrieval system,
without permission in writing from the publisher.*

On the cover: Menagerie Dance Company in the "Big Reach"
from *Symbiosis*; choreography: Mark Magruder,
dancers: Mark and Ella Magruder (courtesy Mary Gearhart)

Manufactured in the United States of America

McFarland & Company, Inc., Publishers
Box 611, Jefferson, North Carolina 28640
www.mcfarlandpub.com

To Mark, my dancing and life partner

Acknowledgments

Special thanks to my family for the support they have provided, especially to my daughter, Mia, and my son, Conan (both of whom sometimes even toured with us when they were young); to my father, Richard Hanson, and my mother, Ella Hanson, who always and in all ways supported my dream to dance; to my proofreaders, Liz Waring McCracken and Dee Waring, for their thoughtful corrections and encouragement; to Catherine Bost of Sweet Briar College Public Relations; to M.J. Stinnette and Tom Marcais of Sweet Briar College for their computer help; to Becky Harvey of Sweet Briar for her work; to Sally Mundy for her assistance; to my pedagogy students Aili McGill and Leslie Price; to Dean Jonathan Green and Betsy Muhlenfeld, former president of Sweet Briar College, for their support; to Suny Monk, Sheila and Craig Pleasants at the Virginia Center for the Creative Arts, the artist colony where I reworked my conception and conducted additional research; to Bill Bevis and Juliette Crump of the University of Montana for their belief in arts outreach; to David and Karen Williams of University of Wisconsin, Stout (formerly of Ripon College) for decades of support and friendship. Thanks especially to Mary Lawson who served on the Virginia Commission for the Arts and who was an early cheerleader for our company and cause, and to Elizabeth Breiman thanks to both women for their indefatigable arts advocacy and sustained encouragement of artists; to Larry Goldstein, our Virginia friend and new vaudevillian, for his welcoming attitude to new performers; to my dance colleagues who gave words of encouragement—Anne Green Gilbert, Marilyn Berret, Sue Stinson, Cheryl Willis, and Jeanne Traxler; to Erica Nielsen Okamura for her generosity; to Lesley Dofflemyer of Augusta County Schools; to my Finnish colleague Eeva Anttila; to my Australian colleague Jeff Meiners; to my South African colleagues Sharon Friedman, and especially to Gerald Samuel who gave me new leads and connections to the world of dance beyond familiar borders; and to the school administrators who opened doors for our dance company; John Trissell, Joe Bunn, Reuben Doss, Ed Hopkins, Grady Davis, and the hundreds of other supporters of dance we met through the years of touring and teaching.

Contents

Foreword by
Lynnette Young Overby

"Never underestimate the power of a dance that springs
off the stage and into the heart and imagination of a child."

In *Dancing for Young Audiences,* Ella Magruder shares her experiences as the co-director of a successful dance company. From beginning to end, the book contains a wealth of material — a road map of guidelines based on lessons learned.

For 20 years Ella choreographed, toured and performed with her husband Mark, in their duet dance company Menagerie. During those years they performed for over 100,000 students and teachers. Through the pages of this book, we view the journey that has enabled her to share firsthand knowledge about creating a dance company designed to perform for children.

The book is organized into parts that show us how to create, produce, and dance in productions for children. I found Chapter 5 particularly interesting, and took copious notes about publicity strategies. By reading the information in this chapter I gained important pubic relations knowledge, from logo development, to press releases, to the rationale for sending mass mailings versus direct contact. Other chapters provided guidance in the development of a business plan, grant writing and dancing in a production. Every aspect of this comprehensive book offers gems of knowledge for both the novice and experienced director.

From 1999 to 2004, I directed a children's dance theater company called "Kinetic Energy," composed of 5–7 university performers. We created performances that connected dance and theater with the K–5 curriculum in the state of Michigan. How I wish I had had access to this wonderful book — a good show would have been even better!

Part IV of the book provides intriguing glimpses into a variety of dance companies from around the globe. Each of the companies uniquely reaches out to children with a clearly designed approach that (1) educates and entertains, (2) includes the audience in the performance, and (3) utilizes a multidisciplinary approach that fuses dance with diverse curricular content, social issues, and cultural knowledge.

If one wonders whether or not building a career around the development and implementation of children's dance productions is lucrative and professionally satisfying, the voices of the audiences, other company directors and the author herself leap from the pages and into our hearts to provide convincing evidence: "Art is a powerful messenger of shared respect and shared emotion. You have a primary and worthy goal if you perform dances that accomplish this for any audience, but especially for an audience of children."

Ella Magruder shares her life's work with us. We benefit greatly from the lessons she learned during this fascinating journey.

Lynnette Young Overby, co-author of Interdisciplinary Learning Through Dance: 101 Moventures, *is faculty director of the University of Delaware's Office of Undergraduate Research Program and Experiential Learning. She has presented and published widely in the field of arts and dance education, and is one of 10 dance educators and 40 arts educators serving on the National Coalition for Core Arts Standards.*

Introduction

This book has directions on how to handle booking for dance, how to write effective grants for dance, how to handle crowds of children in a theater environment for dance, how to keep children's interest high for dance, and how to maintain the support and the appreciation of presenters, teachers, and principals for whom you perform, plus profiles of ten successful dance companies that perform for children, and much more.

The book supplies practical tools to build a career in dance for people who love dance and who enjoy being around children. In addition, the touring and production information within the book can be applied to almost any performing group that uses the medium of dance to deliver its message — from professional dance companies and organizations to university, high school, or studio dance performers.

It is designed to help university students who are planning a dance career, professional dance companies that would like to perform for children, and performing arts educators in colleges and universities who will want to use it as a resource or text for teaching methods of dance education outreach — such as assembly programs, lecture demonstrations, and master classes. It will also be useful to dance studios and to school dance educators and directors of any group that uses dance as a medium for a touring show. It is written primarily for an American audience, but international colleagues in daCi (dance and the Child international) — an organization affiliated with UNESCO — have urged me to write about what we do, so where possible I have tried to make broader international references.

When my husband and dance partner, Mark, and I first began to dream of trying to make a living and provide financially for our own children by doing what we loved, some of our friends, fellow dancers, and family probably thought we were in a state of delusion, although they were too polite to say so. First of all, there is a widely accepted belief that you cannot make any money by touring dance; in fact, you are expected to lose money. Secondly, there is also the understanding that even if you can book a season of performances, you cannot exist financially away from major metropolitan areas like New York or San Francisco or without an agent. And certainly our little area of central Virginia with its mountains, cows, and the occasional town was anything but the center of the dance universe.

Today, nearly twenty years later, at the end of a wonderful dance-touring career with our duet dance company, we're as optimistic and enthusiastic about performing dance for children as when we began. From our "up-front and personal" experience touring dance in schools and in community centers we have seen firsthand the profoundly positive effects that dance has on youth audiences and students who participate in dance experiences. Our schools and community centers need more dance!

This book addresses this need. In it is information gathered through years of experience, from mistakes and successes we have had while dancing for children. My hope is that you, the dancing reader, will benefit from the insights it contains, and confidently step forward to present dance on stage in view of young and old.

Children need to see dance in performance — to share the same space with dancers — in living motion, with colorful costumes, intriguing music, and imaginative sets. Children need *real*, three-dimensional people — "us" — jumping and leaping right in front of their own eyes; they need the embodied "us" far more than they need the virtual images of us as dancers that are televised, digitized, and shrunk into flattened rectangles. Don't get me wrong, I love *Great Performances* on public television, and idolize Jac Venza, its producer. But even he would agree, I think, that kids need to hear the slap of footsteps and be close to the kinetic, fractal explosions of energy that happen with every kick, swirl, and turn.

Why? Why is the immediacy of live performance so powerful? And why should anyone need it? Well, for starters, live dance performance is compelling because it is basic human communication. Children don't need a grown-up's vocabulary or an adult intellect to understand it. That doesn't mean dance is simplistic, far from it. Dance conveys rich layers of meaning instantly, in the same way that a picture is said to be worth place of a thousand words. A child who watches Alvin Ailey's dance *Cry* learns very quickly about nobility of the spirit in the face of adversity, in a way that might take reading an entire book on slavery to duplicate. Dance is immediate and direct. Say the word "no" and a child might ignore you. Dance, gesture, and move "no" and the child will freeze action and instantly stop. That attention-getting aspect of dance is extremely valuable in the distraction-saturated world that we inhabit.

All young children love dance; it is a powerful medium for education. This includes all types of education, not just dance education. Dance can teach concepts like math and science, or concepts of social justice, such as championing the rights of the handicapped, or erasing ugly stereotypes. The book will lead you through the "nuts and bolts" of how to create an atmosphere that fosters the transference of the important messages that you want to get across to your audience through your performance.

Dance naturally makes children enthusiastic. Children love to watch dance; they love to dance themselves and they love to create their own dances. With an epidemic of obesity today facing American children, children need to move more. *Dance makes children want to move.* Most importantly, dance gives children access to joy and transforms their energy into understanding. It helps shape their nonverbal chaotic thoughts into pattern and form. Empathy, shared catharsis, vibrant communication — the list goes on. We know what we love about dance as adults, what makes us continue to dance in the studio and stretch our muscles and imaginations. It is amplified for kids.

What's more, there are some awe-inspiring "spin-offs" from helping children learn how to behave appropriately together in a group, such as an audience must when viewing dance. Good audience skills are essential to a civilized society. Almost everyone benefits some if, say, movie audience behavior improves. Everyone benefits even more, and society benefits in general, if crowds behave well at sports events or political gatherings. What better way to teach children how to regulate their own behavior than while reacting to dance, with its inherent beauty, excitement, and fun? As they watch a performance at school or in a community center, you as a performer can help guide children to respond appropriately, and in the process, hone their aesthetic sensibilities.

If you love to dance and you love children, you have the two most important things you need to begin a delightful journey. Through the process of performing, both you and the children for whom you dance will be enriched beyond measure. As Elizabeth Hayes, the great dance educator from the University of Utah, said, "Never underestimate the power of a lecture demonstration."[1] I echo and add, "Never underestimate the power of a dance that springs off the stage and into the heart and imagination of a child!"

There is a financial market and a clear need for many more companies to perform dance for children. The book that follows is a result of my wish to make it a little easier for dancers who want to do what our company does: tour in order to dance for children who are rich or poor, urban or rural, with varying ethnic, cultural, and social backgrounds, and for general audiences everywhere, and not just in major theaters. In our experience it is not only possible but also feasible, and a great way to live your life as a dancer.

This book gives you, the reader, some suggestions and ways to help you to ride the wave of enthusiasm that dance generates! It provides practical, child-tested ideas for presenting a performance that will interest, inspire, and activate children to learn and stay curious about dance and the subjects that you're dancing about. It is divided into four larger sections: Dreaming and Creating, Producing, Dancing, and Dancing Their Dreams: Ten Successful National and International Companies. The fifth section is an epilogue of advice and vignettes of real-life touring experiences — one of the most eye-opening and informative parts of the book!. This section ends with three appendices. Appendix A has descriptions of dance companies from around the world that work with children. Appendix B is a list of dance professionals and schools. Appendix C is a compilation of helpful dance resources.

The first part, Dreaming and Creating, helps you discover your focus and define your philosophy as a dance company. It talks about why it is important to be able to verbalize and write down your company's purpose and goals. It discusses conceptual solutions that foster success, especially if you plan to perform in an educational setting. This includes how you might format your program for a young audience, and why the subjects you dance about have an effect on how (and if) educators will welcome you. This part has a chapter on the type of choreographic themes that work well for children and general audiences, and practical considerations as you create choreographic material to perform for children. While there are wonderful books on teaching creative dance to children, there are no texts that specifically say what works in a dance performance for an audience of children. This book addresses that need and attempts to present new ideas so that the reader understands what the problems and their solutions are.

The second part, Producing, has chapters on aspects of production, including sets, costumes, music, lights, props, make-up and masks, and how you can enhance the portability of all these things while you are on the road. This second part also covers marketing: creating a mission statement, contacts with arts councils and other support agencies and foundations, booking conferences, grant-writing; publicity: logo, brochures, posters, press kit; finances: developing a budget, nonprofit incorporation; and the hardest aspect of touring, the booking process. The chapter on booking details how to begin booking: find presenters, make direct telephone contacts, write contracts, create teacher guides and bibliographies, and how to arrange tours so you can travel less and dance more.

The third section, Dancing, gets down to the basics of what to expect and plan for when you tour. It lists basic equipment needs, transportation issues, accommodation on the road, communication with your presenter (the organization or person who hires you) regarding schedules and arrival time; what you must deal with on site in the school or theater as far as production element necessities. It raises important safety issues about the hazards of stages to both dancers and audience. There is a chapter on what schools expect from visitors and several chapters on how to establish good contacts to make a school residency run more smoothly; how to seat an audience, and what to do when audience problems arise. Other chapters detail how to develop an effective, dramatic stage voice in our essentially nonverbal art, since this is often a problem for dancers on stage who must emcee their own shows. There is a chapter devoted to performing itself since there are major presentational differences when the audience is young, of varying ages, and/or differently sized. You will learn how to make an effective and controlled audience participation segment in your performance without having the kids careen out of control. There is a chapter called "Don't Be a Drop-In, Drop-Out Company" on how to produce a great artist residency or performance, with in-depth discussion on teaching master classes and how to approach master class discipline and behavior issues. Finally, there is a chapter on assessment and evaluation. It covers questions you need to ask audiences about your performance, how you do it and why you must welcome this kind of feedback from an audience (even if it is tough on the ego sometimes!).

The fourth section, Dancing Their Dreams: Ten Successful National and International Companies, includes descriptions of a number of different types of dance organizations. Each chapter features the history, the mission, and the structure of that particular company. Every chapter in this fourth section concludes with an interview of its founder, artistic director or choreographer. These inspiring dance artists offer all sort of advice on different aspects of their life's work — touring, choreography, aesthetics, philosophy, funding, organization, running a company, outreach, and management, among other things. Generously, they share with you, the reader, many of the unexpected things they learned along the way in their outstanding dance careers. You may fall in love with dance all over again (as I did) as you read about the amazing ways that they use dance to unlock human potential and open doors of understanding for their dancers and for their audiences.

You can read this book straight through or skip around to glean what you need since some parts may be more useful to you than others. You may be just beginning your dance career as a performer, choreographer or teacher, or leaving a professional company to begin your own work. You may even want to start with the epilogue, the final section. It is called *Dancing with the Lettuce Leaf: Things That Can Happen While Touring.* If you wonder about the curious imagery, the answer is here in the epilogue. It has to do with performing in that ubiquitous multi-purpose room, the "cafetorium"— part auditorium, part lunchroom, part stage ... you get the picture.

Everything in the last section is true; it offers cautions, advice and reveals the gory and goofy details of touring! Yet despite the days of aching muscles and long hours of driving, despite the smell of school lunches with corn dogs, baked beans and the limp lettuce leaf, nothing matches this as lifework — dancing for children. Way back when, as we debated our decision and toyed with the "what if we had a dance company for children" dream, we never imagined the richness of experiences that we would come to enjoy in our touring lives. Little did we know that there are so many ways for children to say "thank you for dancing for us" or as many ways for us to feel as grateful as we do to the children, arts presenters, teachers, principals, parents and others who have been a part of our loving and generous audiences over these past twenty years. They have given much to us as dancers in return. It is to our loving audiences that this book is dedicated.

PART I

Dreaming and Creating

All life is but a dream within a dream...
— Calderón de la Barca

Chapter 1

Defining Your Goals

It's odd to begin a book by saying, "You can skip this chapter if you like," but that's just what you are welcome to do. This is a book that can be read in any order. Use each chapter to extract nuggets of information that you need. You are a creative and resourceful person (you're a dancer, right?); decide for yourself what is important to you. Feel free to improvise your way through the chapters and you may enjoy the book and its advice more! Now, with that said, let me introduce this first chapter and you can decide if you want to leap ahead or not. This chapter is about understanding why you want to dance for children and what you want to accomplish. If you know these things already, jump ahead now to the "how to" sections. If you want to spend a little more time thinking about your purpose and goals, then read on. And good luck!

First, define your focus so that you can understand what your dance goals are. What is your purpose for creating a company? What do you want to have happen in children's hearts and minds when they see your company perform? What do you want them to feel, to learn, or to understand? Your starting base might be ballet, jazz, Irish, Kathakali or African/Caribbean. (See Part IV, Chapters 18–27 to explore further the diversity of dance in the field.) Almost any genre of dance has intrinsic value in and of itself, and the sharing of that dance style with young audiences can be a great reason to create a company and to perform.

While there is more to creating a dance company than being a great dancer in a particular technique, the perfection of the skills you emphasize in your technique is very important! To that end, one of your first priorities is to employ very skilled dancers in your company. Another priority, however, is to figure out how best to convey the energy and thrill of your work as you present it onstage for children. To accomplish this, the most important requirement is that the dances themselves be aesthetically sound and meaningful, whatever the style or technique. To do that you must carefully choose the subject material, meticulously craft the movement content of your dances, and monitor the pacing of the entire performance as well as of each individual dance to keep the performance exciting.

When we first began our children's dance company, Menagerie, we had two strong interests to guide us — our love for and skill in modern/contemporary theatrical dance, and, being parents, our love for and appreciation of the wide-eyed curiosity and heartfelt energy that children radiate. Our dance company's goals and philosophy then developed easily from those interests — to create dances that children would love to watch *and* from which they would gain a greater understanding of communication through movement. In addition, we wanted to share our excitement about certain ideas and subjects that interested us — in science and in literature. We always chose topics to choreograph that fascinated or motivated us, believing that if we enjoyed an idea, we could present it through dance so that an audience would enjoy it too. It worked! The audiences loved our shows. We rarely became bored with our dances, and some of them we performed *hundreds* of times!

A Closer Look at Your Reasons for Dancing

What you dance about is as important as how you dance it. From the "what" and "how" you dance comes your sense of why you do what you do and what you want an audience to feel and learn from your performance. This is where an individual understanding of the whole point of why you do what you do — your philosophy — comes from.

We all have a philosophy. It is just that for most of us in the dance world philosophy is felt, not spoken. The content of our art is moved, not written. This poses a problem for the general acceptance of our art form, since historically predominant Western academic philosophers believe that ideas don't exist if you cannot say them or write them down. We, as dancers, and some modern philosophers know that many ideas and philosophies are intangible; yet these "intangibles" prove their existence with every choreographic choice we make. A reluctance to discuss choreographic work is a sticking point for many artists and dancers. They don't want to limit their art form by describing it inadequately — that is, by translating it poorly into words. Nevertheless, it is important for you to articulate your dance company's goals and your philosophy. When you do, you communicate better with others who are outside the field of dance — the people who ultimately may hire your company to perform or may award you grants. Most importantly, though, you direct your own awareness to your very purpose of dancing.

Dance performed onstage is an art, not a contest. You do not win or lose, except in success or in failure to communicate well with your audience. It helps if you can understand and define your goals, *and* understand what you want to accomplish in each dance and in your dancing in general. It makes it much easier actually to accomplish those goals and to communicate them to everyone else, including your audience.

For you this may be an orderly process; you figure out your focus, define your philosophy and then start to create a show that reflects your goals. Sometimes, however, you may have to dance and even choreograph first before you can deduce the "verbal why" of your philosophy. You may have to perform some, get feedback from an audience, and reform your choreography before you accurately can *define* and *refine* your focus and philosophy.

Although considered unusual by the general public, it is quite true that some choreographers and directors must "put the cart before the horse" in their process of discovery. It really does not matter in what order you come to understand your own choreographic work. The most important thing is that after you complete the journey and create dances that communicate with, entertain, and enlighten your audience, you should be able to describe what you have done! Identifying and describing both your company's current work *and* broad goals makes many other aspects of creating a successful dance company easier: such as development (and subsequent improvement of your show), marketing, booking, and grant writing.

Some dancers and performers cover themselves in the cloak of "brilliant, misunderstood, and mysterious artist" with the mistaken belief that this aura of impenetrability makes them greater or more legitimate. Sometimes they take this attitude because they are reluctant to do the important personal reflection necessary to discern the meaning of their own work. Sometimes they believe that verbalizing or trying to pin down themes or meaning in their choreography will inhibit their subsequent creativity. While it is true (and legitimate) that an artist usually prefers not to talk about a work in progress, there is certainly nothing to be gained by refusing to help people understand a dance after it has been choreographed. Moreover, this uncooperative attitude will not help them succeed in the world of children's dance and theater.

No matter what, it is essential for you to understand your goals and to discover your philosophy — whether you begin by verbalizing it or whether you have to work up to that point. If, even after a good attempt, trying to write down or talk about your choreography or company philosophy still proves elusive, then have other people who are good with words watch what you do. Perhaps they will better be able to find the words to describe your work.

Let's say that you have a wonderful group of dances that you want to perform. One

Menagerie Dance Company in "Whimsical Creatures Emerge" from *Evos*. Choreography: Mark Magruder. Dancers: Mark and Ella Magruder (credit Andrewwildsphotography.com).

reason you, as a choreographer, may shy away from a written or verbalized statement or philosophy is that you may feel that it is degrading to your art to translate the powerful thing that you dance about into words. First, you realize that you will never be able to transform the essence or power of what you do into words; and therefore, why should you even try? Well, what if you speak French and have a visitor from Spain? Wouldn't you, out of politeness or necessity, try to learn a few words of Spanish? Perhaps you will communicate using sign language. In any case, most likely you will attempt, out of a basic desire to make yourself understood, to follow through with actions that show a desire to communicate.

Think about the person who will hire your company or award you a grant as someone who does not speak your "language." You need to communicate, as carefully and as clearly as possible, what it is that you do.

Your medium is dance, but not everyone knows dance the way the choreographer and the dancer do. What are you trying to say with your dancing and in your dances? While it is true that thinking and dance happen beyond words, words are all we have as a common ground with people who are not familiar with our work or with the art of dance. Use words to describe your work, your dance philosophy, and why the children will relate to what you have to say.

Dance and theater groups run a gamut from companies formed to promote a specific cause — like drug abuse awareness or to diminish stereotypes of disabled persons, or to promote a way of understanding the world through dance — to companies established to showcase the work of well-known choreographers. One hallmark of all successful companies is that they communicate their goals and philosophies in their descriptive and promotional literature as well as onstage.

Sometimes true understanding of your focus and philosophy comes after you have danced a while — that's OK in the beginning. Often we as dancers and choreographers understand with our kinetic sense. However you develop your focus and philosophy, speak about it, write about it and dance it!

Through time you may discover, as we did, that your company's philosophy comes into focus to an even greater degree as you have more performance and tour experience. This certainly happened to us. We began with an idea of creativity and involvement and those ideas just expanded and deepened. One day we discovered a poster at a school, in a teacher's lounge, that really epitomized our view of working with children: "Tell me, I forget. Show me, I remember. Involve me, I understand." The essence of what we believed — our philosophy — was so eloquently captured in the saying that we adopted it as a primary goal of our company and used it in our brochure. The saying verbally crystallized our philosophy. The ability to sum up our philosophy in a few words made all the difference in the world — in both how we thought about ourselves and how we explained who we were to everyone else.

Structure Your Philosophy into a Coherent and Workable Show for Children

You may love every element of planning and choreography for a performance and have no problem communicating your focus and philosophy. However, there is one more aspect of planning that is crucial if you want to dance and perform for children. That is to arrange your performance in a format that will work for a young audience.

The rest of this book will give you the tools to do that. Keep in mind while you structure your show that the theatrical elements need to be balanced but not overpowered by the educational elements. You do not want to be a boring or a predictable educational show. Timing and pace of the show is paramount. Dance is energy. Energy is the primary focus of every dance presentation, because it excites the imagination of the viewer, especially the young viewer.

Our dance company focused on the involvement of the kids. We also love improvisation, so we developed a two-part presentation with thirty minutes of choreography and one to three dances followed by fifteen minutes of audience participation. In between each of the dances we devised some audience participation improvisation activity that the children could do while sitting in their seats. For example, before a dance that was accompanied by a medley of Celtic music with different meters, we asked the children to clap fours and then to use another body part like their elbows to move in a 3/4 meter.

In another dance, a Native American story/dance with an elk as a main character, we asked the children to imagine that their arms were the antlers and to make their arms as strong as they could to hold up such a heavy load. Not only did these activities between dances give time for a costume change, they also gave the children in the audience a chance to "get their wiggles out." Participation activities are a good idea because they break the tiresome monotony for children of just sitting still and watching.

After we had performed in this manner for a while, we saw how adding more movement for the audience really helped focus their attention more strongly on our dances. If each in-between activity linked to the dance that the audience had just seen or would see next, their reaction to the dance that followed was even better.

Both the pace of the show and how you contrast elements within and between the dances is crucial when you create a show for a young audience. You need to give children a chance to respond kinetically. Create chances for children to clap, to laugh, to be excited and to move in response to the activities on stage.

Will Your Company Perform in a School Setting?

If you plan to perform in an educational setting, why should a school hire you? Often, dancers and choreographers are driven by the sheer power of their love to dance—and to perform. Many times one person's drive becomes the raison d'etre of the company and that drive becomes the philosophy. This is true of the many wonderful dance companies named after their founders: Martha Graham, Paul Taylor, and so on. In a school environment, something more is needed.

Why should a school hire you? You know why a commercially run theater might hire you, because you are entertaining and can sell at the box office. A school is not a commercial enterprise. That you are excellent in what you do is of course the most important accomplishment for your company. However, when you move into a school setting, the criteria change. Institutional time is precious. Resources and money are scarce and not supplemented by box office funds. Many schools are on very tight budgets.

Why should a school principal or head invite strangers into the school? What is

Child's depiction of Menagerie Dance Company's duet *Hawk's Wing*. Choreography: Ella Magruder.

important to children that you have to offer? Explain what you want to perform about so everyone can understand. Principals must know *what* they are asking teachers to attend. Teachers need to know *why* they are being asked to alter their schedule — why is what you do important for children to see? If a person who is in charge of children's welfare and education, parent, principal or other, does not know why you want to perform for children in their charge, or what message you will convey to those children, then why should they hire you? It would be unethical and irresponsible on their part.

Many school boards forbid schools to book performances autonomously. Why? Well, to give an example, our company called one principal who said that his school board would not let the school book performances without the board's approval because for the last assembly program the school had a man who threw Frisbees for fifty minutes. In the next assembly, a person whistled for an hour. Now, Frisbee throwing is a skill and whistling is nifty, but both are tough to justify as educational content or teaching tools, especially at taxpayer expense (most school funding comes directly from local taxes in the United States). Make sure you find and explain the educational link in what you offer.

How is a school supposed to tell the difference between what you and a company of lesser quality do? You must verbalize the differences and distinguish yourself from the whistlers and Frisbee-throwing performers of the world. You must say what you do, express it succinctly and be ready to explain why a school or organization — or any presenters of the arts — should spend their hard earned money on your dance performance.

Take a Vow to Maintain the Highest Quality:
Be Real. Be Excellent. Tell the Truth.

In attendance at all performances for children are adults: parents, grandparents, teachers, principals, and other theatrical, arts, and/or school staff who will judge the quality of your work and will help you establish your reputation as a good dance company for young audiences. If you want to develop a good reputation, your show must reach all ages, even if your focus is for children. Each dance company needs to have choreography that will appeal to an audience composed of people aged three to ninety-three (referred to as a general audience). How can that be accomplished with your artistic work? Figure out how your dance company can maintain the finest aesthetic quality while dancing for children and general audiences.

You must be careful when you are performing for children to recognize, to fully articulate, and to understand — as well as show respect for — the power you wield while performing onstage and conducting yourself offstage. Don't give mixed messages; don't perform an anti-smoking dance and then go offstage and smoke outside the building. You are always in the public eye when you tour, onstage and off. Children learn by behavior they see; one hypocritical action reverberates in a young mind often with unexpected consequences. Be a good role model.

Be truthful in what you present. If you believe, like we do, that the arts offer a chance for each child to learn and practice empathy — to feel sadness from another's body movement, to feel joy from seeing a leap, and to acknowledge the existence of other people and to respect them — then you have a philosophy that justifies your presence. Art is a powerful messenger of shared respect and shared emotion. You have a primary and worthy goal if you perform dances that accomplish this for any audience, but especially for an audience of children.

Chapter 2

Choreography That Appeals to Children… (Is Choreography That Appeals to Everyone!)

The first task is to figure out what you have to say to an audience. This happens naturally after you have trained and practiced as a dancer. As a choreographer it is not so difficult to find myriad topics. What is more difficult is to figure out how what you already have choreographed — or what you soon will choreograph — is best presented to children. You want to have an exciting theatrical performance that will inspire and captivate any audience. Yet the fact remains that your audience is composed primarily of children. Your choreography should entertain children. It also must be age appropriate. This is basic. Yet it is astounding how often these facts are misunderstood and misinterpreted to the detriment of the choreographer, dancers, and especially the children in the audience!

Don't "Dance Down" to Children

Much children's work in the performing arts has a bad reputation — either for the sickeningly sweet, saccharine "Now, kiddies, let's all be quiet and see the sweet little lambs dance" or the crass "Bop them on the head and make rude noises/gestures to make them laugh" — because performers mistakenly think the children are too young to understand (or appreciate) anything but the most obvious gags. Creating this kind of trite work is a huge mistake — theatrically, educationally, and aesthetically. Don't talk *or* dance down to children. Kids have very perceptive "fakeometers." Cutesy or maudlin presentations disgust children as well as some adults who watch. Every child, and indeed every individual, in an audience deserves respect. Every dance you create for children must interest and fascinate you or, believe me, you will rue the day you choreographed it, especially if you're dancing it. In addition, if you choreograph a dance for children that is too embarrassingly dull for adults to watch, then the children will be bored too. Take a cue from successful commercial producers for children. Disney has this all figured out. Each Disney film has a way of engaging universal themes with language and ideas that amuse both adults and children.

With our dance company, we didn't always understand this, but it didn't take long before we figured out that what was interesting to us was interesting to the children and vice versa. The different accommodations that we made for young audiences were all in how we introduced each new dance, not in the depth of topic. We will discuss presentation at length later in this book (see Chapter 14). Right now, concentrate on dreaming up subjects that would work for children and that appeal to your artistic taste.

As examples of what works to hold children's interest, below is a partial list of some of the themes we used over a fifteen-year period, with photographs to give an idea of the "look" of each dance. Many of the themes in these dances directly relate to standards and curriculum that are taught in a particular grade level. Identifying these links ahead of time makes it easy for teachers to be supportive of outside programs and your presentation in particular. However, by no means are these the only types of dances that interest youth audiences. At this point you may find it instructive to skip to Part IV in this book, Dancing Their Dreams, for a look at the descriptions of (and advice from) ten successful companies from across the United States and around the world. These companies are as different as can be — ranging in size, genres, ages and types of performers, and goals. They dance about diverse topics, yet each captures the hearts of its audiences — young and old!

Here are some dance ideas that worked for our company...

Topics in Science:

Stars and Constellations—A visually rich dance about the night sky, with images of meteors, planets in orbit and other celestial allusions, including a Native American story from the Navajo about how the Milky Way originated.

Symbiosis—A dance filled with shapes in trust and support balances about the complexities of relationships between the species of animals, such as the symbiotic relationship between the clown fish and the sea anemone.

Metamorphosis—A dance that focused on changes from one form to another in the insect world, especially those of the praying mantis, chrysalis to butterfly, and flies and their peculiar balances.

Topics in Literature:

The Peacock Maiden—A Chinese folk adventure story about a peacock, with research completed through the privately funded translation of a Chinese dance text. The dance uses extensive Chinese props and costumes, including huge fans, paper parasols, and silk kites.

Rosemary—An Italian folktale. This dance was commissioned by the Walters Art Gallery in Baltimore, Maryland, which hosted an exhibition from Italy called "The Splendors of the Popes." *Rosemary* was based on a story retold by Italo Calvino about a magic rosemary plant that came to life when watered five times a day with milk. *Rosemary* has monsters, a prince and princess, an old gardener, and an evil sister as characters. All the characters were created through the use of masks and costumes with just two dancers. We selected music by Italian composers: Vivaldi, Albinoni, Scarlatti, and Boccherini.

Jack and the King's Girl—An Appalachian story collected by the WPA Writers' Project in the Great Depression about a king's daughter who wouldn't smile and Jack, the boy who made her smile. We rediscovered the story through our research in a WPA collection in the rare manuscripts room of the University of Virginia library.

Other topics:

Cranes—An abstract work based on the complex dance of the whooping cranes, inspired

Left: Menagerie Dance Company in the "Sun" from *Stars and Constellations*. Choreography: Mark Magruder. Dancers: Ella and Mark Magruder (credit Andrewwildsphotography.com). *Right:* Menagerie Dance Company in the "Giant" from *Symbiosis*. Choreography by Mark Magruder. Dancers: Mark and Ella Magruder (credit Mary Gearhart).

Below: Menagerie Dance Company in "Insects Explore" from *Metamorphosis*. Choreography: Mark Magruder. Dancers: Mark and Ella Magruder (credit Lee Luther, Jr.). *Right:* Menagerie Dance Company in *The Peacock Maiden*. Choreography: Mark Magruder. Dancers: Mark and Ella Magruder (credit Mary Gearhart).

Left: Menagerie Dance Company in *Rosemary.* Choreography: Mark Magruder. Dancer: Ella Magruder as the Old Gardener (credit Andrew wildsphotography.com). *Above:* Child's Drawing of the rosemary plant and the pitcher of milk the old gardener uses to free the princess.

Left: Menagerie Dance Company in *Jack and the King's Girl.* Choreography: Mark Magruder. Dancers Mark and Ella Magruder play Appalachian dulcimers (credit Joe H. Bunn, principal, Hillsville Elementary). *Right:* Menagerie Dance Company in *Signs and Signals.* Choreography: Mark Magruder. Dancers: Mark and Ella Magruder (credit Mary Gearhart).

by the birds at the International Crane Foundation in Baraboo, Wisconsin. Teachers at one school told us how the kindergartners, boys and girls alike, ran outside to the playground and made cranes under the trees after seeing this dance!

Signs and Signals— A dance based on nonverbal gestures and communications between people, inspired by a performance in the 1980s of the visiting Russian clowns and

Left: Menagerie Dance Company in the "shoe" shape from *Environs*. *Right:* Menagerie Dance Company in the "house" shape from *Environs*. Both photographs, choreography: Mark Magruder; dancers: Mark and Ella Magruder (credit Mary Gearhart).

their hilarious use of kazoo vocalizations, and also by the secret signals of baseball players.

Bamboo—An abstract dance using long pieces of bamboo in as many symbolic and structural ways as possible.

Jesters—A buffoon dance of kinetic humor and pratfalls based on commedia dell'arte-style characters.

Environs—A dance of morphing forms, where two dancers encased in tubular fabric shift from images as varied as a high heeled shoe to a house. One teacher remarked that her students watched the dance so closely that they saw more shapes than she did.

The Power of the Abstract Dance versus the Appeal of Stories

You may look at the pictured dance topics and think there are some here that would work better than others, and that is true. Oddly enough, in our twenty years of performing for children, we have discovered something unexpected. The dances that are the most successful with children are more often the abstract dances rather than the story dances. Intuitively we first thought the opposite. Of course, all children love stories, right? Well, yes and no. The human mind is rapid. It can guess how a story ends and at that "Aha!" moment, the mind moves on and loses interest. It is actually counter-theatrical if the story is too predictable. Also, if a story is too familiar it is not the best choice for educating or entertaining children. Stories work only if the subject is entertaining enough to fascinate with unusual twists or if the physical movement is stupendous—in other words, accomplished with brilliant technique, very high leaps, multiple turns, feats of strength, and timing. Conversely, we found that abstract dances often were audience favorites. So while teachers sometimes approached us and said, "Why don't you choreograph something the children are familiar with, like the fairy tale of Snow White?" The children came up to us and said, "Oh, I love *Cranes*, the movements reminded me of birds!" Or, "I loved *Environs*, I saw a house, a basketball player, two wise men, and a pair of pants!"

In other words, the mind soars and the imagination leaps through images created by abstract shapes. Children love the play of their imagination. It is their job to develop creative connections, and abstract dance is a vast conduit for this necessary work. The poems, stories, drawings, and new movement that spring from watching abstract dances are overwhelming. Our dance company has volumes of material, the creative outpourings sent to us by teachers from children who have written and drawn after seeing our shows. Here is an example of a beautiful poem that a child composed during a Menagerie dance workshop.

> *Clouds of Silk*
> Clouds of silk dance lightly
> Across an ice silver ground
> There *is* harmony in this world of hatred.
> —*Elizabeth Dattilio (age 12), Augusta County Summer Arts*

Creativity doesn't arise in a vacuum — it usually manifests itself in response to a stimulating environment and an opportunity to play and respond. When a child sees an abstract dance, the music, the visual symbolic energy, and costumes all add together to create what one brain researcher, Mihaly Csikszentmihalyi, calls the "flow" state.[1] I believe that this "flow" state (which is associated, by the way, with human happiness) occurs in audience members who have been able to bridge the divide between mundane reality and exciting theatrical reality. This happens when a viewer has a "willing suspension of disbelief."[2] Children will respond readily to an exciting and moving dance performance. They believe what they see because one half of what a child experiences in a dance show occurs in the child's imagination. In any show, this is true. The combination of excellence of choreography and the ability of the dancers to convey emotion as well as perform in a technically flawless manner creates a portal to the imagination. What a responsibility, then, because you must have great integrity in what you present to any audience and especially to a young audience. It can't be boring, it can't be babyish, and it can't be dull.

Exciting, challenging, and brilliant — these are the benchmarks for your choreography. To achieve this, you must video and critique your work before you present it publicly. Critique it as if a *Dance Magazine* or a *New York Times* reviewer will be there (they may be someday, as we discovered. See following paragraph.). Then perform it for a selected audience (small, friendly, and frank speaking) before you take it out on the road. Rework parts of your performance that need it in response to your own critiquing from the video and in response to your trial performance audience's feedback. And remember Doris Humphrey's dictum "Listen to qualified advice; don't be arrogant."[3]

> At the opposite end of the spectrum, Menagerie Dance Company — a two-person troupe based in Amherst, Virginia — is small in size but not in the number of demands for its dance education programs, vigorously delivered to schools in locations along the Shenandoah Valley and among the Blue Ridge Mountains. Mark and Ella Magruder combine performances with workshops that focus on movement as a creative medium. "While we appear in Washington, D.C., and Baltimore," Mark reveals, "our real circuit

includes small communities like Palmyra, Danville, Martinsville, and Richlands." Under the sponsorship of the Virginia Commission for the Arts, the pair (faculty members at Sweet Briar College) has danced for and with more than seventy thousand students during the last three years. "No one told us," remarks Ella, "that when we received M.F.A. degrees in dance we were going to become Missionaries for the Fine Arts!"[4]

PART II

Producing

Genius is one percent inspiration and ninety-nine percent perspiration.
— Thomas Edison

Chapter 3

Production: Putting the Show Together

Putting a show on the road includes many elements of production that are similar to producing a show anywhere. The main difference is in the attention you must pay to make everything portable and easy to carry. Normally only the largest dance companies employ a separate technical assistant. If you can afford to, by all means hire someone for the road to serve as T.D. (technical director or stage manager). But for most small companies it is too expensive, so here are some tips.

Portability

Make sure you can carry all sets, props, and sound systems and so on without strain. They should be lightweight enough that carrying any of these items up a flight of stairs should not threaten the quality of your performance. Many trips unloading, walking back and forth to your vehicle, are less strain on the body (and actually serve as a great core temperature warm-up) than hauling a couple of massively heavy loads. Handcarts are great, but loading ramps are not always present in theaters or schools. Often a handcart does you no good at all and actually takes up valuable cargo space.

Sets should be made of the most lightweight, yet sturdy materials possible. Large items should be made to be taken apart into pieces that are small enough for the dancers themselves to carry in and out of buildings. That is how the touring usually happens, especially in smaller companies where often each dancer is in charge of a technical aspect (costumes, set, props, sound) in addition to performing.

Sound

Travel with your sound system. It should have a tuner/amplifier and separate speakers. Include: at least three heavy-duty extension cords; an adapter; extra speaker wire; electrical tape; and boxes to protect the speakers. Even if you make an investment in heavy-duty speakers of the sort used for public broadcast — aerobics classes and so forth — realize that touring is extremely wearing on woofers and tweeters (speaker "innards") no matter how much you pay for the system. Cushion them as best you can. No "boom box" will ever compare in sound quality to a separate component sound system. The attention-getting quality of a good sound system — as opposed to most school auditorium built-in systems, or even to the most expensive one-piece unit — is impressive. The first hurdle to grabbing an audience's attention is to make sure they can hear the music, *feel* the music — with good bass and clear, undistorted treble.

Always carry a small public address system — a one-piece box amplifier and microphone. They are useful in situations where you are surprised by an extremely large audience or by awful acoustics. Use your unamplified, resonant "stage voice" during introductions (see Chapter 13), for in-between-dance patter and for conducting lectures. Use a microphone only if it is absolutely necessary. Audiences will listen more quietly to an unamplified voice. Somehow the presence of a microphone and a public address system seems to imply permission for people in an audience to talk louder. Unconsciously, perhaps, people understand that if they talk while an unamplified person on stage talks, others will not hear the stage speaker. At any rate, be prepared for all contingencies and carry a microphone system, since you can never be sure if the venue's sound equipment is usable or in good working order, if acoustics are going to swallow your voice, or if you will have an unexpectedly huge audience.

Sets

Keep sets light. Touring companies have devised a number of light and portable sets — everything from PVC pipes and quilted hanging backdrops to actual "flats." Whatever design you choose, two things are important. Number one: *What an audience sees onstage reflects the quality of your presentation.* Water stains or ripped fabric, shoddy workmanship or inelegant designs send a blaringly negative message to the audience. Number two: *Safety is crucial.* Any set should be portable, yet sturdy enough to withstand a child falling on it or a performer's misplaced kick. Stages are inherently hazardous places — school stages especially so since they are often used as temporary or even permanent classrooms. They may have anything stashed, from stacks of chairs to recycling bins teetering precariously behind stage curtains. Any set should be light enough that if it should accidentally fall, it would not injure anyone on stage. This is not an idle caution. I know of at least one performer friend who was permanently injured when the pipe set was being struck (dismantled) after the show, and a large piece landed squarely on her lower back.

On page 29 is a lightweight set design that will fit into a van or other larger vehicle: This also can be placed in a car top carrier, as we did for several years. The beauty of this simple set is that it is light, inexpensive, and easy to construct. If the fabric is soiled, it can be washed easily or replaced. By changing angles of the hinged wing doors, more or less of the stage space can be covered. It can be used in different configurations: a four-piece panel; or two different two-piece panels depending if you want a wide center screen backdrop or two wings. We experimented with the design through the years; first using light-colored fabrics (too easily stained), a fabric stapled permanently to the set (tough to keep clean), and finally developed a curtained version with detachable fabric that is removed each time the set is taken down. Carefully wrapped around on a cardboard roll or batten to minimize wrinkles and stored in a waterproof bag for easy transport between shows, it is an attractive, versatile, and forgiving set.

Menagerie Dance Company in *Rosemary*. Choreography: Mark Magruder. (Pictured here as the Prince), he leaps in front of a lightweight portable set (credit William D. Watson).

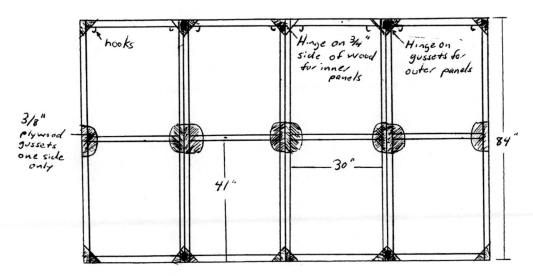

Portable set design drawing (back view).

Use Western red cedar, or other lightweight, strong wood that is strong enough to last through years of touring.

- All wood is 1½ inch by ¾ inches in size
- 12 horizontals (crosspieces) are 30 inches wide
- 8 verticals (uprights) are 84 inches long (7 feet)
- Center horizontals placed at 41 inches from the floor
- All joints are wood-glued and reinforced by ⅜-inch plywood gussets and screwed together.

This design yields 4 finished panels 33 inches wide and 84 inches tall.
Hooks can be screwed into the top horizontals for hanging fabric or props.

Use hinges to attach the panels together either as two freestanding wings (using 2 panels each) or one large center set (using all four panels). If you mount hinges opposite on the two center panels from the outer panels, you will be able to fold the set into a stack of 4 connected panels which can be easily transported as one piece 33 inches wide by 84 inches long and just 5 inches high.

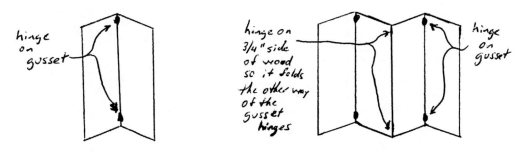

Correct hinge placement on panels creates easily folding set.

Curtain materials needed:

- 4 wooden rods — each 33½ inches (85 cm) long, ¾ inches (2 cm) in diameter
- 4 panels of dark washable fabric with some weight and stretch (polyester jersey is good). Each panel of fabric 86 inches (214 cm) long, 62 inches (158 cm) wide
- Elastic 24 inches (61 cm) length, ¼ inch (5 mm) wide, cut into 8 equal pieces
- Pins or hooks (optional)
- Fabric roll or batten (heavy cardboard or durable plastic)
- Carrying bag for fabric and poles (waterproof)

Directions for fabric stage curtains covering for wooden frame set panels:

1. Make 3-inch (8 cm) hem at top of fabric panels to create pocket for curtain rod.
2. Fold each 4-inch (10 cm) piece of elastic in half to create a loop and sew one loop onto fabric at each end of the top of the four fabric panels.
3. Attach these loops 1½ inches (4 cm) from the hemmed top, 2 elastics per fabric panel. Insert rods into hem pockets.
4. Drape rod and fabric over the top of the set (from the downstage side)
5. Fasten the elastic loops to sturdy metal hooks that should be screwed into the inside top of the wood (on the upstage side). Fabric should hang to the floor in graceful folds and each panel may be pinned together so that edges of the frame will be covered. If you pin the curtains instead of hooking them or using Velcro, you sacrifice permanence for flexibility. It is a good idea to pin the fabric sides together rather than let it hang completely free because as dancers brush past the set, they might open a gap between the fabric panels, accidentally revealing behind the scene. Make sure to mark which fabric curtain matches which wooden frame because sometimes there is a slight variation in measurement that makes a difference visually.

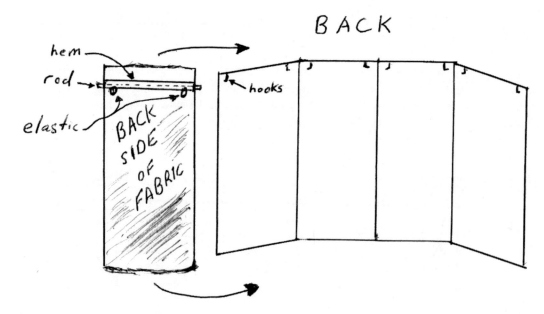

Curtain and rod placement, back view of hooks on set.

FRONT

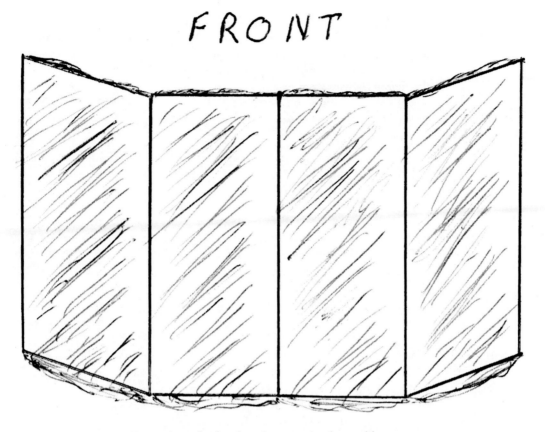

Front view of a free hanging curtained portable set.

The beauty of this simple set is that it is light, inexpensive, and easy to construct. If the fabric is soiled, it can easily be washed or replaced. By changing angles of the hinged wing doors, more or less of the stage space can be covered.

You may wonder, "Why do I need a set at all if we perform on a stage proper?" Well, you cannot ever count on having a usable backstage area. In fact, many school stages have no wings or curtains. There may be huge rips in the curtains onstage. Big immobile storage boxes may protrude into stage spaces, and you may want to hide them from audience view. In addition, occasionally backstage "wing" space is noncxistent and your props and costumes may need more concealment than the stage offers.

Also, you may find a stage that is too small for dancing. You may have to move a performance offstage, perhaps onto the cafeteria floor where there are no wings. Lastly, and unfortunately, you may have to "wing it" in a gymnasium, library, or other alternative space — with nothing that can provide sight lines to keep you from being seen when you don't want to be seen, except the wings or set that you provide.

Outdoor performances at festivals are notorious for lack of the necessary facilities. Our company has performed around canopy tent poles, directly across from "Ronald McDonald" singing "Head and Shoulders, Knees and Toes" (thank heavens for our powerful sound system) and even in windstorms that knocked over our set. Choose your outdoor performing venues with care. Think ahead for all contingencies involving the four elements: earth — mud, sand and dust; air — wind and other sound interference (Will you be able to perform on a boardwalk stage against the sound of crashing ocean waves?); fire — heat, sun, humidity (always carry plenty of water bottles stored behind your set); and water — rain and electrical storms. Outdoor festivals sometimes only allow for a few minutes of strike time in between performances — you may have to strike your own set in five minutes while a drum ensemble sets up around you. By being courteous and moving your set quickly, you will establish and maintain a good reputation for flexibility and reliability. An easily moveable set is a must.

Costumes

As with your sets, your costumes reflect not only the visual image of your dance but also the quality of your production. Costumes illuminate the meaning of your dance through color, style, development of shape, and emphasis on movement qualities (think flowing scarves, the stretch tube fabric, and so on.) The attention to costumes more than repays the time it takes to visualize what you want and then make it a reality.

Obviously, costumes for the road have more demands than costumes that are going to be used only once or twice in a year. The first demand is that the costume must be constructed well enough to withstand multiple performances, perhaps as many as three performances a day — with little or no time for repairs or cleaning in between. This means seams sewn with heavy and durable thread, and fabrics that can stand the tremendous wear and tear of dance movements, from explosive leaps to floor back spins.

The best fabrics always are those which have a combination of movement-enhancing qualities — flowing materials like silk, rayon, chiffon — and light-reflective qualities — satin-type materials and those made with Lycra. Cotton costumes are wonderful to wick off perspiration but awful for light reflection, so choose cotton blends with Lycra and/or other materials with motion- and light-enhancing qualities.

How the costumes are constructed matters as well. While it is true that you can fake a lot of detail — since there is distance between audience and performer, hems can be done sloppily with basting stitches rather than slip stitches and still not be visible from the audience — other details are more important onstage. Underarm sleeve seams need to be constructed with stretch material or gussets — a diamond shaped addition — to prevent rips from the dance movement.

The sketch on page 33 shows the diamond-shaped piece of cloth under the arm. This is known as a *gusset*. Whenever you have a dance costume with no "give" or stretch in it, this is what you need to sew under the arm, out of fabric as close in color as possible to the surrounding fabric. Almost any clothing can be turned into a workable dance costume with this simple little addition. It works on trousers as well as jackets and shirts/blouses.

Hems should have no gaps for a toe to become entangled with, and skirts can be altered to accommodate movement in several ways. Extra panels, called *gores*, can be added for fullness. These (usually triangular) pieces of fabric can be added with triangle point up or down, depending on where fullness is needed.

Dancers need to be able to move their legs with freedom. Kick height should not be impaired by a costume. You can slit the back seams of a skirt to free the leg. In addition,

Drawing of a costume with underarm inserts called "gussets."

elastic waistbands are necessary on skirts and pants, and you should use the type of elastic that is wide, at least one inch (2.54) centimeters wide, made specifically for waistbands, as it minimizes rolling of the waistband. Hems of long skirts and pants should be short enough to clear the floor by at least an inch or two to prevent trips (unless it is a period dress with a long, flowing train).

The issue of whether or not to use leotards and tights or unitards for school performances is one area of controversy. When our dance company first began to tour twenty years ago in the 1980s, leotards and unitards were accepted (although to put it politely, men always have needed to wear athletic support garments and women have always needed bras — preferably the athletic support type). However, since the advent of "good touch/bad touch" educational programs, the religious revivals of the 1990s, and the subsequent expansion of the bounds of acceptable body imagery in the media — unitards became such a cause of negative comment and criticism from schoolteachers that for school performances our company decided to change our costume choices more towards the garb of "regular people" and ditch the leotards. Occasionally we wear a leotard top with dance pants, skirts or even — horrors — sweat pants for some more athletic pieces like our *Signs and Signals.*

Did we "wimp out" to avoid controversy? Yes, in some ways. But the

Drawings of skirts modified to allow for wider range of motion.

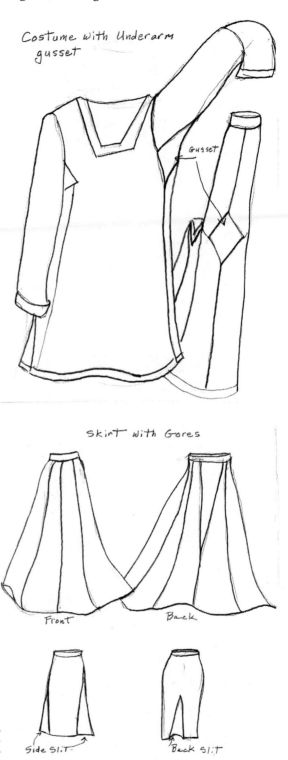

Costume with Underarm gusset

Gusset

Skirt with Gores

Front

Back

Side Slit

Back Slit

straight skirts with slits

Avoid unitards and skimpy costumes

Carefully think through costume decisions for school performances.

positive side has been that school personnel are visibly relieved when we appear in costumes that are not obviously body-revealing. You can see why: the teachers have to spend much less time reprimanding older children for off color comments or nervous laughter. In a society that is drenched in sexual imagery — billboards to television — it seems ludicrous that a unitard could cause so much controversy, but it does.

In addition, most schools everywhere in the United States have dress codes, some of which forbid bare midriffs, short shorts and skirts, or sleeveless shirts. If performers onstage are breaking school dress codes, there is a mixed message for the kids. The schoolteachers and principals, who must make sure the children respect their authority and obey rules, may resent the nonconforming costume and the dancers who wear it. So, in the early 1990s, rather than try to justify our company's right to wear unitards in a school setting, we decided not to waste time with it. In other words, we chose our battle. We decided that it was more important that the children see dance — no matter that we wore pants instead of tights. A leap is still a leap. You may disagree. If so, go ahead and follow your convictions to dance proudly in unitards or tights; but go into the situation forewarned and determined to address it directly rather than try to ignore it. *Clothing, or perceived lack of it, is one of those things that is so "in your face" that it is virtually impossible to ignore, especially when you perform in a school.*

Remember that cleanliness is important for a lot of reasons. Figure out how to wash or dry-clean your costumes regularly. In our dance company we find that when touring, daily washing or cleaning of dance wear is necessary, especially if there is more than one performance a day. If you don't do this, several things will happen. The costumes will start to smell, and the audience's sense of smell is even more acute than its sense of sight. (Also remind your dancers who don't believe in deodorant that the audience should have a pleasant experience "all around." Sorry to be indelicate, but the body odor of a nervous dancer who is not wearing deodorant is in the category of what we, in the United States, will not *willingly* sit still to experience.) Second, if you don't clean your costumes regularly, in addition to odor, the costume fabric will break down under long term exposure to body salts, oils, and bacteria. Cleaning is a way to extend the life of any costume. It is especially important in between touring seasons to store only well-laundered garments.

Hats and crushable objects should be stored in boxes to prevent them from being damaged while on tour. Use hatboxes or other rigid, lightweight boxes to carry masks, hats, and the like. Garment bags that hang are better for transporting costumes if you can hang them up — otherwise carefully roll costumes and pack however you can to reduce wrinkles. For many years we transported our costumes and props in a wooden box that began its incarnation as a bench on stage — part of the set for *Jack and the King's Girl.* The box proved to be so useful as storage and footstool that it became almost indispensable. Carry a portable iron and a small ironing board with you on the road. A steamer will work for light fabrics but a portable steam iron can fix many problems. And audiences *do* notice wrinkles and shoddily kept costumes. Don't let your wonderful dances be obscured by poorly constructed or maintained costumes!

Don't *ever* pin together any costume except in an extreme emergency. Nothing is as painful as dancing with an open pin sticking you. No safety pin has been invented that remains securely in a dancer's costume. Maybe it works for other performers, but for dancers who bend, stretch and sway, a pin is a fast track to disaster. Let my personal testimonial warn you, because you never know your own capacity for enduring pain until you have danced with a safety pin sticking in your waist. Once you are in front of an audience, the show must go on, no matter what! Avoid pins!

More Thoughts on Costumes

Through the twenty years of stage costuming in our company, we have come to realize that if you have costume changes to make, make sure that you layer so that you are never in a completely stripped-down position backstage in the wings. Many things happen backstage in school auditoriums and community spaces.

Once when performing in our early touring years and making a fast change in a cafetorium (with our set upstage, right in front of the school kitchen), I was doing my sixty-second change from one costume to another. At the moment when I had just shed down to my bra and was in the process of pulling up my tights, the kitchen door behind the set opened and a cafeteria lady's arm and friendly face shoved a brownie at me and said, "Here honey, you need this."

Caught in the proverbial moment —"with my pants down"— all in the name of chocolate and kindness — I made a vow never to devise a costume that left me that vulnerable again! Of course the audience didn't see all this, but I had the feeling that they might have been even more entertained when this happened — to see the color of my face as I crouched behind the set fumbling with the paper napkin, the brownie, and my tights — than by what was happening in the dance taking place in front of the set!

Layer over a basic leotard — or, better yet, have a basic costume that you add to or subtract from. You may find yourself in a gym with the world viewing you 360 degrees, or in an outdoor performance with only a portable "john" (W.C.) for a changing room (and you might have to share that with the general public or other performers)! In fact, for outdoor shows it is always wise to call ahead and ask what type of changing facilities the presenters have for your dance company, even if you have sent a prior technical requirement sheet. And, if the outdoor dressing room space they offer is less than adequate for your needs, then pack your own small tent. Of course, for the tent to work as a changing room, you must make sure that you can stand up in it.

Velcro is better than zippers, which rust, break and get stuck. Hooks and eyes work, but Velcro is better still. Emergency iron-on hem is great (it can be found at a sewing or crafts store). Snaps are too unreliable in movement performances. Carry a stapler to fix hems in an extreme emergency. On the road use a detergent that works with cold water and is suitable for hand washing delicate fabrics. After you wash costumes, roll them in an absorbent towel to wick excess water and lay flat to dry.

Props

If you use props in your performance, you add a wonderful new dimension. The props become extensions of motion or add to the believability of the illusion that you are trying to create. Children really respond to the variety of visual cues and colors. Props help children enter willingly into the world you are trying to create. That said, it is also true that props add exponentially to the complexity of your performance. Props must be sturdily constructed with both theatricality and safety in mind. In other words, the beans can't fly out of your beanbags! Props require careful maintenance and must be accounted for and/or counted at the end of each performance before being packed. Props break and have to be replaced, they get lost, lose their luster, or just plain wear out. In the past we have used such props as: a flute, a crooked stick, a Chinese cloth kite, several two-feet-wide fans, ribbon streamers, shiny cloth and paper, twenty-four beanbag sparkling "meteors," hula hoops covered with sequin-like material, a brass pitcher, a wooden bench, bamboo poles, kazoos, birthday party favors (to represent insect tongues), a huge three-

Menagerie Dance Company in *Fog Woman & Raven.* **Choreography: Mark Magruder. Dancers: Karla Booth and Mark Magruder (credit Lee Luther, Jr.).**

foot-wide rubber ball, and masks. All kinds of masks — a sparse bentwood face frame of a woodpecker, masks of monsters made out of felt, Chinese opera masks made of papier mâché, a huge, Northwest Native American style wooden raven mask, a half head latex mask with a wig — and others. The advantage of using masks is that if you have a small company and choose a story to dance that has a lot of characters, it is easy to change personalities quickly, and the children's imaginations fly quickly right along with you.

Masks

Masks introduce two main concerns, however. They cause visibility problems for the dancers wearing them. And they completely alter a dancer's appearance, which can be frightening to very young children who are not expecting dancers to disappear and strangers to take their places.

Anything that impairs vision on stage can be a problem. Masks in particular cause a hazard because they restrict a dancer's peripheral vision. We dancers rely intimately and unconsciously on our peripheral vision. On stage we use it to keep in time with one another without being obvious about it. We use it to judge distance and depth — above and below. When you wear a mask, even if it is a half facemask, all peripheral vision, plus vision immediately above and below the mask, is affected in a major way. Your peripheral vision actually vanishes once you put on a mask.

The person who wears the mask cannot see the edges of the stage. This is especially worrisome because it means that the mask wearer can't see where the front drop-off of the stage into the audience is. This dangerous problem is complicated by the fact that for most school performances you will only have a maximum of one to one and one half hours (sometimes less than that) to set up and have a spacing rehearsal on the stage before your performance. Dancing with a mask can be *very scary* under those circumstances, and even more so if you haven't even gotten a chance to try out the stage at all — due to tight schedules, unexpected delays on the road and so forth. One way to help all dancers in your company heighten their sensitivity toward the problems that masks pose is to have every dancer wear a mask sometime in your rehearsal process, even if they don't have to wear one onstage for their character or part. This instantly helps them understand how much responsibility they will have to take in spacing, leading, and timing for the masked dancer, who is really dependent on whomever he or she dances with for all of those things. Unison movement especially is a challenge with a mask on. As you choreograph and rehearse, make sure to stagger the depth of the dancers onstage so that the masked dancer is never directly beside another dancer with whom they have to move in unison.

Another problem that we have seen with performers who use half head masks is that sometimes dancers and other performers neglect to hide the tie or elastics that secure the masks to their heads. Always use ingenuity to hide the fastenings — put it behind your ears or under your hair. Or fluff your hair over the tie. Dye the tie the same color as your hair or cover the back of your head entirely with a hat or cap. Why is this important? Well, if you think about the mask as an illusion, the answer becomes clear. You have a spherical head. In the mirror the mask may look convincing — but what you don't see on the back of the head may not look so good. A bird in front ... a person with rumpled hair in back?

Menagerie Dance Company in *Peacock Maiden,* **Choreography by Mark Magruder, Dancers Mark Magruder (Evil Advisor) and Ella Magruder (Peacock Maiden) dance in masks that obscure their peripheral vision (credit Mary Gearhart).**

The other big issue with masks is that they can frighten very young children. How a mask is introduced makes all the difference. One of our performance nightmares happened in a school when we arrived late, after a flat tire. We didn't have time to roam out in the audience before the show and introduce ourselves through our presence in costume and with friendly conversation with the children — nor did we have time to introduce the masks before the show. When we came onto the stage in the first mask, a child became

How to wear a mask....

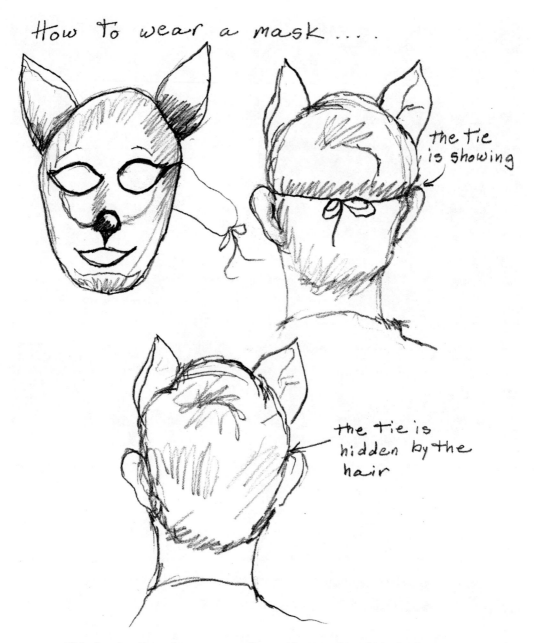

the tie is showing

the tie is hidden by the hair

This drawing shows how to wear a face mask correctly to hide the fastenings.

so terrified that she ran screaming from the auditorium. Since it was a fairly innocuous costume and mask, the child presumably had some other issues that she was dealing with; nevertheless we felt awful. After the show was over, we took a lot of time to try and reassure the child — who was cringing in her teacher's lap. But it was of no use, the damaging moment had occurred and she was inconsolable.

A lesson in this — the masks you wear should always be introduced to the youngest members of your audience before the show. Young students, pre-school through kindergarten, usually arrive first because they sit in the front rows; they are the ones for whom this is important.

Before your show, as the audience is filing in, take the mask from backstage. Bring it out casually in your hand and then show it to the children *held away from your face.* Then ask the children to raise their hands if they know what it is. Most children will answer when you call on them — they will say that it is a mask, a coyote, something like that. Initiate a discussion about how and what it is made of. Talk about how when the dancer wears it she is "pretending." All children understand this.

My line usually goes something like this, after they tell me that they know it is a mask of something. "Yes," I say, "I'm glad you're old enough to know it is just make-believe, because some of the little three-year-olds we perform for think that it's a REAL _____ and they get worried. But YOU know it's just us dancers behind the mask — that we're just PRETENDING to be a _____!"

Of course, they will, at age four or five, feel quite superior to the little imaginary three-year-olds whom I bring up as examples. Almost all of the youngest then proudly (and with comically studied and deliberate casualness) — because they are "in the know" — relax around the mask.

There will still be a few children who will need to be reassured. I usually bring the kindergarten teachers in on this so the timid one gets the teacher's lap. Then, at the last moment before you leave the children to go talk to the other little ones elsewhere in the audience, hold the mask up to your face and take it away quickly. Be prepared still for an occasional apprehensive reaction from one or two of the children. And let this be a reminder never to underestimate a mask's power to focus attention and feelings. From the earliest recorded use of masks (17,000 B.C.E.[1]) to the present time, they have been used so that a performer could completely change character. Masks work, and sometimes they work more powerfully than you can imagine ahead of time.

Make-up

Make-up is, of course, necessary for any stage with lighting. Stage lights threaten to obscure the basic features of a performer's face — unless the features are emphasized by make-up coloration and line. Traditional performing arts like Kabuki and Baharata Natyam use make-up even in daylight to enhance visibility and establish character. The rule of thumb is that the brighter the lights or the larger the auditorium, the more your facial features need to be reinforced with make-up. However, since you may be out in the audience greeting the children as they enter into the performance seating space, you will have to wear make-up that can go from the everyday look to the stage. This means you may want to forego the "clown white" between the eye lines, or even the eye lines!

In general, for stage make-up you attempt to emphasize the expressive features of your face. For women that means pencil eyeliner, some brown or gray shadow above the crease of the eye, and eyebrow pencil if necessary. Blush in two tones, pinker on cheek-bones, darker in the hollows, lipstick that is redder/brighter than you would normally wear, lotion first and then a base for skin make-up under it all that matches your skin tone. Remember to blend your make-up down your neck. All this is easily removed after

correct

"beady" eye

How to use theatrical stage make-up to "open up" eyes.

the performance with commercial baby wipes. Don't draw lines to bottom tear duct, it makes the eyes appear small and beady. Start midway under the lower eyelash.

Remove all jewelry (unless it is part of your costume) and hair fasteners that shine (you can always tape over rings that won't come off). Cover tattoos. Always use transparent powder over all make-up, let it set for two minutes and lightly brush off. This prevents make-up smearing or perspiring off. Hairspray is necessary for a professional look.

For men, the situation changes. If the male dancer is going to go out into the audience at all, then probably a bare minimum to no make-up should be used — due to the negative stereotypes of males in dance in the U.S. (no matter that male TV anchors and reporter regularly wear make-up). For male dancers with obvious make-up on, children's blunt comments can be overwhelming and distract attention from the performance itself.

Stage make-up, applied heavily, is at best startling to children (and adults, too, when seeing it up close) and at worst frightening to children. So, modulate it accordingly. One caution, unless it is a part of a monster/alien or other character —*never* wear blue or green eye shadow on stage if you're trying to look like a "normal" person. It looks garish and amateurish.

Lights

Lights can make or break any show. Our company chooses to use what each facility has, rather than lug heavy lighting instruments from site to site. We made the choice because it seemed to us that while most stage spaces had some type of fairly adequate illumination (and some even had very good lighting), fewer schools and auditoriums had satisfactory (or any) sound systems. To minimize the pre-performance stage set-up time, we chose to bring our own sound system and spend the pre-performance time preparing a rich sound environment. To ensure that schools realize that we rely on their lighting to be in good working order, we send a technical requirement sheet to schools beforehand. In it we remind schools to have lights in good working order. (See Chapter 7.)

The worst possible lights to dance in are fluorescent, because they cast a green hue on faces and diminish shine and sparkle of the costumes and props. However, viewers tolerate minimal lighting better than bad audio. Go ahead and establish your own company priorities, according to what you're willing (or have time, vehicle space or technical assistance) to haul around. No matter what else they don't have, the good news is that all performing spaces have some kind of lighting, ranging from primitive to state of the art. Some old stages even have footlights. If you can, always use them when they're available. (Remember that old vaudeville performers always insisted on "foots" because they were so "kind" to aging faces!)

The school janitor usually knows the whereabouts of all lighting control boxes and how to work them. Make contact with the janitor(s) immediately; they are the key to clean floors, working electrical outlets, and lighting systems. Be extra polite to the school janitors in the short amount of time you spend at each site. Janitors and secretaries make schools function and deserve respect for that, and praise, too, when they help you. Often these folks are the lowest paid workers and all they have is their dignity. In return for a polite manner to all school staff members, especially custodians and secretaries, your company will be rewarded with a smooth performing and teaching environment.

Chapter 4

Marketing:
Don't Sell Yourself Short

Our company has accomplished a lot by marketing in many different ways. We have learned what works for us and what doesn't. You can listen to what our approaches have been and come up with marketing strategies of your own; ones that work for you uniquely. There is no one formula to getting your name out and booking performances. You will have to experiment before you find the best methods for marketing your dance company.

Dancers and Marketing

The first hurdle is to get over is an aversion to the word "marketing." This was the hardest thing for me to do personally. For years most of us train as artists, we have our carefully honed technique; we work on creating choreography and refining our artistic purpose and philosophy. But *selling* ourselves — ugh. Isn't that like prostitution of our art? After all, what does true art have to do with "filthy lucre"?

If you look about, however, you know that art is big business. In 2000, according to Dance/USA, nonprofit dance companies added $350 million to the economy in the United States. It has even been asserted that art is the U.S.'s biggest export (music, films, television). There is a reason that art is big money, and the reason is not that the artists have great agents and marketing strategies (although it doesn't hurt!). People want and need art. They are willing to pay for it, and what's more, they are willing to appreciate and support individuals who create what helps them, as viewers/listeners/audience members, feel more fully alive. It is simple. Art makes you feel and appreciate your humanity — you laugh, you cry. The divorce between doing and feeling is annulled.

Just think of how exuberant, thrilled and moved you are when you have seen a fantastic dance company perform. You know you are alive right down to the kinesthetic tips of your nerve endings — all from watching the glorious performers and the illusions they create onstage. If you are a performer, a talented dancer who has honed her skills with hard work, it is a wonderful chance to accept a great honor and perform a worthy duty, to dance for audiences who want to share your vision. It's the process of figuring out how to get you there — in front of that needy and appreciative audience — that is called marketing. And while dance can be trickier to market than some of the other arts, with careful planning, it is possible for any size company.

First, you have to justify the "why" of marketing. Basically, "why" has to do with the worth of your company's vision and who has a right to experience the beauty and energy of your program. Is it only your family and friends? Don't children in a poor neighborhood, or children whose parents can't afford to take them to live performances at Lincoln Center or the Kennedy Center have a right to see your work? Won't they learn from it? If you thought that a child, a young Alvin Ailey, who sees your company, will find inspiration from the experience — wouldn't you fight for the right to have your company seen? I have, and I can tell you that the personal rewards are unbelievably rich. Children who have seen our company perform in Appalachia and elsewhere, have approached us after the performance and said, "I want to be a dancer when I grow up." In a grocery store a child says, "Oh Mom, it's *them*!" Or a child solemnly comes up from behind, tugs on your arm and says "You done good."

Even if it doesn't come to pass that the child escapes the poverty, just that moment of hope, that moment of personal inspiration and encouragement to the child is priceless. It enlivens the child's spirit and imagination and extends children's dreams. Many times I have seen as a dancer and teacher, that natural talent is a minuscule part of a dancer's success. The talent that develops — from dedication to perfection of expression and technique — and above all the will and desire to succeed, makes all the difference for an aspiring dancer. But the will and desire are usually the result of the person first seeing an inspiring performance — a dancer who transported that individual into the exciting world of energy and dance. Don't you remember seeing a performance that inspired you to want to dance? You can be the instrument of that inspiration, and if marketing is necessary to accomplish it, then market like crazy for a great cause! Be a missionary for your art, the great art of dance!

Basic Groundwork Before You Begin

Once you have fortified yourself with the necessary business attitude (you know why it's important to tour) and before you begin the actual time-consuming process of booking your company, there are several things you must do. First, ask yourself what groups you want to perform for. Will you dance for public or private school assembly audiences in primary, elementary, middle or high schools? For children in libraries, at summer outdoor festivals, in museums, or in other community centers like hospitals? Or through traditional matinees and evening presentations in established theaters with formal performing arts seasons? Will you dance for one or two or all of the above? You should think about this carefully, because to be effective you must tailor your performances for a particular type of audience, and that in turn affects how you market your company and whom you contact in the booking process. I confess that our company has tried to be as broad in appeal as possible and we have performed in almost, but not all, of the above venues. This is possible because we are flexible in our approach and have devised a number of different presentational formats for our show. You can, too, or maybe you can't — and this is the time to figure out just how accommodating and open to alternatives you are willing to be in terms of what audiences and where you are willing to perform.

Next, define how far you want to travel in any touring period. (More about this later in Chapter 7.) Get a map. Decide what your geographic area will be — a tri-state, one state, regional, or metropolitan area? What are the constraints that might stop you from being a national company? How flexible is your life? This is determined by whether or not you have another job (most of us do) and what that job is. If you are in a relationship, does your partner intend to tour with you? Do you have children? What will you do for child care if you have to spend several days to a week on the road? Once you answer these questions you will better be able to answer the geographic question, "how far?" Factor, too, into this decision what the lives of the people with whom you are going to be dancing require, if you are not touring solo. Once you figure this out, make sure you get a good detailed map, one that has all roads, county/city lines and elevations of terrain noted (more about that later in the book).

Mission Statement

Then you must develop a short verbal description of what the artistic goals and mission of your company are. The person in charge of representing the company (probably you) should memorize this. It also helps if you *write it down*. This short mission statement has multiple uses — it can be used in all types of situations, such as for booking your company — by telephone or through brochures, on videos, in press releases and for grants. It can be elaborated on, enlarged, compacted, stretched — but still focuses on the essentials of your company. It's the basic five W's.

> *Who* are you?
> *What* do you do?
> *When* are you available for performance?
> *Where* do you perform?
> *Why* do you dance in this way?

Here is an example of our company's mission statement:

> Menagerie Dance Company is a duet dance company which involves the audience so that they see, hear and feel the joy and artistry of dance and motion. Our company tours throughout the year under the sponsorship of the Virginia Commission for the Arts, and has performed for over 100,000 children and adults in Virginia and throughout the United States. From the abstract to tales and legends, Menagerie provides a fast paced and educational program that will both entertain and inform.

Further detailed elaboration on the mission statement includes this more specific information:

> In each school performance, the audience sees 30 minutes of original dance followed by 15 minutes of creative audience participation where children gain first-hand knowledge of basic movement skills and creative problem solving through motion. Menagerie also offers residencies that include both performances and workshops. The company performs on a stage or in a gym or multipurpose room and provides its own sound and set.

Other issues will come up such as cost, technical needs and so forth, but those are not necessary to enumerate in the beginning.

Once you have defined whom you want to perform for, the geographic area where you want to tour, and have refined the concise verbal description of what your company is, then you are ready to begin in earnest. Marketing means that you let people know you exist as a dance company and that you have a worthwhile show that they might like to present. (The people who hire you are called "presenters" because they present you to their audience.) You can get the word out to presenters in a variety of ways.

One of the most effective ways is through liaisons with local arts councils and/or state/provincial arts councils. Affiliation with an arts council brings many benefits, such as clearing the way for your company to become eligible to apply for grants from the sponsoring council. Grant money makes it financially more feasible for nonprofit organizations like schools to hire you. Also, many for-profit corporations have philanthropic foundations associated with them or have set aside money to support worthy causes. Many of these corporations identify funding the arts as a worthy cause to support. Other philanthropic agencies, associations and clubs exist that may want to support your work so that you can present your performances to audiences who would otherwise not be able to afford your presentation.

Another good marketing tool is to attend booking conferences where you can set up a booth to distribute information and show videos of your work, network with other performers and company managers, and learn about vital issues to performers and presenters. Direct calls to individual presenters, while time consuming and nerve wracking, are perhaps the best marketing tool of all. Less effective but more traditional marketing means are direct mass mailing, employing an agent, and through paid advertising.

Arts Councils

The National Endowment for the Arts was created in the United States in 1965 and state arts councils subsequently were formed to help expand arts outreach across the country — so that not all arts activities would be concentrated only in major metropolitan areas like New York, Chicago, and Los Angeles. This act has had the transformative effect of nurturing a broad spectrum of arts across the U.S. As one professional writer, the late Jo Carson, said, a person doesn't have to be located in a major metropolitan area to be able to earn money from art.[1] That is certainly the case for us, because our company was able to tour from rural central Virginia. We were able to do this because of the extraordinary support of our state council, the Virginia Commission for the Arts (VCA). The VCA and its citizen advisory committee are responsible for bringing the arts to every corner of the state.

Some state arts councils are extremely proactive. For example, Ohio actually helps to book performances, provides lists of presenters, and offers lots of advice and encouragement to dance companies. (In North Carolina, Maryland and Rhode Island, dance has a place in school curriculums, so that dance companies have an easier time making contacts for fruitful residencies.) Some arts councils award outright grants after a review process. Other councils award grant money in a pool from which presenters of dance companies may receive up to fifty percent to help offset the dance company's fees.

Every state has an arts council. Lists are available at www.arts.endow.gov (the National Endowment for the Arts) and http://www.americansforthearts.org (Americans for the Arts). Every region has its arts council and the umbrella organization for all the arts councils in the U.S. is the National Endowment for the Arts, an organization that has accomplished a lot of good since its inception. The NEA funds activities that make it possible for children from diverse backgrounds and regions — such as inner-city children and children from poor rural mountain areas — to see dance. After performing over fifteen years through the sponsorship of the NEA, I include it high on the list of organizations that really have made a difference in the lives of children across America.

Investigate all arts councils — metropolitan, regional, national — and any others that can help you get your dance company seen. They are listed in many different directories, including the yellow pages. Some arts councils even sponsor yearly conferences where you can network with other performers. At these conferences you will inevitably meet and make friends with other performers, who will give you advice and maybe even leads for booking contacts. When we first appeared on the arts scene in Virginia, we met a mime, Larry Goldstein, who was really helpful and kind to us at a Virginia Commission for the Arts meeting. It was the beginning of a long and wonderful performing friendship. We have exchanged performing information with him through the years and even have been fortunate enough to be able to work together regularly in a yearly summer arts program. The benefits of having close, non-competitive relationships with other artists who perform for and work with children — across all the arts disciplines — are delightful as well as numerous. You learn a lot whenever you are around good art and good artists. You are very likely to meet these great folks if you attend conferences and other activities sponsored by arts councils.

Conferences and Showcases

Regional and national arts councils and organizations sponsor conferences on a large scale. They bring together performers and presenters in a trade show atmosphere, complete with opportunities to perform or "showcase" your company. Some examples are the Southeastern Arts Conference in Atlanta and the Northeast Presenters and Performers conference, held in different cities in the northeastern U.S. There are children's arts organizations like the International Performing Arts for Youth (http://www.ipayweb.org). IPAY is headquartered in Canada but has an active U.S. chapter. It hosts regional conferences and one national conference — heavy in theater company participation, but some dance companies participate also. Young Audiences (YA), an umbrella-type organization that acts as sponsoring agent for presenters to contact artists, is dedicated to bringing the performing arts into schools. YA has chapters in twenty-three states. In 2007 an astounding 5,260 artists performed for 7.5 million children in 22,000 performances through this organization. Its website is http://www.youngaudiences.org.

Normally, you must send an audition tape with your application before you will be invited by the sponsoring organization or arts council to "showcase" before a live audience at the conference. When you showcase, you are given anywhere from ten to thirty minutes of performance time in front of an audience of presenters — theater season managers, performing arts seasons sponsors, and similar people. Some large county school systems have their own separate booking conferences — such as Fairfax City, Virginia, in the Washington, D.C., metropolitan area. The advantage of marketing yourself this way is that you can expand your tour base, introduce your company to new audiences, and have a chance for presenters, including principals and teachers in school system conferences, to see you

Menagerie Dance Company in "standing" shapes from *Environs*. Choreography: Mark Magruder. Dancers: Ella and Mark Magruder (credit Andrewwildsphotography.com).

live rather than rely on video, website, or verbal descriptions of what you do. Remember, with dance, live is always better.

Always choose to showcase the very best part of your very best dance.[2] Make sure it is not your "greenest," (least rehearsed) work. The performance jitters are sure to move in when you are in a conference pressure cooker, where competition is keen, so help your dancers do their best. Ask them only to dance what they do best, even if it is not your latest work. All conferences, including the biggest of them all, the American Presenters and Performers Conference (APAP), held in New York City every year, rely not only on showcasing but also provide booths and tables to set up your informational posters, brochures, and videos. Find information at http://www.artspresenters.org. Most important, APAP provides a place for you (or your company representative) to station yourself and make direct booking agreements on the spot.

These conferences are wonderful venues to publicize your company. Unfortunately, as with most things that are wonderful, there are fees for attending and exhibiting at these conferences. Fees range from hundreds to thousands of dollars, depending on the size and clout of the sponsoring organization. "Yikes!" you say. However, used judiciously, these conferences are useful and excellent ways to market your company, especially after you have established a good track record locally and want to expand your touring area.

Agents and Agencies

You can hire an agent to represent you at conferences and to be in charge of booking your performances. However, to be represented by an excellent agent — one who knows how to promote dance well — you must be a hot item, with major reviews and performances that the critics are raving about. Don't waste the money on an agent if you are just beginning. Ivan Svoboda of Pentacle Arts Agency, one of the most reputable agencies representing dance, gave us this same advice early in our careers. It was excellent advice, because while it is true that you work harder and longer hours at representing yourself, you save on agent's fees and/or percentage cuts and can arrange your own tours and finances. In our company's case, after being courted by an agent, we agreed to be represented by his New York agency. But it never worked to our financial advantage; in fact it was the opposite. As a company we valued staying in the black financially. If we had counted on this particular agency to complete the booking for our season of touring, we never would have survived those years as a fiscally sound company.

Make sure if you do employ an agent, that you stipulate percentage basis — that is, the agent gets a percentage cut of each booked performance. It is unwise to enter into a financial agreement with an agent who requires you to pay other obligatory fees or preconference costs. If you are on a percentage basis only, this means that the agent must get you a booking before he gets paid — which is an added incentive for the agent to find you work. If you do decide to have an agent represent you, shop around and compare rates. Ask other performers in your area who are represented by agents or agencies what the going rate is before you sign any contracts with an agency. Rates vary from locale to locale and year to year.

A good agent takes the pressure of booking off a company director or choreographer. Not to have to worry about arranging performances can be an enormous relief and a gift of valuable time for the creating artist. It is difficult to do it all — choreographing, managing, dancing, and so forth. However, downsides do exist in working with an agent. When you must give an agent a percentage of your performance fee, sometimes you are forced to raise your price per performance, and this may have the bad effect of pricing your company out of the market. In addition, an agent may be unwilling to reduce your fees in a situation where you might want them reduced, such as a benefit performance for a cause or for a poor school, because the agent's monetary share would then decrease (or vice versa). Be careful and keep the lines of communication open. Call the presenters back who call you personally, even if you have an agent. There may be questions that only you can answer, or confusion with some important part of the contract. Don't relinquish your responsibility for communication with everyone concerned with a booking or residency of your company.

Finally, if you do decide to sign on with an agency then do your share to help the agent who is doing the booking for you be successful. A good agency works hard to promote and book all the performing arts groups that it represents. Provide all the booking promotional materials, photos and videos, and the like in the timely manner that the agent requests from you. Provide a clear sense of your best time schedule for performances. There is really no such thing as a hands-off approach to booking and marketing yourself, even when you have a good agent. As the old guy said, "Ain't nobody get something for nothing" and "You work with me, I'll work with you." You get the idea; a performer/agent relationship is ideally a partnership to everyone's mutual advantage. If it doesn't work, cut the apron strings and get out — quickly. Find a better agency or do it yourself. Booking on your own is possible; and you can survive it. You may even become friends with some of your booking contacts and presenters!

Chapter 5

Publicity

Development of good publicity material for your company must take place in several stages. The first stage is the preparatory one in which you must gather together photos, written reviews, and a short written description of your company and purpose. The prose style of your description needs to be energetic and upbeat, something that would want to make the reader come to see a performance of your work. Photos should create the same excitement in a viewer. Likewise, you need to choose the best things that people have said about your dance in published reviews, letters, or written comments.

Next, you need to seek out the most innovative graphic designer you can afford to help you design a logo, brochure, and poster for your company. These media materials are useful in myriad ways. You can use them as direct mail tools and as part of your press kit. Some companies have in house desktop publishing talent among their dancers and directors. However, if you know only a modest amount about graphic design, then this is an area where using a good professional really pays back the money that you invest.

How do you find a graphic designer? Most printing companies, especially the larger ones, have graphic designers on their staff. If you live far away from a sizable metropolitan area, you may have to do extra research to find the quality designer you want. Always opt for the best quality in all your printed materials. Photocopied brochures look shoddy and reflect poorly on your level of professionalism.

To find a good designer for our publicity materials we looked around for printed materials that caught our eye. One design that captured our attention was our state arts council touring guide. The images were bold and energetic and the layout had innovative use of photographic images. We did a little detective work and discovered the name of the graphic designer, who happened to live in a city two hours away. We made an appointment with the designer at her company and began a wonderful artistic relationship. We supplied the designer, Lisa, with all the photos that we had and the text for the brochure. Many telephone calls, faxes and visits to her office later, we had a logo, brochure and poster design that was great—in marked contrast to our first foray into the printed representation of our dance company. Our first graphic design adventure was a short-lived waste of time and money: we came out with a result that dismayed us and worse, a design that became unusable.

Logo

This is what we did wrong the first time. We went to a small design studio in a very small city near us and gave the designer our information. Then, rather than producing

Logo design for Menagerie Dance Company.

anything original, the designer "lifted" a design for our logo directly out of a famous children's book (unfortunately this is accepted practice among some unimaginative graphic designers!). We were shocked and protested against what seemed to us to be blatant plagiarism. The designer assured us that the book was public domain and that there would be no problem. This might have been true, but the unimaginative "borrowing" of a logo design gave us nothing original to represent our company with. Although the logo and the brochure looked slick, they really were not good marketing tools. So we eventually discarded them and started over. The second time around, we knew better than to stay too local in our search and also, we emphasized from the beginning with our newly chosen design firm that we wanted an *original* logo. We got it, and have always been proud of the result, seen below. The irony is that both logo designs — unoriginal and original — cost about the same.

Brochure

A brochure must represent as much of your range of choreography as possible, pictorially and thorough written description. However, when producing a paper representation of your company, pay attention to the seemingly small details. Make sure that the layout is done carefully and professionally in order that the entire document is aesthetically pleasing. This is where poor print quality or smudged ink is ruinous; it spoils the artful message that you are trying to convey about your dance company.

Pay attention also to the type of paper on which the brochure is printed. The tactile feel of the paper — its weight, whether it is coated with a gloss or sheen, and the actual fiber of the paper also reflect on the quality and worth of your show. Everyone has seen poorly photocopied flyers and usually judges the event or information accordingly.

A brochure should have fine quality photographs and/or very skillful drawings because the old adage "a picture speaks a thousand words" is true. It is usually much cheaper to use black-and-white photography or drawings, but color is eye catching. Realize, however, that the excellence of the photograph is primary. Do not use a color picture if the composition or details of the photo are poor or unclear.

The written text in a brochure should include a well-worded brief description of your company and the type of work you do. Use any short, positive quotes — even single words — from reviews that your company has received, to accompany your logo, photographs, and/or drawings. Include all contact information, like mailing address, telephone number, web pages, and email address. Remember to use a very legible font *and* a letter size that can be read easily. Remember the brochure must be perfectly edited and proofread. Always have two or three readers check the copy for mistakes before printing.

A brochure serves as an introduction to your company but does not substitute for the personal contact that your booking manager or you make by phone or in person at booking conferences. Most people will just glance at a brochure. Make sure your brochure is distinctive and that your reader/viewer can understand quickly what you are saying, and sees only the best visual representation of your dance company.

Poster

A poster needs, first and foremost, to have a large, eye-catching image and, second, just like your brochure, to be clear and legible. The difference is that a poster must be read from a distance. A startling and intriguing picture will demand attention and dance photo graphics instantly can accomplish this if the photo is of a leap or an "on the edge" movement.

A poster must grab the attention of a passer-by instantly, deliver a written identification of the company, and give a place where the performance — with location and time — will be held. Usually, most dance companies create a single poster for general distribution with a blank box where the details of each show can be handwritten or printed in — usually by the presenter.

If you leave this blank spot for writing in the pertinent details, you can send copies of your poster out in the mail ahead of time, and the organization that is hiring your dance company can fill in the time and place and be in charge of advertising your show.

Menagerie Dance Company poster. Poster Design: Lisa Cumby (credit Mary Gearhart).

In the case of a school, having a poster of your company before your performance generates excitement and expectation among the students, teachers, and staff. In the case of theaters or community venues, the sponsors need your posters to help bring in the audience.

Although you *can* send a copy of your poster on computer disk or through email for your presenter to print, it usually is considered the responsibility of the dance company to provide physical paper copies of posters due the expense of printing (and the risk of crashing your sponsor's email with a file that is too large if you send it via the Internet.) It is really to your advantage if you have your own posters printed up because then you control the quality of your image. If you do not provide a poster, you may be alarmed, shocked, or disappointed at what dance images your presenters create on their versions of posters that represent your company.

Website

A website is a great resource *IF* it can be accomplished without a lot of time or money and *IF* the result still looks professional. Poor coding (often resulting in images that overlap) represents shoddy quality in the same way that smudged ink on a brochure does. Many companies are available that can help with web page development. Always view the work of an individual designer or web design company before you choose them to do your web design. There may be nonprofit resources in your area through your local, state, or regional arts council. In the UK, the national umbrella arts council does a wonderful job presenting dance company links and web pages.

However, never create a website and think that it will do your marketing for you. It is merely one more convenient resource, a place for you to refer interested presenters and grant agencies that want to learn more about your company, to see pictures in your gallery, or to view your best filmed dance clips. Few people will bother to take the trouble to watch a video of a dance company that they are not familiar with, even on the web, unless previously contacted by phone or direct contacts at conferences.

Promotional Material Distribution — Pros and Cons of Mass Mailing

You can distribute press kits and information about your company in many ways — through the postal service, by fax, through email, or via social media. Your web page can be designed so that those interested in booking your company can download information. If you plan on using any mail or electronic form, make sure that the correct person is identified and that you spell the name correctly (the person to whom you are sending your press kit). All mail and promotional material sent out without a personal note or letter to a specific person is wasted time and energy. This takes research on your part. Even if you use a computer program that automatically personalizes your letter, be sure to write something relevant to the intended recipient, such as the name of a nearby school where you will be performing, the dates when you will be performing in the area, or even that you went to school at a nearby college — anything that makes you into a human being and not just another annoying piece of junk mail.

An important note: Do not send unsolicited promotional material through email. Most spam filters will catch your unsolicited email anyway, and there are legal restrictions on electronic information. The fastest way to upset your future presenters is to crash their email because you sent a picture, poster, or other material that blocked their mail access. Technology changes quickly. What is today's favorite mass mail distribution method may be outdated in an instant. (This is a major reason continually to transfer your performances onto the next technological advance in electronic format.) As these venues change and develop, you must keep pace, but don't assume the presenters you are attempting to reach will be up to date. This is one raison d'être for actual paper mail.

However, the same cautions hold for unsolicited brochures sent through the postal service. In fact, brochures unaccompanied by a personal letter or not preceded by a telephone call often end up in the circular file. You have to be around the dance world a long time and have an established name before presenters will seek you out — if even then. However, if you develop a website, the contents of your press kit (see below) should be on your site, as well as your relevant promotional materials.

The Press Kit

A press kit is something you need in addition to posters, logo, and brochure when you actually are set to begin the process of booking a tour. Most companies include their poster and brochure as a part of the press kit folder that is sent out to prospective presenters (ones whom you have previously contacted by telephone or at a conference). However, to save money, you can do as some companies do and eliminate the brochures and posters altogether. Concentrate on making a press kit that supplies lots of written information and actual photos of the company. The reason that this saves money is that you do not have to pay a graphic designer or incur the expense of printing good quality brochures.

There are two different approaches here; you must judge what type of written material is needed to help persuade a presenter (or principal) that your program will be suitable

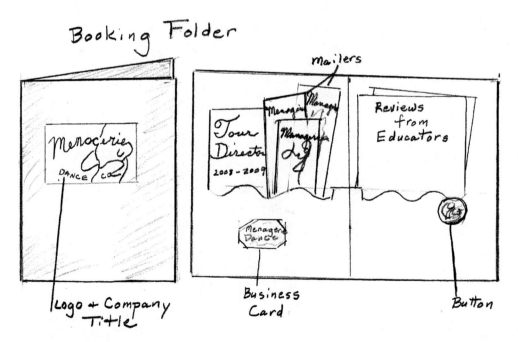

A dance company booking folder and contents of a press kit.

for their particular venue. In general, for the longer residencies through arts councils — or for multiple bookings of any kind — a full and complete press kit (folder style) is best. For a single school contact, a phone call with a follow-up cover letter and brochure is sufficient — as well as being a lot cheaper to mail. A press kit costs more to mail because it contains a number of items in a folder — perhaps even a video or DVD.

However, a complete press kit is essential to hand out at booking conferences and for booking larger residencies with multiple performances. In these instances more people are usually involved in the decision making process on whether or not to hire your company. The more information that you provide, the better able you are to compete with other companies that have more marketing resources than you have at your disposal. Also, the committee that makes the decisions for a residency or for a season of performances has more material on hand to understand and to evaluate your suitability for their needs.

A good press kit, first of all, looks professional. Its overall appearance and contents reflect you as a company, so take time to develop it. Press kits usually are compiled in a pocket 11 × 13 inch color folder. The cover may be shiny, matte, textured — anything that distinguishes yours from a stack of other folders. It is best to have the company name and logo somewhere on the outside of the folder. This is most easily and reasonably accomplished by sticking on a label that you have preprinted. The label should be printed on peel-and-stick paper so that you can prepare the folders ahead of time or create them as you need them.

More Detail About the Contents of the Press Kit..

Inside the press kit folder should be a separate page for each of the following:

BROCHURE AND/OR DESCRIPTION OF THE COMPANY This should include a focused, positive, and lively couple of paragraphs about who you are. The description is a short synopsis that introduces you and your company. Make your descriptive language "dance"— although exaggeration and hype turn people off. On the other hand, if you write the description like a lab report, you make the idea of your performance tough to sell to anyone! This must be, above all, a kindly and persuasive introduction — something that could be read on the radio and make people want to see your show.

COMPANY HISTORY Put all your interesting information about when and where and why the company was founded, as well as information about who founded it, on this page. Include background information about places where the company has performed and the dates, anecdotes about what motivated the founder to want to create the company, any special awards, and other pertinent and interesting facts about the company. This is actually fun to do, and it will make you feel proud about yourself and your dance work. Don't include too-personal material though; this is a marketing device, not a family or seasonal newsletter.

WRITTEN ENDORSEMENTS AND REVIEWS You can include formal newspaper reviews in their entirety or just use quotes. Clearly identify what publication published the review and who wrote it (remember to italicize the names of publications). Written endorsements are important too, quotes from teachers or principals who have liked your performance, thank you's from arts council directors, etc. But you say... "I haven't toured yet, how can

I have quotes?" If you have danced on stage, chances are that someone has written something about the show and better yet, you in particular. If not, as I mentioned earlier, do some free shows and hand out after performance evaluations to generate honest and praiseworthy remarks.

BIOGRAPHIES OF DANCERS AND CHOREOGRAPHERS It is always important to let your presenter — whether PTA president, principal or chair of a performing arts center — know where you are from, what schools you attended, and what companies you performed with or worked for. This helps people in professions that may come into contact with performing artists only rarely understand more about who you are and why you value dance. In addition, the information can be used as a "handle" to connect you to your presenters in other ways. Perhaps you attended the same college or have the same hobbies. When you work in educational environments such as schools, it is especially important to reassure your presenters that you have credentials, just as they do. Even if you are fresh out of college and are setting up a new company, it is important — even doubly so — to give yourself a niche, so to speak, in the arts, in dance, and as a human being.

DESCRIPTION of your current touring program — This should include a written summary of the subject of each dance or program, listed in the order that you plan to tour. List only the dances that you are willing to maintain in your repertoire. If you are planning to tour one program in fall and another in spring, then clearly indicate that. If you link (or are willing to link) your program with current standards of learning in education for the state in which you are touring, this is a great place to feature this — or to make note of this aspect of your performance so you can use it as a "selling" point in your telephone sales presentation. Schools often must justify any activity or expenditure in terms of its relevance to educational standards or its benefit to particular educational goals. Since the arts are included as core subjects in the American national educational goals for children, it is important that you understand how your program fits in the National Standards for Dance Education (http://www.aapherd.org/nda). If you think that your program relates to other core curricular standards, like those in science, math, or language arts (and dance is so broad — it must fit into at least one other curriculum category) or if it has a special mission such as education about a particular issue, like racism or violence, then describe how. Arts Edge is a web-based educational resource produced by the Kennedy Center for the Performing Arts where you can find everything from standards and lesson plans to job notices in the arts. It's a real treasure chest of creative ideas. Find it at http://www.artsedge.org.

A LIST OF WORKSHOPS OR TEACHER IN-SERVICE THAT YOU OFFER What can you teach? A residency can include classes as well as performances. Our company's list included children's workshops in creative dance, since that is a primary area of our expertise. We further divided our offerings into creative dance for individual grade levels, disabled/special education, identified gifted and talented children, and children interested in dance and drama. We offer workshops in different lengths — one forty-five-minute workshop in a large space like a gym or dance studio or three fifteen-minute workshops in the classroom, with creative dance activities that the children could do seated and while standing beside their seats. This latter format is an excellent arrangement for schools that have limited spaces for movement classes. This is also a good place to state how many children you will allow in a workshop (see Chapter 14). Our maximum is forty. Fewer students mean a better learning climate for students involved in the workshop. Over forty directly diminishes the experience. If you have no choice but to conduct a class or workshop with over forty children, then insist that the classroom teachers be present to assist with discipline. This is something you can impress on your contact person in the telephone prior to the performance.

Other workshops in dance technique are also great to offer. Outside of arts magnet schools, only a limited number of school systems have dance teachers, and schools rarely offer dance classes except in a few instances in music or physical education. Visiting teachers are a valuable opportunity for a principal to engage children who crave movement. Often children who suffer when confined to a desk really enjoy and appreciate a chance to leap and jump in a dance master class.

PRESS RELEASE A press release includes the five W's — Who, What, When, Where and Why. You supply who, what, and why and leave blanks for the when and where. All this should be included in the first paragraph. The second paragraph should have other details elaborating the facts in the first paragraph, and the third paragraph should have information that, while important and interesting, could be cut without damage to basic information by a newspaper editor who needed the extra column space. Your release should have the words *For Immediate Release* printed on the top of the page. You send the press release with your promotional material to demonstrate to your prospective presenters that you will supply them with the necessary back-up materials later, which will include a short video clip, additional posters and photos. In addition, if they offer you a contract, the presenter will have enough basic information to proceed with his promotion of your program — for a season or residency.

PHOTOS It is traditional to include black and white glossy 8" × 10" shots in each press folder. Lately, some companies have begun to include color photos (which also can be sent in digital form on the Internet) since more and more newspapers and other news outlets print in color. Make sure the black-and-white photos have high contrast, as gray tones and muddy images do not reproduce well. Each photo should be labeled on the back with the name of the dance and/or choreographer, the name of the dance company and the name of the photographer.

POSTER A poster is optional until after the booking is in place. Presenters of evening shows and matinees need multiple posters. They appreciate seeing what you have and are prepared to send them in advance. For school performances it is a nice touch to have a poster that can be displayed centrally to give a visual introduction to your performance ahead of time. (Refer to the poster advice earlier in this chapter.)

You can post the information from your press kit on a web page. Remember, any type of publicity is only as good as its distribution and follow-through. A brochure, videotape, DVD or web page does little good in marketing unless it is accompanied by real human contact through telephone calls, sales presentations, conference contacts, and the like.

Mass Mailing versus Direct Contact

There is really no substitute for person-to-person contact. Since most dancers are accustomed to communication through movement rather than through words, the direct method of marketing seems excruciating at first. Personal contact — through direct telephone calls and visits — is more effective for booking a tour than any other method: more effective than mass mailing, being listed on an approved arts council touring roster, going to a booking conference, or having an agent book you. It is with this method that I recommend that a dance company, new to the field, begin marketing. The next chapter details how to do this well. However, I want to introduce the concept now, along with all the other methods and processes of marketing.

When our company first began we made a thousand telephone calls. The telephone bill was massive (long distance, before cell phones and nationwide calling plans), but not as expensive as the bills for printing extra brochures, stuffing hundreds of letters in envelopes, and otherwise wasting postage through direct mail. In our company experience, for every ten to fifteen calls, one booking usually results. For every *two hundred* mailings (brochure in envelope plus personalized cover letter with handwritten note), *one* booking materializes.

In addition, it is through direct contact that you learn valuable information that may be useful now or later (such as who hires for assembly programs in city or county school systems — or whether the local school board forbids principals to book independently or without prior school board approval.) You learn if a particular principal knows of another school that might be interested in sharing a day or two of performances. This is to everyone's benefit. The schools save money through multiple performances (under these circumstances it is important to always give price breaks as a good customer relations gesture). The dance company saves on extensive time and travel costs. It costs less for a company to perform one show in the morning and travel to another school in the afternoon than to go out on two separate days. Also, it is even more cost efficient for the dance company to have one school host another school. The performance site should be the one with the best theater facilities.

Chapter 6

Finance

The decision of whether or not to incorporate as a nonprofit organization is one that all dance companies should weigh very carefully. There are several advantages and several disadvantages. In our case, we had no choice if we wanted to apply for a grant from our state arts council, which required nonprofit status before awarding grants or even considering grant applications. That requirement has since been relaxed, but is still in place for some granting agencies.

Nonprofit Incorporation

The advantage of nonprofit status is that it sends a message to prospective presenters of your company that you do indeed have a primary and previously demonstrated mission to serve the public, rather than just commercial goals. In addition, incorporation offers legal protection to your dance company. If you are involved in teaching and/or performing and someone (say, a student or audience member) is injured, and then the injured person files a claim to sue, the company can be sued but it is more difficult to sue individual people involved. This was our primary reason for maintaining our incorporation status even after our state arts council dropped the requirement. Since there were many instances in our performances where children would be entering and exiting the stage during the audience participation, and we toured not only performances but also children's and teacher's workshops, incorporation protected our personal finances. Fortunately, after fifteen years of touring our company, we never have had cause to use the incorporation as a defense. Nevertheless, having the protection was reassuring.

501(c)(3) nonprofit incorporation gives the advantage of making the company tax-exempt from U.S. federal income taxes. The company must still pay its employees' federal Social Security FICA, as well as state tax (if a state has an income tax). This is because nonprofit status means that while your company can make money to pay expenses such as employee salaries or to purchase needed equipment, like sound systems and costumes, the company cannot "go public"—that is, make excessive profits and/or sell shares to investors. You cannot make contributions to religious or political causes that are outside your company's mission.

The disadvantage is that once in the federal system as a corporation, either as commercial or nonprofit—you must file quarterly 941 forms and pay quarterly Social Security taxes on any wages paid. This is serious stuff; not to pay or not to file is to risk serious fines and major consequences. This is definitely extra work for whoever takes care of the company finances (or at the very least requires extra money if you have to employ an accountant because you don't want to deal with this type of thing). However, since most companies have a season and thus a limited number of pay periods, it is easy to file a form using zeros during the off season. If you are willing to read and follow the directions on the forms, you can actually decipher the tables and requirements without an accountant. At any rate, if you pay wages to your company members, you will have to pay tax in the U.S. even if you are not incorporated. In addition, in some states (like Virginia) there is a state incorporation fee that has to be paid each year.

Once you decide to obtain nonprofit status, the next step is to initiate the process, which is detailed and requires legal help. Since most beginning dance companies are not flush with cash, it is good to know that less costly legal help is available. There is a wonderful group called Volunteer Lawyers for the Arts (VLA), http://www.vla.ny.org, that offers legal workshops and also maintains a list of lawyers who are willing to serve the arts by doing pro bono (free) legal work. Professional and competent, this organization is an extraordinary resource. VLA found us a wonderful lawyer who was located only three hours' drive away from our rural area. He drew up all the necessary legal documents. We had to appoint a board of directors, whom we chose individually and carefully to make sure they understood and supported our mission. This is a group of people who have remained in the background in our company, but some companies select their directors so that they become an important source of fundraising, grant procurement, and business advice. Yearly meetings of the board are required, but they can be as minimal or as detailed as your organization needs.

The Board

One of the important issues of nonprofit incorporation is that you will be expected to name members to your dance company's board. These members must be selected carefully for their strengths and expertise. A multi-talented board can be an asset if you need to make contacts, to get advice, or when you need to raise money, or perhaps to cover start-up and ongoing expenses that your company incurs. Basically, the people who serve on your board should have — at the very least — dual roles of cheerleader and fundraiser for your organization.

For example, depending on the financial strength of whom you appoint to your board, these members themselves may wish to support your company through their own tax-deductible donations. Anyone can donate time or money to your dance company, even if you are not incorporated. Board members will be enthusiastic and supportive and may want to contribute to your company's financial stability. 501(c)(3) status just gives a donor assurance that the money is being spent on worthy dance company expenses rather than on personal expenses of any one individual.

In addition, in selecting your own board you may choose very useful individuals who will be able help you in supportive ways: with fundraising events such as auctions and dinners or with publicity by helping you get access to press coverage. In some instances board members even can give you astute feedback and advice about your show. Of course, the relationship between the board and the director can be difficult to navigate if there is a power struggle of any sort. The arts world is rife with stories of clashes between organization boards and directors. Therefore you may choose to circumvent these sorts of future problems by selecting members of your board from your trusted friends or even capable, co-operative family members so that you always will retain final say in all artistic and business decisions. Weigh the need for outside help with your own talents to help you decide how to appoint your board if you receive nonprofit status.

Some dance companies ask local, regional, or even national celebrities to serve as honorary members of their boards, not for the services they might render, but for the name recognition and status that these important people confer. The payback for the honorary members is that they can use their names to further a good cause, like your dance company! Theoretically, by linking your organization's name to a famous person, you establish legitimacy for your dance company in the eye of the public. Of course, for the good of your company this means that your honorary board member must be above reproach, and definitely out of the gossip headlines.

Developing a Business Plan

Your company needs a business plan. This can be elaborate or informal, written on the backside of an envelope or on the computer using a big spreadsheet. However you like, just make a plan. An informal plan might be: "We have X money to spend: this much can be for marketing — including marketing tools and media like brochures, posters, conferences; this is how much we will pay for each dancer for rehearsals and shows; and this is how we can make it all happen." By figuring out what your bottom line needs to be for production, marketing, and payroll, then you can determine how much you need to charge for each show and how many days and weeks of touring you need to meet your basic expenses.

Look at what other dance and theater companies who work in your area charge. If their fees are high, is it because they're larger, more experienced, or in demand? What can you charge to make yourself competitive as a company — in other words, what can the market bear? Where does your market come from? The answer will help you understand how to set the price for your fees. As we have discussed at the beginning of this chapter, your market most likely is composed of schools and theaters, but may also include arts councils, museums, libraries, festivals, and such. None of these types of venues are flush with cash. Even commercial theatrical venues have a bottom line. However, schools and PTAs do set aside money for enrichment because it is a vital component of education. Principals usually have small budget lines to use for worthy activities and projects at their schools. Funding sources for local arts councils that sponsor work in the schools and in theaters are donations, grants and government funding, and are especially earmarked for art. In the United States the folks at these institutions and agencies struggle to get the most from their limited dollars since government subsidies do not even begin to touch the monetary needs of schools, theaters, and arts-sponsoring organizations. (And no matter what pro-arts plank any one politician runs on in a particular election, this situation is not likely to change anytime soon. If history is any indication of the future, in the United States, the arts will *never* be well funded through government sources.

In other words, money always will be tight for your presenters and for your dance company. However, you must pay your dancers, or you won't keep them long! Keep in mind that your goal is to make sure you are the best quality performance group that the presenting organization has the privilege of hiring for their school or theater. Of course there are some exceptions to the "must pay performers" rule. For instance, if you have a student group, the young people who dance receive training through performance and are not usually paid for performing. The students' compensations are the wonderful experiences of travel and the personal growth gained from dancing.

Creating a Budget

To begin the process of setting your fees, figure out as precisely as possible (closely estimate) what it is going to cost you to produce your show. Then, once you figure out what your costs are you can determine what to charge for your performance — keeping in mind what other, similar companies charge. Factor in any grants you think you are likely to receive. (Although if you receive corporate grants, remember that they sometimes come with strings attached — you may end up wearing the commercial sponsor's logo. This in turn may involve you in a moral dilemma. Should you hawk commercial products? If you must to receive money from a company, are these the type products that are appropriate/healthy/non-exploitative of children?)

Allow for emergencies and cost overruns. Keep something in reserve so that under all circumstances you can stay in the black and out of debt. Debt is discouraging and is a red light to granting agencies. Debt signals that you have trouble with money management. If your company does have financial confusion, why should granting agencies risk their precious dollars — whether public or private — on you? *Stay in the black.* Fiscal responsibility: maintain it and make it your mantra. In truth, you will likely to end up using your own personal funds sometimes, but don't ever leave any other company or person unpaid. Nothing spoils a reputation like unpaid bills.

A detailed business plan is very useful and is worth the trouble it takes to figure out. It should include a line-by-line budget, similar to the one that is presented here:

Proposed Budget for a Dance Company

Proposed Revenues and Expenses for [Year–Year] Tour

Revenue from tour*	25,000.00
Total Assets	25,000.00
Debits from Tour	
1 Director/Dancer/Choreographer	7,500.00
1 Booking Manager/Dancer/Choreographer	7,500.00
Per Diem for Dancers	1,000.00
Child Care	1,000.00
Transportation	2,000.00
Heating	400.00
Motels	700.00
Electric	250.00
Postage	250.00
Video Production	1,000.00
Xerox	100.00
Arts Organization Membership	50.00
Costumes	400.00

Office Equipment	525.00
Telephone	600.00
Commissioned scores (music)	500.00
New Brochure & website maintenance	1,225.00
	25,000.00

*This budget is based on 15 full-day residencies, 3 evening performances and 4 single performances.

Grants and Grant Writing

All types of grants are worth applying for since money is always tight for the presenters of the performing arts. Corporate sponsorships are another avenue to fund your company. Our dance company's first grant came from the corporate world. The Green Giant Company believed that our performances and workshops in dance would benefit its workers' children who attended public school in the township of Ripon, Wisconsin, and funded us for that reason.

The best time to apply for a grant to help support your dance company is actually *after* your company has done some touring, unless your program is based on a special project concept that has a definite beginning and end and can only take place if you have a grant. The reason you should wait a year or so is that then you will have a good track record of both sound money management and performance accomplishments.

To begin the process of procuring funding through grants, first you must identify the sources through which you wish to seek a grant. These sources are usually obtained through information provided to you by the arts councils, dance and performing arts umbrella agencies and resource sites (listed in Appendix C at the end of this book), or through your own web searches. From this information you will have a list of national, state, and regional resources such as philanthropic organizations and businesses that contribute money to either community projects or arts-based proposals. Contact the organization that you are interested in obtaining the grant from to ask for the grant proposal forms or simply download them if they are available online. Sometimes the forms easily can be downloaded from websites, other times the forms will need to be faxed or mailed to you. Once you have the forms you can begin the business of writing a grant.

Carefully research the type of funding that the granting agency has given in the past. Make sure that your application fits with that organization's philanthropic mission. Failure to do so means wasted time for your organization (because writing a good grant application takes many, many hours, days, and even weeks on occasion). With a good understanding of the type of grant that you are applying for, it is more likely that you will be awarded the money.

Never wait until the last minute to begin the process of writing a grant. We found out the hard way that burning the midnight oil and rushing applications is a surefire way to lose grant awards. Last minute, hastily completed application forms usually look thrown together, are filled with clerical mistakes and omissions that reflect negatively on your performance company. If you are too lazy to spell correctly or to use proper grammar, then the grant reviewer will assume that you will be oblivious to the important financial details that are crucial in careful use of grant money. Likewise, a poorly put together grant with incomplete information indicates to the granting organization that the aesthetic quality of your program may also be lacking.

Below you will find the components necessary for a fundable grant application — "a good grant." Detailed instructions on how to create many of the components listed below are found throughout this book. Please refer to those chapters noted below in the chart for information.

A good grant includes:

1. A clear mission statement with detailed information about how the grant proposal serves the goals of both your company and the granting agency (see Chapter 4)
2. A detailed description of the proposed project and how and when it will take place (include company and project goals — see Chapter 1)
3. Narrative history of your company (include brochures, press materials — see Chapter 5)
4. Biographical information for the director/artistic director and financial manager (resume and/or written narrative)
5. A proven track record, such as a recent tour that has multiple bookings
6. Clearly proposed budget with realistic line items (reflects actual costs and prices)
7. Evidence of well-managed current operating budget for current fiscal year (see section just prior to this one in Chapter 6)
8. Reviews or written praise of your past work from school system or newspaper
9. Evaluations, fan mail from children/teachers/principals/arts administrators
10. High quality video/DVD of your best choreographed and produced work

When you write a detailed description of your project begin by restating the goals of your company. This is the case of having to "translate" your work for "foreign speakers" who may not have had experience with dance or any of the performing arts. *The grant readers may or may not know who you are, may or may not have a favorable view of the arts.* Depending on the granting agency, frame your application project description to be relevant to what that grant reviewer may understand.

For instance, if you are applying for a grant from a corporation, know the product that the corporation produces and who produces it and where. Then carefully describe how your proposal relates to the grant agency goals. (As in the previously stated example of our company's first grant, in an application to a food producing corporation we described how the children of the workers would benefit from seeing our performance.) Next you must carefully specify how this will take place, (performances and workshops, perhaps); where (what cities, states, provinces, schools, libraries, or colleges); the timetable for beginning and ending (actual dates including months and year); and finally how you will track and evaluate your project.

Are there benchmarks to gauge your progress toward fulfilling your grant goal? Think of how you will evaluate your project. Include this in your project description. Plan this with careful thought. Collaborate with psychologists or others who can help you track in a quantifiable way, for instance, and clearly state how you will accomplish this in the description of project section of the grant application. It is very important to the organization that will be the source of your grant — the philanthropic foundation, arts council, or government agency — for you to have a measurable way to learn if your project is on track or is a success. If they have this type of information, they can track benefits or results of your progress to see (and you can prove to them) that the grant money has been well spent in the service of *their* philanthropic or corporate goals.

One way to accomplish this is through surveys given to children or participants both before and after the project is complete. In our second grant application for funding (the first was rejected because it was hastily put together) we administered before and after surveys to the children with the help of our college grants officer and a professional psychologist on the college staff. (We discovered some very eye-opening data. For instance, boys went into our dance performance with an unfavorable attitude, but they came out almost 100 percent wanting to leap and jump — in other words, they wanted to dance after seeing a dance performance.)

Finally, remember project descriptions for grant proposals must include what journalists call "the five W's" — who, what, when, where, why. Carefully write the parts of your proposal to include each. Summarize the project in the first paragraph of the project description saying who will be the target audience or target group, and the types of activities that the target group will be involved in, as well as who will lead the project. Give the dates when these contact activities will occur, and where. Discuss why the project is important in terms of what goals and outcomes are involved. Then in the subsequent paragraphs of the project description provide every detail that you possibly can that explains each of these five W's in greater depth.

Make sure to scrutinize and recheck your submitted budgets before you send them out in your grant application. The spreadsheets or forms should line up in neat columns and be clear, coherent and free from mathematical mistakes. It is surprising how numbers can get bounced around — sometimes with disastrous results. Check your arithmetic.

You can volunteer free performances and distribute evaluation sheets — for the teachers, principals, and other audience members to fill in after they see your show — to get some written critical reaction to your program. If you have no newspaper reviews, it is critical to have outside evaluation of your work. (New graduates from colleges and universities can use peer reviews from student or faculty performances, for example.) Use letters or emails that extol your performances or your previous projects; this is the time and place to use them as recommendations. Or if you have dependable people who are willing to write positive recommendations, give written comments, and/or have their email addresses or telephone contact information made available, this is a great way to assure grant reviewers that you and your project proposal are worth the public or private philanthropic money you request. (Before you give out any contact information, make sure you have permission of the person whom you are listing or using.)

The resumes and biographical information of company director and of the manager should be current and professional. (Use action words — create, manage, run, organize, and so on.) List most recent positions and activities first and then go back in time. Be truthful and do not exaggerate your past. However, if you are just starting out in your career, do not forget that choreography is a leadership activity and that arts management is notable even if you were a student when you choreographed or produced a concert. List your competencies, education, work, and choreography, directing, managing, and performing experience. Grant application resumes do not need to be one-page documents. A resume of three pages is perfectly acceptable.

With grant applications, longer is better. In fact, there probably is a more favorable view on lengthy grant applications than on short ones. This makes sense if you regard the activity. You are asking for money, which you have not yet earned by work accomplished. The granting agency needs to be assured that you are dependable, have a strong track record of fiscal responsibility, and are competent enough (on the basis of your previous work) actually to accomplish your proposed project goal/s.

Have several different people read through your grant application before you submit it. It is amazing what computer software spelling and grammar checks will miss. In addition, just as with artistic matters, an outside eye is valuable. What is perfectly clear to you may not be to someone else and it is much better that that "someone else" be a friendly helper than the grant reviewer who is left puzzled as to what you are talking about. Try and choose one reader who is inside the performing world and one who is not, to get as many different perspectives as possible. If you know someone who is a spelling and grammar expert — use her.

Finally, before you mail your application, make sure to have your videotape cued up. Never expect any viewer to fast forward or rewind a tape — whether it is for a grant application, showcase, conference, or a single booking. And use your best video. By "best," I mean that you should try to avoid an empty screen filled with tiny, two-inch people dancing in a void. Print the identifying labels for the videotape on the computer, don't handwrite them. Place chapters in any DVD and make sure your DVDs are playable on different machines. Always send a copy, not your master video/DVD and include a stamped, self-addressed video mailer envelope with each tape/DVD. However, expect the rate of returned videos to be one in ten videos returned. (Sorry!)

Fundraising — Beyond Car Washes and Bake Sales

Sometimes a dance company needs to raise some money (capital). For example, this might be to pay for the start-up costs for graphic design, costume purchases, or even to pay for a set designer for the next show. If the revenue from the performance fees or from grant monies has not yet begun flowing in, or if extra expenses arise, here are eight tried and true methods for raising funds. (This is when having the help of active board members, willing associates, supportive friends, and family is a great advantage.)

1. Silent auctions — Often run as a part of a catered dinner. In this method as many people as you can find donate items that are then put out in a room or hall (sometimes with a starting monetary bid). Attendees are given numbers. They then view the objects and write their bid and number on the tag. The winner is the highest bidder.
2. Skills auctions — Organizers ask people to make gifts of things they can do that are valuable. For example, a lawyer could donate the drawing up of a will; a gardener could offer a lesson on herbs and supply the materials for a planter garden; or a mechanic gives a car tune-up. Using an auctioneer, skills are sold to highest bidder.
3. Lottery events *(where legal — make sure to check with local laws)* — A limited number of tickets are sold ahead of time, for a significant price and each printed with a number. At a dinner, held in a private restaurant, lodge, or club that is reserved for the evening, all the ticket numbers are put in a big bowl and drawn out, one by

one. Winners receive prizes that have been donated, and in some instances bought with pre-sold ticket funds. This can even be done with cash grand prizes coming from the advance sale ticket proceeds.

4. Fundraising dinners — Flyers and advertising are sent out about the goals of the fundraiser. The information also describes the meal (donated at cost by a person who is either a professional caterer or good enough to be one). Tickets are sold ahead and at the door. The dinner always should include a short performance, or actually may be scheduled to precede a large gala performance with preferential seating for dinner patrons at the theater.

5. Local festivals — Almost all areas have street fairs, food festivals, and other types of events where vendors can set up canopies and market crafts. Often you can talk with organizers who are happy to provide a space free or for a tiny fee. Using all the craft skills of your company members — which might include face painting, shoulder massages, selling costume hats, or running children's games and crafts — your company can earn money and have a booth that promotes your artistic goals with posters, T-shirts, and brochure. This is a wonderful way to open your company's goals to your community.

6. Pledge drives — Familiar to almost everyone who watches public television or listens to public radio in the U.S., fundraisers contact people on a list of identified possible donors and directly ask for money. This usually involves professional fundraisers or highly skilled and informed volunteers. This may also include ticket sales to a season of performances.

7. Advertisement through program ads and private donations — Someone from the dance company who is likeable, articulate, and persuasive, with a positive attitude, can visit local businesses and sell ads for your dance company's performance program. This involves getting the correct information and graphic layout of the ad such as the logo and wording. Someone from your dance company must designate ad size per amount of money donated prior to the sales. Another approach that works for private donors as well as businesses is to establish giving levels in which those who donate more are listed in the program in the order of the amount of their monetary gift — sponsors, patrons, and friends, for example.

8. Sponsorships — While being sponsored by one business can be lucrative because that company agrees to help out your dance company by giving money or supplies, there can be serious dilemmas involved. Just about everyone has heard about the perils of sponsorship. Some of the best sponsors of dance are tobacco companies, for instance. What does a sponsor require? Their logo on your set, wearing hats with their business logo, or just placing their name in your dance program? You must make sure you are comfortable with the businesses that offer to sponsor your company and understand what their sponsorship entails.

Chapter 7

Booking

Booking Materials List

To begin the process of booking, you need the following items:
- Map of state or region you plan to tour
- Multi-year calendar
- Logbook (sturdy blank notebook with easy-turning pages)
- Pens/pencils
- Telephone
- Lists of schools, performing venues and contact persons (see below)
- Uninterrupted and regularly scheduled time during the daily working hours 9–5

Optional but extremely convenient are a computer with Internet access, a quality printer, a fax machine, and an answering machine or voice mail system.

Finding Presenters

To begin, you need to get the names and addresses of schools and theaters or other performing possibilities such as libraries or festivals. One important source for larger venues is the American Presenters and Performers (APAP), http://www.artspresenters.org, and the International Performing Arts for Youth (IPAY), http://www.ipayweb.org/; both are mentioned in the section on conferences. The following section will focus primarily on finding lists and contacting schools since it is the intent of this book to encourage the most inclusive and broadest possible outreach for dance companies that perform for children. Performances in schools are where this broad reach is most possible and most effective.

For school contacts, each state has a department of education or DOE usually located in the state capital, and accessible on the Internet through their respective websites. The DOE has lists of all schools in a state (public and private), telephone numbers, and names of principals and headmasters. There are independent school associations such as NAIS (National Associations of Independent Schools) that provide information for private schools. The information usually is available to the public free or for a small charge if you are receiving printed books or listings.

In this information are lists of all school districts with all educational supervisors, including arts or enrichment supervisors; school superintendents; and the names, telephone numbers and addresses of every school and its principal. You can try contacting the top brass in a school system first if you wish. Occasionally you will find receptive administrators who are willing to contact for you the individual schools and principals within their school district to arrange performances of your dance company.

However, a better strategy is to contact individual schools directly and to ask to speak with their principal. If you contact the schools directly you can begin the actual date setting process, without waiting for a middle person to make arrangements for a performance. In addition, many individual principals are on the lookout for extra enrichment and are eager to find additional ways to improve their students' learning experience. Most principals realize that a good quality performance or assembly program also can be of tremendous motivational value. That is where you and your exciting dance company are welcome to enter the picture!

One way that you can contact a principal is by sending out a "sales representative." However, this is expensive and/or time consuming since you must either travel from school to school yourself or hire someone to travel and to represent your company. The more cost effective method is directly to call the principal. This method is known as "cold calling" and means that you personally telephone a prospective presenter (a principal or other person who may hire your company to perform) to introduce yourself and discuss what your company offers.

To do this efficiently, you need a good geographical sense (that is, a map) of where the presenter whom you call is located in your state or region (so you can build an efficient tour with less travel time between performances); a multi-year calendar and projected sense of when specifically you can tour in a given year, month, week and day; and, most importantly, a sturdy notebook to keep a log of the numbers you call.

In this logbook you need to record the telephone number, name of school, name of the contact person, and an abbreviated summary of your conversation. In your notes it is helpful to use codes, something short that you understand, such as:

N/A — no answer — so that you know to call back
ANM — answering machine — so you remember that you have left your information
TS — talked to secretary — so you remember that you need to call again
TPR — talked to principal — with result of conversation and any pertinent points that
    you discussed in the conversation

If you begin cold calling by telephone, remember that *persistence and a thick skin are important virtues.* (More about the thick skin later.) First ask to speak to the principal directly. It is important to have a list so that you can ask for the principal by name. If you know the name of the person to ask for, you appear more legitimate and less like an annoying salesperson to whoever answers the telephone. The secretary may connect you and then you can begin your introduction — otherwise known as your sales pitch. (You will see an example of a dance company "sales pitch" in the next section of this chapter.) More often, the secretary will ask your name, figure out that you are trying to sell something, and either tell you that the principal is unavailable or ask to take a message.

If you get this off-putting response, above all, be pleasant to the secretary. Secretaries have the responsibility to protect principals from harassment or unwelcome demands on their time. You can let the secretary know that you are performing at a neighboring school (if this is true) or touring in the state and then ask when will be the best time to call back the principal. Don't bother to leave a message; it is a waste of your time and money. Messages are returned approximately 1 percent of the time. Just call back at another time. Besides, a brief chat with the secretary can help you quietly check to see if you have the right pronunciation of the principal's name. This is crucial if you want someone's respectful attention. Remember how you feel when telemarketers mangle your name during those annoying dinnertime solicitation telephone calls? Try and get these details accurate if at all possible. And make a note of the phonetic pronunciation in your logbook for the return call.

Cold calling is most successful when you have an actual (and perceived by the person you are talking to) legitimacy behind you, such as a sponsorship by an arts council, a booking at a nearby school, or if you can give the name of the person who recommended that you call this particular school principal. Cold calling is more difficult in the beginning, but once you have made one booking in an area it gets easier. In my experience cold calling seems to have better results in the morning hours on Tuesdays, Wednesdays and Thursdays. Mondays and Fridays are just not great days for anyone! Use your afternoons, Mondays and Fridays for other office/dance tasks such as writing contracts, answering your mail, email, or rehearsing.

The Telephone Contact

The most important element of booking is the direct contact telephone call. (This is daunting to many dancers who would rather move than talk.) Each company needs its own personal sales approach, which may range from personal visits to email contacts, but direct telephone calls remain the most effective method of marketing dance to schools and other presenters. Below is a framework where you can begin once you have acquired a list of prospective presenters. Notice how useful the advance definition of your company's goals and the description of your program are.

Some notes before you begin: Never cradle the telephone between your head and neck. Get a hands-free telephone or just practice good posture. The quality of your voice will sound more assured and professional if you're not contorting your vocal cords by trying to hold a receiver with your neck and shoulder. Do not use a speakerphone. Most speakerphone conversations have a tinny quality, and they suggest to the person on the other end that you are only addressing them with half your attention and/or that they may not be engaged in a private conversation with you.

Never type on a keyboard while talking on the phone. The person can hear you and, for all they know, you might be answering your email or be in a chat room instead of listening to them with undivided attention. Etiquette is crucial in a sales situation, as it is in all human relations. If you want to be taken seriously, you have to create a situation on the telephone where you are not just a flat, disembodied voice but a real person. Roll your shoulders, find your dancer's "center," take a sip of water, breathe deeply, relax and dial.

Now that you know what not to do when you are making a telephone call to a presenter, next read a sample script that gives an example of what you should do. It is a good idea actually to write out your own script. Then practice saying it until you have it memorized in order not to sound like you're reading it. Practice talking out loud. It makes a big difference in terms of nerves and preparedness.

The framework of the call:

Dial the number. Once you make it through the "fortress" of the secretary (as detailed earlier in this section) then begin...

"Hello, Mr./Ms. _____, I'm _____, from [your dance company]. I was given your name by _____ [or] we tour under the sponsorship of _____ Arts Council [and/or] we will be touring in your area _____ in *month* of next year" [*brief pause to catch your breath but not to invite comment*]. "We have an (educational) assembly program [or] evening concert for children, that deals with _____ [*standards of learning subject such as science, music, specific culture, Native American folktales or etc.*]. "May I send you information about our program?" [**If Y then ask:*] "Would you like to learn more about our program?" [*If Y then ask:*] "Is this a good time to discuss it?" [*If Y, then continue with more description of your program, etc., and to answer the principal's specific questions.*

If the principal seems open and receptive, ask: "Would you like to receive more information through the mail?" [*If the answer is Y, then carefully make a note of all the pertinent contact information, such as name, title of the person to whom you are speaking and mailing address so that you can be sure the company information reaches the right hands.*] *After concluding the call, mail a full press kit with a personal note indicating how much you enjoyed talking with the person and how you look forward to the chance to work together.*

When you mail it, put To the Attention of Name of Contact Person on the envelope to assure that the specific person gets your information, otherwise a secretary may just throw it away. If, better yet, the answer to your previous question is an almost unheard of] "Yes, I'd like to arrange for a performance RIGHT NOW!" [*Then make sure to get preferred dates and times and begin the process of sending promotional material, press kit and contracts immediately.*]

[*If the answer to your previous question* "Is this a good time to discuss it *(the program you offer)*?" *is N then politely ask*] "When would be a better time to talk more in depth about the program that we offer?" [*Note it. Check to make sure you have the correct address of the principal and school. Then thank the principal for his/her time and attention and hang up.*] *Make note of the pertinent information in your logbook. Each calling session should include not only cold calls, but return calls to principals who were out when you first called and principals who have received your information and might be reading to give you a firm yes or no.*

At the end of your calling session, you must complete the necessary office work that is needed to follow your timeline for mailings (see later in this chapter) and keeping in contact with the people with whom you have talked during this session and previously. This will include mailing out press kits to interested principals and other presenters with whom you have talked during your calling sessions this time, returning calls to principals and contacts with whom you had left messages or who couldn't talk on the day you contacted them but still wanted you to call back, writing contracts as you make verbal agreements with presenters, sending extra information that a presenter asks for, such as more

---

*If the answer to your first question, "Would you like to learn more about our program?" is "no," remember to say thank you before you hang up, also make a note in your logbook, and read the next section, When the Answer Is "No."

brochures, posters, videos, and answering email. A calling session may last anywhere from fifteen minutes to three hours; the time to stop is when you are too exhausted to sound enthusiastic about the dances that you tour. A workable time plan is to use the telephone for one to two hours in the morning and spend the remainder of the day doing the mailings, or rehearsing.

When the Answer Is "No": The Emotion of Rejection, or Why You Need a Thick Skin

Before you go any further in this process of booking, you must steel yourself for the word "no." It is odd how you can think that you are tough, resilient and flexible until you hear "no" applied to your dance company's chance for a performance opportunity. A rejection can make the proverbial "great pit of despair" well up in your heart until it totally obscures your sense of self-worth and future chances for success, especially if you are the choreographer or dancer in your own company!

However normal a reaction it is, to be successful in booking, despair cannot be allowed to take up residence in your psyche. It is OK to feel discouragement momentarily, but it is not OK to let it take over your job and love of dance! Think of it this way; a "no" is just a quick way for you to learn that it is time to go on to the next, better opportunity. A "no" is not a personal indictment of your company's ability to put on a good show, or a "put-down" of your personal dancing/choreographic ability. It is primarily an indicator that funding is tight for the arts in schools and other settings. Perhaps when you call again in the following booking season, things will be better financially for that particular school or performance presenter.

Surprisingly, this "better luck next year" scenario is often the case (especially if you have been cordial and persuasive in your first telephone presentation). Just remember, that while there is a story behind each rejection, you do not have to take ownership of that story, unless you have forgotten to do something crucial, such as making sure your communications are clearly presented to the principal. Being refused an opportunity to perform is not your fault unless your company previously has failed to establish a good reputation for quality work or for being prompt or polite when touring. Barring those possibilities, a "no" is a signal of someone else's difficulty (usually financial). You just have to go on booking until you find the right match—where children will have the chance to enjoy dance and your company will have the chance to perform! That thought is the shield to put around your heart when it is under "disappointment attack'" from a "no"!

For every fifteen calls you make, you will be able to get through your speech in only about six of them before you hear the word "no." Of those six, you will be a lucky person if you have one person say he is interested in talking more about a performance. This is the average: one "maybe yes" in fifteen calls. It sounds awful, doesn't it? Consider the alternative. One "maybe yes" for two hundred full publicity mailings. Unsolicited mailings (usually a cover letter and the press kit) cost in postage, time and effort, not to mention that most unsolicited mailings are added only to a school's circular file. Even if you receive a "no" from cold calling, chances are, the next year the principal or presenter will remember your name and listen a little more carefully. Perhaps he/she will even give you leads to pursue, if not try to find sources of funding to host your company, especially if your company has performed successfully elsewhere in the same or neighboring school system. Do not take a "no" personally. Booking is like perfecting a difficult dance step. When did you ever dance one perfectly the very first time you tried? You just need discipline, persistence and a thick skin!

When the Answer Is Yes: How to Arrange Performances into a Tour

The shape of a tour is part design, part chance choreography. The design part comes from you, the chance part from the presenters who hire you. Before you begin to settle on a specific day to perform in a school or theater, you must have a clear idea of when it is actually possible to gather your dancers together and set off "on the road." If you have been working with other dancers beside yourself, you have an established rehearsal time and you will need to have a commitment from your dancers for a period of time in which they are available.

With this specific knowledge, you begin to lay the foundation of dates on a calendar as you negotiate with schools and other presenters. This is completely dependent upon your dancers' freedom and availability of time. Are you setting aside three consecutive weeks in May and/or October? How about spreading the performances out every other day to help prevent dancer injuries?

Much is also dependent upon whether you plan to travel in a close radius or farther. If you are touring in your immediate area and your dancers are flexible with time, your touring schedule will not require overnight stays in motels. This cuts down on your overhead costs for lodging and allows you to go in different directions from home/rehearsal/studio base each day. If, on the other hand, you are planning to tour at a greater distance, you must arrange the performances to minimize the amount of driving time in between performances. Dancers get stiff and exhausted the longer they ride in a car, which in turn affects their performance. Long drives with a lot of backtracking miles on the road waste time, energy and gasoline. Plan the sequence of bookings carefully and listen to the advice of principals and presenters about the logical sequencing of particular performance locales.

Another thing to think about in the beginning is the question of how many performances and/or workshops your company can perform in a day. If you have a show that has few props and not much set, and your dancers are young and full of energy, depending on the length of performance, your company may be able to offer multiple performances a day. The most our company ever performed was three forty-five minute performances in one day, with two back-to-back performances (one at nine and one at ten) in the morning and the third performance in the afternoon. Large schools prefer this type of schedule since they can get a lot of children in to see your performances and not have to book two consecutive days or choose only one group to see the performance. Or they may want to split a day with neighboring schools. However, this is terribly grueling for dancers, with three complete setups, performances and strikes (takedown) of the sets. A day with three performances should be at the most an occasional exception rather than the rule because it is very difficult to sustain without the dancers developing injuries, exhaustion and/or depression. Try to negotiate a two or more day multiple performance residency with the school. Offer substantial discounts to encourage a residency rather than try to cram in all the performances in one day. Your company will fare better in the long run from a health and emotional standpoint, and your financial bottom line will actually improve. Another day in the motel is easier to pay for than training a brand new dancer in mid-season to replace an overworked, exhausted, and injured one.

A full but workable daily schedule is having two back-to-back performances in the morning and a workshop in the afternoon. Schools often prefer to have one performance in the afternoon and one in the afternoon. This set up is actually harder for the dancers because it means that they have to warm up twice, put on make up twice, *and* change back into cold and damp costumes. (If you cannot avoid this, at least encourage the dancers to dry out their costumes during lunch!)

The third common booking schedule is to travel between two schools during the day, with one performance in the morning and another in the afternoon. If you book this way, make sure the schools are very near one another and you have a personal guide or perfectly clear directions. (See the epilogue, Chapter 28, to read some of our fantastic tales of travel and touring between shows.) If a principal offers to make contact with another school for you in order to receive a discounted price (full day discount rather than the higher-priced individual performance per school) then by all means agree; everyone wins in this situation. Just make sure you personally contact the other school to double-check the arrangements and be clear about contracts and publicity with the second school.

How to Create and Exchange a Contract

When the answer is yes, and you have made an agreement to perform in a school or other venue such as a children's theater or library, then the next important step is to legalize and confirm the agreement by an exchange of contracts. A sample contract is shown next:

Sponsor Contract

On [day, month, date, and year] our organization will have [*Your Dance Company*] in residence. [*Your Dance Company*] will provide [3 (three)] functions that day. Our organization will pay [*Your Dance Company*] [$1200] on the day of the residency. The [state] Commission for the Arts will reimburse [$600] to your school. The details of the residency are as follows:

[2 performances 8:45 and 9:45 A.M. and 1 workshop 1:00 P.M. for grade 4]

The performances will include dances appropriate for the age group. Maximum number in each audience is not to exceed 350.

Schools will provide clean (damp mopped or vacuumed), well-lighted performance area with access to electrical outlets and dressing room (with appropriate ventilation/heat). Schools must clear performance space of all desks, risers, chairs, etc. at least one hour before performance is scheduled to begin. Performance floor—if wood—must be free of splinters—if carpeted—must be free of staples or sharp objects.

In the event of cancellation due to inclement weather or unforeseen circumstances, the performance will be rescheduled for another date.

Please sign and return to:

                                            (Signed) _____
[Your Dance Company]   Representative, *[Your Dance Company]*
Box 123
City, State Zip   Date: *[month, date, year]*
[Tel. #]   (Signed)_____
[Email address]   Sponsor Organization Representative

                                            Date: _____

By signing this contract both parties agree to the above terms.

                                            [School Name]
                                            [Street Address]
                                            [Town, State, zip code]
                                            Contact person: *[Name & tel.#]*
                                            Email: [_____]

This contract is contingent on full funding by the [State] Commission for the Arts
_____

You will want multiple copies of the contract, all to be signed by both parties: one for the principal/presenter to keep for their records; one to be signed and returned to you; and a third may be required by granting agencies before they can release funds. Each contract needs to have a clause to allow for unforeseen problems (sometimes called an "Act of God" clause) such as ice and snow, floods, war, or other disasters. This also addresses the problems of what to do if a booking has to be cancelled. It makes sure that once a party has agreed to a date, that it will be rescheduled rather than cancelled permanently.

During our fifteen-year touring period, our company faced a number of postponed performances due to snow and other issues. Only rarely have presenters actually broken contracts. Usually cancellations are due to loss of funding revenue — such as drastic budget cuts. Under these conditions, since they happen very rarely (only three times in fifteen years for our company) the best thing is just to accept the cancellation and let the presenter know that should the funds be restored for the next year you would very much like to perform for them. Usually schools and presenters are embarrassed and apologetic and give plenty of advance notice so that you can fix the hole that has been created in your touring schedule. It is discouraging if you have allocated part of a grant for that presenter. Normally, however, state arts agencies and other funding sources will not count this cancellation against you in future funding applications. This is a legitimate concern because some states arts councils only allocate funds directly to presenters, who then pay you the grant proportion of the funds plus their share of the performance fee. In this instance, if you have designated funds that are unallocated from one year, the next year your company may not receive as large a dollar amount as it did previously, due to a perceived lack of work (appeal or viability) on your account.

We were lucky as a company never to have a presenter fail to pay us after we had performed, although some did delay payment too long. (That is why we began to ask for payment on the day of the performance.) The worst instance of contract breaking that we know of happened to a prominent children's-theater company in the school touring circuit. After a week's completed residency of multiple performances each day, the arts council that hired them claimed that it had no funds and could not pay for the already completed residency. This was a contract loss in the thousands of dollars, for a fine and reputable company with four performers and a large support staff. Even though the theater company had a legal signed contract, they decided not to sue the arts council presenter, figuring that they, the theater company, stood to lose more in a lawsuit by developing a litigious reputation. Also, they believed that the arts council director was not malicious, just a poor money manager. The theater company chalked it up as a donation to the arts!

Our most troublesome incident concerning a contract occurred as we literally were walking out the door to begin a three-hour drive to perform an evening show, for which we had been in heavy rehearsal for three weeks. The telephone rang and a nervous voice identified herself as second in command at the _____ Chamber of Commerce, our evening presenter. The voice then assured us that the newspaper coverage, publicity, and everything else were ready for us that night, except for one problem — there was no theater.

Dumbfounded, we listened in amazement as she then told us how the head of the chamber of commerce was away at a photo shoot and no one at the facility where we were scheduled to perform knew anything about opening the building. According to her, the building's alarms were set; no one was authorized to turn them off and no janitor could be reached. The weeks of heavy rehearsal and the knowledge that we had exchanged contracts sixteen months previously (plus kept up timely contacts) loomed over us. This was the closest our company had come to ever being stood up.

Thinking fast, we told the second in command to keep looking for the "chief" and an available janitor and to call us back. When she called again in half an hour, we had thought of an alternative plan. When she again told us that nothing had changed, we presented her with an alternative. We instructed her to put a sign on the door of the facility saying the performance was cancelled due to "problems with the facility." Then we told her to arrange a daytime school residency at the local elementary school in that same town.

This was an inconvenience to us, to have to rebook a tour event, but more than fair to the chamber of commerce. Better yet, it served our artistic mission of outreach to the children. We completed the performance later in the month, and the chamber of commerce, apologetically and embarrassedly, paid us. Anything and everything can happen in touring, but usually with some flexibility, matters can be resolved.

Establishing a Timeline

Once you have made the first contact and negotiated a performance day, you need to set a clear sequence for the remainder of the publicity, contacts, and so on to support each booking on a tour. It should look something like this:

1st week	Telephone call and first contact Mailing press kit if requested
Same week	If needed, second telephone call to discuss or confirm dates or relay new information

ASAP/Next day	Contract exchange
2nd Week After Receiving Signed Contract	Send publicity packet, posters, technical requirement sheet, and teaching guide if you are performing for a school (with instructions on how to distribute it to teachers)
2 months	Letter requesting directions and maps, and to detail payment protocol (if grant agencies are involved, there may be different ways you will receive funds other than by one check from the presenting organization). Confirm receipt of teaching guide.
1 week to 3 days Before the Performance	Telephone call to confirm your performance date and time(s), answer any last minute questions, to remind them of your technical requirements — such as a clean, clear stage space, well lighted (the janitor may need to change light bulbs if they do not have theatrical lighting instruments). Ask questions again about stage curtains, wings, and type of floor surface. Give your estimated arrival time and specify if you need help unloading.
Day of	Arrive early at space to set up

Teaching Guides for Schools

For schools, you need to prepare teaching guides to send to each school well ahead of your performance visit. With these guides teachers can prepare lessons or use them to relate your work to their classroom topics. You do not want to be a "drop-in, drop-out" company that comes and does your work (extraneous to the topics taught) and is quickly forgotten.

Every dance has a theme or idea and usually it relates to the standards of learning or curriculum goals in one area. At the very least the librarian could use the material to select books for a school library display. Creative teachers (and there are many whom we have met in the public and private school systems where our company toured) can take a study guide and "run with it." After these teachers use your guide, their students will arrive to your performance so well prepared for the experience that it will be a sheer delight to perform for them. These children will ask thoughtful and relevant questions. You will feel that you are performing to an eager, expectant, and educated audience of children and adults.

Teachers and principals, on the other hand, will be amazed to see how readily the children take an interest in science or literature concepts when they are presented through dance, as a result of a thorough preparation for your performance and the performance itself.

Our dances *Symbiosis* and *Metamorphosis*, two works that took inspiration from the science concepts, were wildly popular with children and with adults alike. For our teacher guides we used the relevant science topics to spin off many suggestions in our guides for teachers.

Here is a sample teacher activity guide for our dance, *Symbiosis:*

Ideas to Explore Before Our Residency

Symbiosis is a give-and-take association for the mutual benefits of two different species. In this dance we will be showing this relationship by using trust and support to do many different lifts and balances.

Menagerie Dance Company. Dancers Karla Booth and Mark Magruder in *Fog Woman & Raven*. Choreography: Mark Magruder (credit Lee Luther, Jr.).

Your class might study the symbiotic associations in nature like the wrasse and moray eel, crocodile and crocodile bird, or the clownfish and the sea anemone. These are amazing relationships in nature and often very important ones. When all the cleaner fishes (wrasse) were removed from a reef in the Bahamas, in two weeks almost no fish were left in that area. The fish that remained were left in poor condition.

Shape is one of the focus points in this dance. The human body can make many shapes. Talk about the joints in the body: gliding, ball and socket, and hinge. Use sculpture or paintings — talk about positive and negative space. (The body is positive space and the voids around it are negative.) Talk about symmetric and asymmetric relationships.

Some references on symbiotic associations are: *The Fishes, the Plants and the Birds* by Life Nature Library, *Wonders of Nature* by Linsemaier, *Fish Do the Strangest Things* by Hornblow. An excellent series of dance films is available through the Virginia Museum: *Space, Shape, Time, Energy* and *The Body as an Instrument* by Murray Louis.

Scientific aspects of dance are a rich source for teacher guides. All well and good, you might say, if you are using those topics as inspiration or subjects for your dance. But what does science have to do with dance if you are not dancing cellular division, for instance? Well, just consider this. A number of years ago Professor Kenneth Law published a book called *The Physics of Dance*.[1] This is a case in point. A partnered lift in any form of dance is a study in force, levers, inertia, mass — in short, it is filled with educational "handles" to bring in to your performance presentation and to help teachers find a topic they can teach from your presentation that relates to their state-mandated standards of learning.

Social and historical topics also are rich sources for teacher guides. Dance, in itself, is a powerful conveyor of social bonding.[2] With predictable and delightful regularity, a predominant culture encounters traditions, through immigration and other forms of assimilation, that are different ways of both living and dancing. This usually results in some form of "cultural fusion."[3] Blending of cultural art forms has given us many new dance forms — for example, break dancing or hip hop. These types of dance are fruitful educational topics for teacher guides when presented with sensitivity and flair. In any case it is important to examine your own choreography from as many angles as possible so that you can present useful and informative guides for teachers.

The Teaching Guide must contain:

A. Before and after — a synopsis of each dance to educate the children before they view the dance, topics for discussion that pertain to some aspect of the dance, and a list of movement activities to do beside the desks or even while seated at a desk, such as an "energy pass" while standing or sitting, using different types of energy and movement qualities,

B. Bibliography — of books, videos and websites that relate to your program. For instance, for our program *Stars and Constellations*, we listed the books *365 Starry Nights*, by Chet Atkins,[4] another book about the Navajo legend of how the stars were put in the sky; and a NASA website of planet Mars pictures. Also included in the bibliography were several texts that we found particularly good guides to help teachers introduce movement and dance into their own teaching, by authors Anne Green Gilbert,[5] Susan McGreevy-Nichols,[6] and Sue Stinson.[7]

Sweet Briar College Dance Concert, *Society of Insects*. Choreography: Mark Magruder. Dancers (from top to bottom): Natalie King, Mark Magruder, Angel Milone (credit Andrew wildsphotography.com).

C. Biographies of the choreographer and dancers in the company — brief bios of the performers help the teachers and students find things in common with the visitors to their school. This may help inspire a child to think — "I can become a dancer." Knowing more about the hard work a dancer has had to do — such as attending college and majoring in dance (or other subjects) — and where the dancers have performed helps foster an attitude of respect for the people who are onstage.

D. Cover letter for the teaching packet — With the teacher guide mailing enclose a letter that explains how the guide should be duplicated and distributed to all teachers whose students will see your show.

Technical Requirement Sheet for Schools or Theaters

Enclosed in the same mailing that contains the teacher guide should be a technical requirement sheet. This is a page of requirements (like a clean, clear performing space) that your company needs to make sure the performance goes smoothly. It is useful to have one minimal type of technical requirement sheet for schools and a more complex one for theaters. Examples of both are shown in the following section.

A sample technical requirement sheet for schools:

Technical Requirement Sheet for Schools   *[Your Dance Company]*
[Telephone #] [FAX #] [Email address]
Contact: [Name of Your Dance Company Representative]

Our company will arrive one and a half hours prior to performance time to set up. Please have someone who is familiar with the performing space available to direct us to the electrical outlets and lighting control. Check the electrical outlet ahead of our arrival to make sure it is on. Our company is a contemporary modern dance company. Most of the pieces of choreography will be performed without shoes. Please ensure the dancers' safety in your school so that they can provide the best show possible. Schools will provide a performing space that is:

1. Safe — If the performing surface is wood, it must be free from splinters or any sharp protrusions. All dangerous surfaces must be sanded or securely taped with duct tape. If carpeting, all staples, etc. must be removed.
2. Clean, vacuum and/or wet mop, and then dry the floor before *[Your Dance Company]* arrives.
3. Well lighted (burned out bulbs should be replaced.) Make sure all lighting instruments are in good working order and are focused to give general illumination throughout the stage.
4. Free from obstructions — All risers, desks, band music stands, P.E. equipment, etc. should be moved prior to the company's arrival.
5. Access to a dressing room, or teacher's lounge.
6. Drinking water — Water fountain access, pitcher of water with 2 cups or two bottled waters available near backstage.

Our company can and has been flexible as regards stage dimensions, but smaller than 20' by 25' diminishes the theatrical effect. Side wings are needed, although the company can bring portable wings if there are none.

The company brings its own sound system.

Please call if there are questions or problems with any technical requirements.

Next is a second sample technical requirement sheet that has been modified from the one above. This one is for performances that will take place in theaters. Notice that although the requirements are much the same, in this second sheet there are more detailed instructions that would be useful to a theatrical technical designer. Professional theater personnel expect specific technical requests that are individual to each company:

Technical Requirement Sheet for Theaters   *[Your Dance Company]*
[Telephone #] [FAX #] [Email address]
Contact: [Name of Your Dance Company Representative]*

Our company is a contemporary modern dance company. Most of the pieces of choreography will be performed without shoes. Please ensure the dancers' safety in your theater so that they can provide the best show possible. In addition it is important that the theater be ready for technical rehearsal at the scheduled time and that there be enough technical personnel to accomplish this before the rehearsal so that rehearsal time can be used setting lights, sound cues, and all the activities which help achieve a smooth performance.

Presenter will provide a:
1. Safe
2. Clean
3. Well-lighted performing space
4. Free from obstructions
5. At least 20' by 25'
6. One light board operator and one sound operator (if sound system is part of the theater equipment) and at least one backstage person for rehearsal and performance, and ushers.
7. A clean, well-heated or ventilated dressing room
8. Drinking water
   A. The best surface is either a wooden floor or a portable dance floor. If the performing surface is concrete, then the presenter must provide a portable dance floor and secure it firmly in place with duct tape. If the performing space is wood then it must be free from splinters or any sharp protrusions.
   B. All dangerous surfaces must be sanded or securely covered with duct tape.
   C. Please vacuum and wet mop the floor before the scheduled rehearsal time.
   D. Make sure all lighting instruments are in good working order and are focused to give general illumination through out the stage. The more complex the capacity to set lighting cues, the longer the rehearsal time should be.
   E. All risers, props, previous sets for theater productions or any obstructions must be removed prior to rehearsal by presenter's staff or theater technicians.
   F. *[Your Dance Company]* can and has been flexible as regards stage dimensions, but smaller than 20' by 25' diminishes the theatrical effects. Side wings are needed, although the company can bring portable wings if there are none.
   G. The company also can bring its own sound system if the theater does not have one, however if a house system is in place, it usually sounds better. All sound is on CD.

Please make sure the dressing room temperature is comfortable.
Water fountain access, pitcher of water with two cups, or 2 bottled waters should be available near backstage.

*Please call if there are questions or problems with any technical requirements.

Menagerie Dance Company in theater performance of *Symbiosis*. Choreography: Mark Magruder. Dancers: Mark and Ella Magruder (credit Mary Gearhart).

Our company toured for years without technical requirement sheets. However, much confusion is eliminated if you communicate your needs ahead of time. Technical requirement sheets certainly do not eliminate all problems, but they go a long way toward making load in and set-up much more efficient and pleasant.

Directions to the School or Theater

In the cover letter that explains how to distribute the teacher guide and mentions the technical requirement sheet, you may decide to insert a request for detailed directions and/or a map to the school. You can request the directions later in a separate mailing or telephone call, but if you request them when you send the teacher guide and technical requirement sheet, you save on postage or telephone expenses. If you are doing a sizable residency that includes more than one school, sometimes the arts council or residency sponsor will provide a person to guide you from school to school. This is especially important if you are on a confusing or poorly marked roadway. Even with a good map (online or with GPS), directions can be confusing, so always ask for help rather than driving on and on.

Programs and Public Service Announcements

School performances do not need paper programs, but performances in theaters and for adult viewers do. Paper adds a gravitas to the non-verbal phenomenon of dance. As mentioned earlier in this book, for many people something does not exist unless it can be described in words. Words not on paper are easily misunderstood or forgotten. That is why titles of dances are important. A title gives the audience member a door through which to step into an alternate but no less real experience — the transcendent metaphor of movement that is dance.

A program must identify everyone correctly: choreographers, dance performers, and composers for the music you use. It is commonly and incorrectly assumed that you can list the musicians or group who plays the music. A program needs to identify the actual composer. This may take a little digging, but with a good amount of web searching you can find the composer. Make sure you follow copyright law for music and have permission to publicly use the music for your dances in performance.

Program copy can be sent via email to your presenter. Usually presenting organizations prefer that you send them your program information in order for them to embed their logos and performance season information in the document that they will distribute to the audience. However, check on this as early in the booking process as you can. Sometimes it is the other way around and the presenters expect the performers to provide the actual paper copies of the program.

Public service announcements or PSAs are an important way for presenters to publicize your performances. Whether for a school newsletter or early morning school announcements — for a theater to publicize on radio, local television, or on their website — a short description of the performance and your company (use the 5 W's here too) is great. Better yet is a short (fifteen to thirty seconds) DVD clip of your most exciting dance along with the written description. In general, the more you can do to help fill the house or create a fun level of anticipation and excitement about your performance, the better. Agree to all requests for radio or television interviews. Always make time to talk with newspaper or journal writers who want to interview you. For extra publicity, agree to do (pre-performance) short "teasers" — little two-minute mini-performances in areas like cafeterias or in courtyards where there are lots of people.

PART III

Dancing

How do you tell the dancer from the dance?
— W. B. Yeats

Chapter 8

Touring: Basic Equipment, Checklist and Travel

Touring is like Murphy's law: anything that can go wrong, does. The first and foremost thing to do to keep "Murphy" at a distance is to remember to phone ahead one to three days before each show to talk with the principal, secretary, or other contact person. With this phone call you should confirm your arrival time and check to see if they have any concerns, questions or confusion regarding your arrival and set-up or any last-minute problems with your technical requirements.

Also, once you know the general "shape" of your tour, make sure you arrange your departures and arrivals so that you have a reasonable amount of time traveling between performing sites. Then, get an early start in driving. Our company's rule of thumb was never to drive more than two hours before a morning performance, as mentioned in the previous section. Dancers are more prone to injury and the performance quality suffers if they spend more than two hours cramped inside a vehicle. Even if you have a significant warm-up time before the performance, something detrimental and irreversible seems to happen to joints, flexibility and circulation. Choose a motel if you are more than two hours from a morning performance site. When driving to performances at other times during the day or in the evening, make sure that you get out of the vehicle to stretch and walk at least every two hours.

In the following chapter are the basic components of the tour itself: necessary equipment, transportation issues and accommodation on the road.

Basic Equipment—the Vehicle

The basic equipment includes both what you will need for the performance site and what you will need while actually on the road. The first thing is to have a suitable vehicle in which to travel (or a means of travel). The vehicle(s) must have enough room for the dancers and for the set, costumes, props, and sound system. You need to plan with considerable thought towards how all the pieces will fit into the vehicle. Most companies own a van, RV, station wagon or sports utility vehicle; other companies rent.

In fifteen years of touring we went from a small car with a large car-top carrier to van to station wagon and then back to a medium-sized car. This worked for us because of the small size of our company and because we learned how to compact our set into a smaller form through the years. We rented a vehicle only when we experienced car trouble. And although sometimes convenient, renting a vehicle is expensive and certainly is no guarantee that the car will be in good mechanical condition. We learned an unfortunate lesson when we first toured out of New York City. It was early in our dancing careers when we were members of a different dance company. The brand-new rented vehicle we were driving literally blew out its engine in an explosion on the New Jersey Turnpike — not a pretty picture. We were on our way to Mississippi, traveling on a tight schedule with tons of electronic equipment and props — all in the day before cell phones. This incident made us leery of rented vehicles for years.

Whatever vehicle you drive you should have a travel emergency kit that includes an aerosol can that temporarily reinflates most flat tires long enough for you to drive to safety (a marvelous invention!), motor oil, transmission fluid, water for the car radiator, a bottle of granules designed to stop leaks in the radiator, flashlights, emergency flares and large plastic bags (to use as emergency blankets, rain covering, a mat to lie on while looking under the car — you get the idea!). Carrying all this may seem like over-preparedness, but in fifteen years of touring, we used all but one of the above at one time or another.

While it is certainly no fun for you to have your engine blow on the road a few hours before you are scheduled to arrive for a performance, remember the most important thing is to keep in personal communication with your presenter, principal or other contact person where you will be performing. Remember that you may not have cellular phone reception everywhere, so act accordingly — find ways to contact schools should you have difficulties on the road.

Final caution: Keep your touring vehicle in good mechanical shape and if (horrors!) you should have to fly, leave the day before and send your equipment ahead by car. Airline baggage restrictions are prohibitive and the costs are enormous for hauling odd-shaped props and sets.

Basic Equipment— the Checklist

Before you go, make a checklist of items you need and then check it off as you pack your vehicle. On the list include:

- Lighting/sound equipment
- Costumes
- Props
- Musical instruments
- Food
- Water
- Directions (with names and telephone numbers)

It is easy to forget equipment that is not packed in boxes or in suitcases. Make sure you have not forgotten the odd-shaped prop that does not easily fit in. Be careful to remember the hanging bags that might be in the closet. It is better to group everything you need to pack by your studio door and check it off the list mentally or actually with pen and paper. Always send one person back to check the studio after you are sure you have loaded everything into your vehicle. It only takes one panicked call or trip back for a forgotten costume before you realize the importance of a checklist and one last-minute look before you go. In our experience as a company *it is not possible to be too paranoid about forgetting things*, either before you leave home or when you pack up after the performance. Have a double-check system: before leaving the studio or performing site, one person should check after another has already made the final sweep. A packing checklist is vital, but even with the list do not become complacent — props and undergarments have a clever way of vaporizing after shows!

As a dancer, you should always carry an extra bag to put your street clothes in so that when you exit from the dressing room (a.k.a. teacher's lounge) you do not have the embarrassing incident of dropping underwear out of the bundle of clothes wadded under your arm as you rush toward a warm-up on stage.

Also, even if you're a modern dance, African, Native American or classical Indian dance company and are used to performing barefoot, carry an extra pair of shoes that you can perform in because, believe me, there are some surfaces that are so hazardous that it is dangerous to walk on them barefoot. There are stages with condition problems that range from twelve-inch splinters to broken metal staples sticking up out of the floors, from sharp-edged, uneven tile floors to risers (created platform stages) with two-inch gaps between the platforms. Sure, you could refuse to perform under these conditions (and you *should* if broken glass is scattered about) — but under other conditions, if you can manage to dance with shoes on then do it. Think of the kids in the audience who will benefit and will not care if you wear shoes or not.

Use the best maps that you can buy (by this time everyone understands the problems with relying completely on web map search engines and GPS) — and still, despite what the best maps and your common sense tell you, understand that your presenters usually give the best directions. Even if you think you see a shortcut on a map, don't take it until you have quizzed your presenter about it.

Once when touring in the Appalachian Mountains we looked at our nationally recognized, "trusty" road booklet of maps and saw what seemed to be a much shorter route to our destination. Even though the presenter's written directions said to keep on the interstate highway, we turned off onto the "shorter" road. Four hours later we arrived at our destination (the "longer" route by the interstate would have taken us two hours). The road started out as a nice two-lane for the first hour or so. It climbed up a steep grade and became a one-lane. After an hour of travel over hills and up mountains, it turned into a gravel road, then a dirt lane and finally to grassy lane indentations. As one principal informed me when I wanted to book a morning performance in one valley (where his school was) and an afternoon performance in another mountain valley, "Baby, you're talking distance."

Of course the best of all worlds is to arrive the evening before and scout out your performance destination ahead of time. Sometimes presenters are so well organized that they provide you with explicit directions or even (in the best situations) a person who will serve as a guide to each school in a multiple residency. One of our favorite arts councils always did this, and it made us loyal to them even when they overworked us!

Hotels/Motels

If a performance is far away or if you have a residency situation call ahead of time to book your hotel. Try to obtain a recommendation from the presenter/principal. They usually will let you know what hotels are nearby, clean and reputable. This is important. After you have spent one night in a "shady" hotel with thin walls and who knows what going on by your ear, you will appreciate any recommendations. If you have dancers in your company who require nonsmoking rooms, try to choose a hotel with a ground floor nonsmoking room (because smoke rises) and windows that actually open. In addition, hotels that offer room with breakfast (more than doughnuts and coffee) will really save you time in the morning. Fumbling around an unfamiliar town looking for a cup or coffee for your caffeine addicts is not a great way to begin a performance day. Fortunately, many hotels have coffee makers in the room.

One way to cope with the breakfast hassle is to carry your own food — granola bars, fruit, yogurt (which needs no refrigeration), juice, bread, and plastic utensils, cups and paper napkins. Some dancers swear by a portable hot pot — a beverage-warming container for tea, instant hot cereal, and other such things, but clean-up is an issue in hotel rooms. Remember that the maids who work for the hotel are paid to clean up normal messes, not extraordinary ones. Be considerate. Besides, you may need to return to that hotel again and want to be welcomed back.

Occasionally you will be offered housing at the home of a presenter — or a member of the organization that arranges your performance (arts council or other). This can be a delightful experience or a dismal one. It really depends on the circumstance and how many days are involved. For one night, staying in a home may involve too much "guest responsibility" to make it work for performance circumstances (that is, how pleasant can you be at 6 A.M. before a 9 A.M. show time?). If you are staying longer, it can be delicious after a long day of performing to come back to a home filled with amenities like gracious hosts and home-cooked meals.

One of the most incredible performing experiences we ever had was during a week's residency in southwestern Virginia when we stayed with the arts council president's parents. They entertained us more than we could have ever imagined possible on tour through interesting conversation (they had traveled all over the world) and healthful food! Being with them was a lesson in how to enjoy life fully; they were both spry older folks who played tennis before breakfast every morning! Our stay with them has become one of our fondest touring memories.

Sometimes small, privately owned hotels and bed and breakfasts are perfectly fine and even charming. However there is always the possibility that problems can be harder to deal with when there is less competition. Once, when performing near the ocean in a small town with only one motel, our company ended up having to stay in the same room where someone had recently been cleaning fish. The moral here is always book ahead on the presenter's recommendation — and carry a room deodorizing disinfectant aerosol spray on tour!

Wherever you choose to stay, see if you can park your vehicle within sight of your motel window. In addition, remember to pack a blanket of some sort to cover any equipment visible through the windows of your car at night. In questionable areas remove any temptations to thieves. Go ahead and unpack your equipment and bring it into your hotel room. Better to be safe than sorry. In all cases it is worth carrying in the sound system and wake up with it than without it. In general, be savvy to the feel of a place. If the area around the hotel is well lighted and the hotel chain seems responsible, great, lock the door, cover your equipment and make sure you have parked the vehicle within sight of your hotel window. Otherwise, find another motel or bring in your valuable and unique equipment. Always lock everything. In most large metropolitan areas do not leave anything in your vehicles and use an enclosed parking lot with a 24-hour attendant.

Some motel chains have corporate discounts. Dance companies count as businesses, so always ask if the hotel has a business or corporate rate! In addition, some chains have membership discounts that you can obtain by filling out an application. It is usually worth it, although you first may have to endure a sales pitch for credit cards. A discount in hotel rates is one benefit of qualifying for membership in Dance/USA. (See Appendix C.)

Other Important Items and Reminders

Food — Bring Emergency Supplies

Never count on 24-hour convenience stores or groceries being available. Restaurants serve only during certain hours, plus you lose valuable travel time if you have to wait for service. One of the best modern inventions for traveling dancers is the supermarket with a complete salad bar and deli — often the food is fresher, more convenient, and cheaper than restaurant food. For dancers with food allergies or restricted diets, grocery stores are often the only sure way of avoiding reactions to unknown ingredients or finding the foods with the right ingredients. It goes almost without saying that you need your own source of water (both for the car radiator emergency as well as yourself!) Finally, our advice about restaurant eating on tour follows the old rule of thumb. If there are few or no cars in the parking lot of the restaurant, take that as an eating guide and choose a different, more visibly frequented place. The food will probably be better. When entering the restaurant, if you see insects, leave the place, even if it looks clean and otherwise acceptable.

One of our worst dining experiences occurred in an outwardly trendy restaurant — a restored mill with big prices in an historic downtown. By the end of the evening, I had swatted six flies — one of them on the sleeve of my dining partner, who then laughed so hard he aspirated the peppers and onions from a chicken

"None shall pass"

Restaurant warning!

fajita. He nearly had to have the Heimlich choking maneuver administered (grabbing the choking victim around the waist from behind and giving a sharp squeeze upward to dislodge the blockage). It was a memorable evening, one that I would not want to repeat.

In Between Performances

At a single location, sometimes you will be invited to share lunch with the children. This is usually a raucous affair with the children swarming over the dancers they have just seen onstage. This is a great chance to experience school lunches again (even though corn dogs might not be your favorite, perhaps the homemade rolls will tempt you). However, your dancers may prefer to find a quiet street or safe park near the school to quietly eat and rest away from the echoing chatter and doting attention of the children.

Sewing Kit

Touring bags should also contain a sewing kit with different colors of thread, several needles, safety pins, Velcro, buttons, small pliers (for zipper repair) different kinds of tape, a small stapler (for emergency mid-performance repair of hems) and a dry cleaning sponge or cloth — *this is very useful.*

First Aid Kit

Every touring vehicle needs a fully equipped first aid kit. Add to the usual Band-Aids and the like a triple antibiotic ointment like Neosporin, Vitamin E (for burns), ginger capsules for motion sickness, Pepto-Bismol (great for preventing intestinal reactions to strange water), tweezers for splinters, and Vitamin C for colds. Remember Benadryl pills for emergency allergy reactions, eye drops for contact lens wearers, a box of moist towelettes (for hand washing and removing grime and make-up from the face), and extra sunglasses for driving.

A separate portable first aid kit for use during performance emergencies should contain the usual first aid things but also should contain chemical ice packs which are activated by a sharp blow, aspirin and ibuprofen, an Ace bandage, and ankle and knee braces. Always remember the acronym PRICE. It stands for prevention, rest, ice, compression and elevation. When ice and compression have been applied within the first 60 seconds of an injury, I have experienced healing of minor injuries that have been up to six times faster than untreated injuries. Ice should be applied directly to the sore area and massaged in a circle for five minutes only. This is the equivalent of twenty minutes of an ice pack.

Trigger point massage is another great cure for sudden muscle spasms — apply increasing pressure for five seconds and then slowly decrease the pressure for five seconds with a finger along the length of a sore muscle. This helps release muscle pain that results from overuse and the sudden unexpected use of muscles. Tennis ball therapy is a wonderful way to release muscle spasms — especially for the back. Lie down of the floor and place a tennis ball under the back and gently roll the ball underneath the area in spasm. This will hurt at first, but then will release the tensions of most spasms.

Aaahh...

Using a tennis ball to alleviate back pain through "trigger point" massage.

REMEMBER!!! Immediately inform your presenter of any delay. This is crucial if it has the potential to delay your show. One of the angriest principals we ever talked with told us the story of how he waited for forty-five minutes in an auditorium filled with three hundred bored and hyper kids on a Friday afternoon for a storyteller who never called to let him know she would be late! That behavior is unforgivable. While everyone understands that accidents happen, no one understands (or should be expected to) when performers keep them in the dark about delays.

Chapter 9

In the School and Theater:
Check-In, Set-Up and Safety

First Things First: The Check-In

At the school, first you will need to check in at the school office. Wear a clear emblem of your dance company so that you can be easily and quickly identified. This can be a shirt or coat with your logo, a button, or even a uniform. Never go directly to a stage area in a school without first sending a representative of the company to identify the presence of your group and to receive the school's permission to enter the school to begin the residency. Because of school safety concerns, you want to make sure everyone knows who you are immediately. This way no one has doubts and your presence causes no disruption to the teaching climate of the school.

You will need someone official to guide you to the performing space, unlock any necessary doors, show you the lighting controls, indicate where the designated dressing room for the company is (usually the teacher's lounge in schools, but sometimes you get lucky and have a real dressing room). At this time (or later before the show) you can ask the principal who will be introducing your company onstage, and then give information that you would like to have included in that introduction to the audience. While your company no doubt will have its own in-house introduction, it is always best to have a principal or designated person call the audience to order. The principal or person in charge should introduce the company by name (names of the dancers is optional), a brief description of the performance, and where the company is from. At this time you also can request that a sponsoring arts council, if appropriate, be recognized in the introduction.

In schools, wear nice clothes. Make sure no one appears in tattered, sloppy dancer attire. This will mean no grungy "on the road" dancer gear when entering the school or walking down the halls. All adults are role models, and most schools have teacher dress codes as well as student dress requirements. Artists are not exempt.) Most schools have all individuals buzz in, sign in, wear a school visitor badge, or even have a previously arranged and completed earlier background check. This is for the safety of the children to make sure that no threatening unidentified strangers lurk in the hallways. When identifying yourself, go to the door marked "school office" and walk in. Ask the secretary to let the principal know you are there and have someone show you the performing area, the best place to unload, and unlock doors. You can do a quick scan and when you return to your vehicle give the information to your dancers.

Menagerie dancers "in uniform" during a Q & A session with students. Uniform clothing immediately lets school personnel identify who you are and why you are in the school (credit William D. Watson).

Getting Ready for the Show

Take a Safety Check

Beforehand, on your technical requirement sheet (sent with the contract) and in your telephone conversation with the principal on the day before your arrival, you have requested that the stage be clear and free of obstructions (swept and, if appropriate, vacuumed) and wet mopped. This may or may not have been done before you arrive. You may find risers onstage or other furniture that needs to be removed. The most useful person to befriend is the school janitor. Let the janitor know any needs and help if heavy hauling is required. A little cooperation with the janitor will go a long way to making a smoother residency. Always carry a push broom and dustpan with you on your tour. It will prove valuable to you when you are in a place with overburdened janitors or in schools where floor conditions are not ready for you. In this realm of thought, duct tape is a dance company's best friend. Tape over splinters, broken-off staples, uneven platforms or holes in the floor. Carry a dance floor if you must, but add a sufficient technical crew and more hours onto your set-up time, as well a larger transport vehicle.

Next, make sure backstage objects are not precariously stacked. They may fall onto the stage. We have had tables and chairs fall onto the stage during performance — fortunately no one ever got hit, but this was just sheer luck. We have now developed a policy to thoroughly check all towers of stuff looming behind stage curtains. In addition, make sure you take care when you put up your own set.

Stages are dangerous places. Have dancers check all exits and stairs, and the angles and heights of steps from audience to stage (if any). The stage surface may be slippery for movement or in some cases — and even worse for dancers' knees — too sticky (resistant). Ceilings may be too low to accommodate the lifts that have been choreographed and the lifts (or use of the props) may have to be changed on the spot. Things like film-screen pull chains, rope handles, or fluorescent lights may hang just above the dancers' heads. Ropes can be pushed over fixtures, but readjust jumps and leaps to avoid the fixed obstacles.

On stages with dangerous surfaces, dancers should don shoes or change the type of shoe to accommodate stage surface problems. If you go into the audience area as a part of your show, make sure you investigate how the stairs or exits will be lighted during the show. Also, if you have a large drop-off between stage and audience, figure out how you will have dancers maneuver their entrances and exits. To dancers who are used to working in large empty studio spaces, a small or uneven surface may be a real challenge.

If you have audience participation, determine how children will get on and off the stage safely. You may have to enlist the help of teachers to "guard" the drop-off during the times when kids are moving on and off the stage so that no one tumbles over the edge of the stage. Make sure that all your electrical cables and extension cords to speakers and sound systems are taped down with duct/gaffers tape if they are placed where dancers or children could trip on them. Tape electrical plugs into the wall if a passing dancer or child could dislodge them during or before the show. If you are in a theater situation with extensive lighting rehearsals, double your safety consciousness. Unfamiliar stages in the total darkness between lighting cues are treacherous. If you talk to veteran performers, chances are that you will hear many stories of near and actual stage catastrophes.

Dancers fall off stages in a variety of ingenious ways. In our company alone, one of us has danced right off the edge and discovered too late that cartoon-like attempts to reverse the pull of gravity don't work even if you are pumping the air like crazy. Another of us (all fingers point to this author), caught stepping down off an unfamiliar stage by a careless lighting technician's unannounced blackout, fell four feet down on her head. No broken bones resulted, but that was just sheer luck. Too many horror stories abound about dancers who were not as lucky. *Be careful on stages.*

As mentioned previously, even if you dance barefooted, have shoes to wear backstage or for walking in the halls or audience. On cramped stages we have stepped on each other's feet and on our own feet, given bloody noses, knocked out contact lenses, dropped and kicked one another, gotten splinters of a myriad of materials in a myriad of places (no more floor spins on the back without checking the floor surface ahead of time). The hidden drama can be agonizing! Sometimes it is hard to have to hide these types of incidents with a "show must go on" demeanor. You must, though, to be professional. Just keep your insurance current. It's a risky business.

Be on time. Whether you are performing in a rural mountain town or in a big theater in a major city, never be late. You need preparation time. You need to be professional and not inconvenience other people — principals, presenters, janitors, and lighting technicians — who are waiting for you. No news travels faster in show business than the news of late arrivals by performers. Not only will other presenters hear about it, but other performers will hear and resent you for giving dance and all the other performing companies a bad name. Be a model company. Arrive on time with a positive attitude. Also, even if conditions at a school or auditorium are not exactly what you requested, remember that it does no good to throw a temper tantrum or shout. Control yourself. Be friendly and ask the janitor or other appropriate person for help in correcting a problem with stage or seating. Usually, miscommunication and misunderstood needs are the problems, not deliberate unhelpfulness. It even may be the fault of your company management or the boss of the person who has seemingly let you down. Your goal is to produce a wonderful show. Don't waste time on the negative. Concentrate on the performance, because that is where the dance lives and where your work is remembered.

Chapter 10

Good Liaisons Make
Good Residencies

This is a short but important chapter. Even though you have called ahead the day before your residency to talk with the principal (or technical director if you're in a theater), when you arrive at the performance site, make it a point to talk with the principal (or technical director) again. Check to see if the performance time has changed and that you have the correct schedule. Schools may ask you to begin earlier than you had arranged when making the contracts. This is usually due to problems with scheduling school lunch times for the children, since performances alter class schedules. Principals have certain federal and state guidelines and requirements about mealtimes that they have to follow. Some principals are willing to stretch things five minutes one way or another, but others are not, usually because they have a strict school board or superintendent of education to whom to report.

Before school performances, remind principals that it usually takes at least ten minutes to move one audience out of an auditorium or performance space and another one in. Occasionally you will have a principal who wants to end a performance before you are finished! This is always distressing, since it is usually due to poor planning on the principal's part. This is one reason why it is good to have an audience participation section and/or a question and answer period built into the end of your performance. That way, if the performance has to be compressed, the children will miss none of the actual dancing.

When you talk to the principal, vice principal or arts council coordinator who will be calling the children to order and introducing your program, give them a quick verbal reminder of who you are and ask that they introduce your performance giving all credits to organizations that made your performance at their school or site possible. This may include parent/teacher organizations, the local arts council or even the National Endowment for the Arts. It is important to give acknowledgment to arts support in every way you can. Even if it is lost on the children, the teachers hear it. When the subject of funding for the arts comes up, they will recognize the worth of these organizations if your performance was a good one. They and their students will have directly benefited from PTO, state or corporate funds put to use in making dance accessible to them.

During larger residencies, well-organized arts agencies that have booked your company for a week or more will give you a written itinerary with names and directions to each school. Often, in difficult-to-navigate regions, the council will have a person to lead

101

you from school to school, as mentioned before. This can be a real benefit, but just in case, always have written directions available.

In the initial discussion with the principal/contact person when you arrive at the school, make sure to ask if the teachers have been given the teacher guides that you sent previously. Always carry extra teaching guides in instances where the teaching guides have been misplaced or lost. Children will let you know right away whether the teachers have received the guides or not by saying when they come into the performance space, "Hey, what are you going to be doing today?" Our hearts always fall at that question because it means that either our teaching guides didn't arrive, or the teacher has not used them. Sometimes this problem results when an arts advocate, who is located outside the school, does the booking. Distribution problems come up when the person outside the institution has your press kit and/or teaching guides and then either forgets or neglects to send them on to each school. For that reason, it is a good idea for both big residencies or for small ones handled by an outside the school system person, to get the name and address of each school principal so you can make sure the teaching guide gets into the hands of the teachers who need them.

Chapter 11

Teachers Who Help,
Teachers Who Hinder

On site, in performance, you may encounter — as we have — teachers who become your personal role models and heroes and, conversely, a few teachers who should not be near children. Great teachers will reveal themselves to you in multiple ways. You may find their students well prepared and asking really pertinent and thoughtful questions about dance and the things that you are dancing about. You may receive wonderful letters and poems with evidence of obvious teacher guidance. (What a great time to teach children to write a letter — when they are excited about a performance that they have just seen and have something they really want to say to the performers!)

Great teachers come in and direct their children into the performance space gently but efficiently. They sit and watch the performance and join in the audience participation. They actively model the behavior that they want children to learn. They show respect to the children, to the performers, and to the principal by simple courtesies. They don't talk during your shows. Nor do they sit on the sides and grade papers. This can be very disconcerting to the performers. However, don't take this behavior as an indictment of the quality of your show.

Teachers are proverbially overworked and underpaid. They always have a backlog of work. Sure, it's really rude of a teacher to ignore a performance. In fact, it so infuriated one of our friends who toured his own solo mime performance that he incorporated a special chase scene into his show. About halfway into his show, if he saw a teacher obviously grading papers on the side, he would grab the papers from the unsuspecting teacher and the children would be entertained hilariously as he mischievously resisted the teacher's attempts to recover the papers! This approach takes guts and a flexible, improvisational show structure to make it work. While we are not recommending (or even condoning) this, it's probably the most effective teaching method for remediation of teachers who forget to model appropriate audience behavior!

Worse yet are the serious professional circumstances, thankfully rare, when you see or hear an adult — teacher or teacher's aide — yelling at students. It is odd that certain teachers just don't perceive the incongruity of yelling at children to be quiet. A wonderful teacher, Bonnie Craig — who is a gem of a physical education teacher that we met and became friends with while performing at her school — barely whispers when she teaches her inner-city classes. Her pupils come close to hear her. She then directs them in movement activities and assigns attention-needy children special tasks to keep them focused and emotionally fulfilled in her classes. You can learn an extraordinary amount about crowd control and effective teaching methods from master teachers in the schools. There ought to be a performer's "teacher hall of fame." After touring for twenty years we have a lot of candidates to nominate!

On the other hand, we hope you never witness direct verbal or physical abuse of a child in a school setting, or anywhere for that matter. But if you do, you have a duty to report it to the principal or other authority in the school. Sometimes you may see or hear things that, while not criminal, are certainly wrong. Address these situations too.

Once on tour a group of middle school kids was shooting basketball in the gym where we were to perform. When I asked the teacher to let them help us unload (as much from desperation to free up our performance space as anything else) the teacher agreed. But later another teacher told me, "These kids are bad. You don't want them anywhere near the performance or the other kids." After the so-called "bad" kids successfully helped us load in and load out, one of them came up to me and said in a sad and plaintive voice while pointing to the disapproving teacher, "Hey, tell him we're not bad." I did.

All people, young and old, live up or down to expectations. Teachers are there for the long haul. Your dance company is in a school only briefly; but while you are there you can inspire children, complement the educational goals of a school, and as much as possible deliver a positive message to teachers and children — some who need something (or anything) positive in their lives. Art is a powerful medium and delivers a powerful message. In every interaction with a child you deliver a "thumbs up" or "thumbs down" to them. Use your brief but powerful influence carefully and judiciously.

Chapter 12

Arranging and Seating Audiences

In many auditoriums and performing spaces, the audience arrangement is permanent and fixed. However, even in these situations it is possible to create a better audience seating arrangement than if you completely leave it to chance. In other, less formal audience spaces, the seating arrangement is entirely open, subject to the traditions of seating arrangements in previous performances or to what you as performers request.

In all situations, the best view for dance is from the center. Most choreographers choreograph dance with the idea of the shapes and movements being seen from straight ahead. Dance is a sculptural art form and both the individual shapes of dancers and configurations of groupings of dancers look different from different angles of perspective. In addition, most stages are rectangular, with wings or side areas where dancers change costumes, grab props, and/or wait to make their entrances. Therefore the first way in which audience seating arrangements should be modified is to move viewers toward the center, away from the edges of the audience (far right and far left). This can be done in auditoriums by placing a rope or signs along the seats at the far edges — or in the case of schools, simply directing the principal or teachers to seat the children in the center and not on the far edges. In schools where the audience size is too large to get everyone seated if the edges are not used, then at least the children from the far edge, side two seats (in rows closest to the stage) can be seated elsewhere. This usually causes little disruption to the flow since it at most will affect four to six children.

In a space such as a cafeteria or gym that has an open seating arrangement, many elementary schools have the children sit on the floor, flanked by teachers seated in folding chairs on both sides of the audience. This is the better arrangement for an audience. It is easy to monitor sight lines merely by adjusting where the teachers place their chairs.

Some schools will not have figured this out and will insist on placing cafeteria tables and benches or folding chairs for the students to sit upon. This is the worst possible seating arrangement. Fewer students can be seated, and other students' heads get in the way of the students being able to see the performance area (especially if the stage area and seating area are on the same level). Students at tables farther away from the front of the stage and the children in back are likely to become bored and disruptive if they can't see what is happening on stage. This is a seating arrangement to avoid at all costs. Sometimes principals insist on this seating because the floor is simply too dirty or cold for the children to sit on it. This is a shameful situation, but as in all cases of performance dilemmas, the show must go on. This is one reason our company usually has a portion of the performance where the dancers "break proscenium" and dance out in the audience — this brings the physical immediacy and excitement of a dance performance right out onto the edge of the stage and beyond — right into the space of the last row of the audience.

Another thing to watch for and try to prevent from happening is seating children so close to the lip of the stage that the front row audience members have to bend their necks back just to see the dancers' faces. This reminds me of what happened in a large civic center that doubled as an ice hockey rink, during a performance of a popular Irish dance troupe. Folding chairs were placed on a huge mat that covered the ice. The chairs went right up to the edge of the stage. The people in the most expensive seats — closest to the Irish dancers — saw the dancers only from the waist up. This was an exasperating situation, especially since feet are really the most important feature of that style of dance. Don't let the same frustrating thing happen to the audience that views your program — make sure you sit on the floor and look up at the stage before the audience arrives to make sure the front row will actually see more than your heads!

Be on guard for teachers who insist on sitting with their classes and place themselves in front of small children who then can't see over the tall teacher's head. Although the

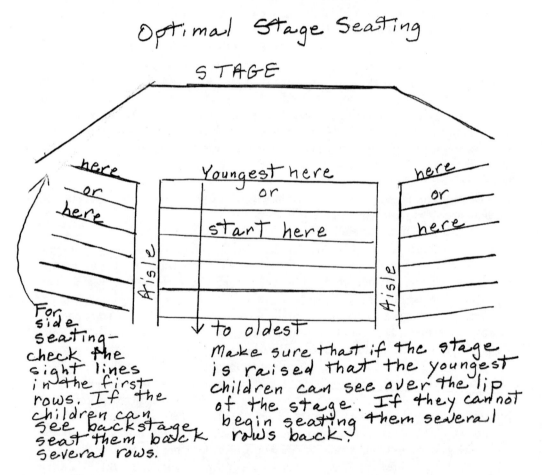

Sketch of best seating arrangement for children in a school audience. Note the aisle placement.

teachers need to be near their classes for control and for dealing with particular behavior problems, often the teacher can move to the outside edge of the audience space rather than be in the center. Sometimes it is not worth the time lost to readjust and you can have the child who is seated directly behind a taller person just change seats or shift slightly to one side. Where you can, create aisles in audiences that are seated cross-legged on the floor. This is necessary for a number of reasons. First, if you have an audience participation time built into your program, when you bring students onstage with you to try different activities (either during or after the show), then you need aisles so you can move children from their places onto the stage and back again without having feet and toes stepped on in the process. Aisles can be maintained most easily by placing orange cones (almost all P.E. teachers have them as standard equipment — or you can carry your own) where you want the aisles located. First, tell the principal or person who is directing audience traffic where you need the students to sit, and find out what their normal procedure for seating is. Then, if you need to modify the seating arrangement by creating aisles, changing placement, or widening aisles — quickly before the children come into the auditorium — place yourself and other dancers out in the empty audience area exactly where you want the aisle. No one can sit where you are standing, although you may have to move forward rather quickly as the rows fill up with children.

Schools that have frequent assembly programs usually have an efficient method for moving children in and out of performance spaces that takes about ten minutes. If you go into a school where they rarely bring the children together for school events, you may find that chaos and lengthy delays ensue, unless you actively direct and guide arrangement of the children in the audience. Be prepared for either contingency and also be prepared to shave off a few moments at the end of your show if the filling of the auditorium or performance space is so slow that it negatively affects the length of the show.

Sometimes lunch or even the final school bell will ring before your show is complete. This is another situation to avoid at all costs. Build in a five-minute cushion at the end of your program, such as a question and answer period or a final movement activity that can be sacrificed without compromising the main integrity of your performance. If you find out that you must direct the seating of children, make sure to seat the youngest and smallest in the front. This way, if you have masks that have to be shown to the younger set, you can do this more easily since the youngest children will be together instead of being spread throughout the performing space.

The most important thing to remember is that someone from the company should be in the auditorium waiting for the children to arrive. The reasons for this are many. Children behave in a more civilized way if there are adults present in each new space. Without an adult present, sometimes the children will enter into an empty space like champagne uncorked. Teachers usually keep order, but sometimes are delayed by a problem in the hall or in their classrooms. Also, if the dancers in your company are wearing garments that might seem funny to the uninitiated — ballet slippers, a tunic, or a historical shirt or skirt — this is a chance for students to ask questions and familiarize themselves with the difference before they see the dance.

We usually make sure to circulate and answer individual questions about the performance before the show. This is an especially important thing to do with the older grades who, with their "weighty" role as the oldest of the school, will often suffer "sophistication attacks" which manifest themselves as a bored, blasé attitude. If you send a dancer back to share some pre-performance conversation — perhaps an inquiry as to whether they can see the stage from where they are seated — then you can alleviate the blasé "cool" and turn these older students into a willing audience. All it takes is a few polite words from you to show your respect for them as individuals. They will become much better audience members because they view you as people who care about them, not just "talking heads" or in our case, dancing legs.

Chapter 13

Your Performance Voice

Discovering the most effective voice to use when addressing an audience is essential to the success of any performance. Verbal language is something that almost everyone can access, while some in your audience may never have seen a theatrical presentation of dance onstage before. The tone, timing, timbre and ease of your speech — in your introduction, in between dances, in audience participation, and in Q & A sessions at the end of your show — make a profound difference in how your company is perceived and received.

The first mistake most people make when addressing a large crowd is to speak too rapidly. Slow down and pause between words more than you normally would in conversational speech. In addition, acoustics differ dramatically from auditorium to multi-purpose room, which further affects how an audience hears your speech. During your stage setup period, make sure to test the sound environment with your voice as well as with your amplified musical equipment. The hand clap or practiced sentence "Hello, my name is _____" projected into a space will quickly teach the speaker about inherent echo, acoustically absorptive surfaces like carpet or cavernous overhead "fly" spaces that obliterate spoken words and eat up the decibels of your voice. Listen for distracting underlying noises — loud fans from air exchange systems or the slamming of dishes in a nearby kitchen, a particular auditory hazard in the cafetorium setting when the kitchen workers may be cleaning up from one meal such as breakfast while preparing for another during your performance time. You easily can ask permission to close kitchen doors during the performance, but it is often much more difficult to control the background buzz of fluorescent gym lights since you need the lighting and yet it is irrevocably associated with a loud hum.

Harder still is coping with the outrageous cacophony of an onstage air-conditioning system. Unfortunately it is the current trend in HVAC (heating, ventilation, air conditioning) to install these units over the stage! Yes, in the very place where large numbers of people gather to strain to hear the words of (usually) just one person speaking at a time. HVAC engineers seem to ignore the profound predicament they create for public speakers. Yet this silly placement of loud machines over stages is happening everywhere, not just in schools K–12, but in colleges and universities too! However, apart from private (or public in this case) ranting and raving there is not much a performer can do except to see if the principal can turn off the fans (if the weather permits), speak louder, and use a microphone where necessary. (More about microphone usage later in this chapter.)

So what if you test the acoustics and discover a problem? Instead of the crystal clear acoustics of the ancient Greek amphitheater, such as the one at Epidaurus where a person's

Menagerie Dance Company using voice and gesture in the audience participation portion during a school performance in a gymnasium. Dancers: Mark and Ella Magruder (credit Joe H. Bunn, Principal, Hillsville Elementary).

voice can be heard clearly from an astounding distance, you find your voice is absorbed or echoing and the microphone doesn't help much, perhaps due to bad connections, reverberations, or a "tinny" quality. You know you must speak louder. As a dancer you know how to solve a similar visual problem — if the back of the audience can't see subtle gestures, you just direct your focus beyond the last row of chairs and dance "bigger" with more accented energy. It should be similar with the voice, right? Well, yes and no.

Projection of the voice does involve focus and speaking out to the far corners of the auditorium audience, but the timbre and resonance of your voice has to be carefully focused as well. It is important to develop a resonant (diaphragmatic) stage voice. When people unaccustomed to speaking from a stage do have to vocalize, many mistakenly equate "louder" with "yelling." This too often becomes screeching.

Keep your voice timbre resonating from your chest, not higher up in your neck — there is a "ringing" tone to a resonant voice. You know it as a teacher's voice, the one that rings across the vast gym or studio and reaches the ears of the intended recipient loud and clear. This also is the voice of the stage actor. Cultivate it by practicing.

At the end of a daylong residency with several performances and master classes behind you, your throat should be a little tired, but not sore or hoarse. If you find you are losing your voice after performance, take advice from the late F.M. Alexander, the Australian actor who kept losing his voice.[1]

He found that many people, himself included, tightened the muscles of the back of the neck, pulled the back of the head down and lifted the chin up while speaking. This is a habitual nervous response that has to be overcome, or a performer is guaranteed to lose the voice. Free your neck and breathe! If you can't accomplish this on your own and continue to stress your voice on stage, find an Alexander teacher and try a lesson.

The next major voice element is tone. When speaking to any audience, but especially to an audience of children, keep your voice lively but not "cutesy." Do not talk down to children or talk in a cloyingly sweet or fake happy voice — the "Hey, kiddies!" syndrome. Remember that children have highly enhanced "fakeometers" that sometimes are a lot more accurate that most adults. Adults forget how much they hated being treated like babies when they were young — and somehow think that they have to put on a baby-talk voice for elementary age kids. This is the fastest way to alienate a young audience. It is absolutely imperative that anyone addressing teenagers heed this advice.

Talk to teenagers as if you are talking to adults. While their emotions and behavior might not always be mature, their perceptions often are quite highly developed. The key word is respect. Remember what a blessed relief it was to be respected when you were in high school? Tone of voice is a major conveyer of underlying message. A tone that says sincerely "I love to dance and can't wait to show you our program" is a different tone than "Here I am with a bunch of adolescent idiots who won't get what I'm trying to say but I have to act 'hyped' up anyway." If you're not sure what your voice tone conveys, practice your onstage speaking parts with another person ahead of time. Videotape or audiotape yourself and try to listen objectively. This will gain you a great measure of control over the audience reactions to your show and save you from embarrassment.

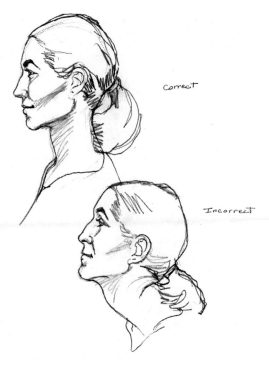

Head position affects vocal quality and volume.

When you are creating the onstage introduction, *make sure that you engage the audience without asking open-ended questions that call for a verbal answer* like "How are you today?" Don't leave pauses that encourage a verbal response from the crowd. What happens when you ask open-ended questions or greetings of this sort to a crowd of quiet and attentive children is that they usually scream back an answer like "Fine!" or "Good morning!" and suddenly your crowd is no longer quiet or attentive. Then you have to respond with time-wasting attempts to regain the attention that was yours a few seconds before. Once you lose control of a large group of children, a mob mentality takes over, and it is not pleasant.

If you want response from an audience, what you say to them should prompt the children to respond physically, involving them silently, without verbal response, unless you specifically evoke that type of response, such as in a Q & A session. Many creative ways to do this exist. The most time-honored method to get a response without losing control is to preface your question with "Raise your hand if you are having a great day," or better yet, "Raise your elbow if..." Another way is to say "When I raise my hand I want you to continue to sit in your seat but grow a little taller." (More about that in Chapter 15, which covers audience participation.)

Finally, the microphone issue. The rule of thumb is, in audiences over 350 children, use one. In audiences under that number, if you can (no loud buzz lights or other disturbing noises), don't use a microphone. Microphones are wonderful for people who are soft spoken; but oddly enough, with a group, the use of a microphone can be an excuse for people not to pay attention. The rationale goes something like this. A child in the audience thinks, "Oh, they're using a microphone, it won't matter if I talk because the microphone's speakers are loud and my voice isn't."

A microphone is also a solid object and like all props has to be dealt with. It has to be put away before you dance. Cordless microphones are easiest, but still have to be put somewhere. Microphone stands have to be moved. And even if you have a small, cordless, clip-on microphone, you still have to wear a power pack strapped or hooked to your costume. I remember a dancer at a festival performing beautifully, but the power pack bulge around her waist was very distracting visually. All these things also are disconcerting to an audience as well as hard on the dancer who has to cope with extra details.

Sometimes loudspeakers go out unexpectedly or develop interference. You also have to be careful to avoid aiming your mike toward the stage speakers or you will get feedback — squeaking and squawking. Proper microphone technique means you have to enunciate your *P*'s and *T*'s softly to avoid loud bumps of sound coming from your speakers. And last but not least, someone must turn on and off the microphones. You, the speaker, must remember to do this or whenever you put the microphone down any sounds will be broadcast over the speaker system, such as feet pounding. This is OK and even desirable in tap or clogging, but far from ideal for a lot of other dance forms. If someone else controls the microphone on and off button, ask yourself, "Will they get it right?" with short or nonexistent rehearsals? And then, ask yourself if it is worth it enough to have the volume of the mike be out of your control.

Menagerie Dance Company surrounded by curious students. Dancer Ella Magruder holds a dulcimer that she played in performance, used here as a teaching aid during a master class (credit Joe H. Bunn, Principal, Hillsville Elementary).

However, as mentioned before, even with all these problems, it is usually best to use a microphone for an audience of over 350. In addition — oddly enough with teenagers — microphones used in a lecture demonstration format make the speaker more "cool" somehow and are very valuable in countering "sophistication attacks." Always test the equipment before the audience arrives, bearing in mind Murphy's laws of amplification that say, "If you really need it, it usually won't work." So practice your stage voice, even if you plan on using a microphone.

While this last section is not exactly voice advice, it is associated with effective public speaking. If you want to reach more of your audience, use visual props. Props can illustrate what you are introducing. We have used African drums and different masks, and we have seen other companies use projections and written outlines (on easel or dry-erase board). The more senses you involve, the better the chance that the children will remember what you say.

Important: During introductions and explanations (unless narration is a part of the show) all dancers onstage should look at the dancer who is speaking to the audience. This encourages the audience to pay more careful attention to the speaker's words. Often people who are on the stage don't realize that they should focus on the stage speaker, and they wind up diverting the audience's attention away from the speaker. It is comforting for those nonspeaking others onstage to have a definite focal point too, because often they feel foolish just staring blankly out into the audience while someone else speaks.

Chapter 14

Performing for an Audience: Numbers, Cautions and Facts

The wonderful and fateful event itself is in progress. The children are enthralled, the dancers mesmerizing and into a "flow" moment. Art is happening and the indescribable essence of dance is there in the space — the magic between audience and performers, the thing that sustains us as performers and inspires children — the same thing that probably inspired each of us to want to dance in the first place.

This happened for me at age seven. My parents took me to see José Limón's company. I saw *Missa Brevis*. My cloistered child's world suddenly expanded. A young child, transformed and transfixed, forever changed by a dance and its dancers ... it's there in my memory. It's here in my grown-up heart. You as a dancer, if you're lucky and talented, may have the same effect on a child watching you as José Limón had on me and countless others. How can you create and sustain this beauty and the power of your art?

First you must treat every performance as the opportunity that it is. When you dance for children, you dance for the future of our art. Doesn't everyone have a similar moment of inspiration? If you do, and most of us have one, you have a calling to dance and a responsibility to respect the young audience as you would any other.

Statistically, a surprisingly high percentage of the children in the audience will find employment in the arts. What do you want them to remember and treasure from your performance? Probably the beauty and integrity of your movement, full-out dancing, and a theme in your choreography that may touch them in a profound way. Certainly, when you are dancing in a school, the environment may not be conducive to show your dance at its best. You may have an uninformed audience. Live performance may be so alien to some children in your audience that they won't have a clue, but some will get it after you dance. And that's the point. Touch one heart.

There are things that you can do both when you plan this moment and while in the dance itself to help sustain the magic. First, beforehand — in your booking conversations — you will have discussed with the principal or the arts presenter the optimum audience size. Three hundred to three hundred and fifty is the benchmark for school performances. At and below this number children will still feel like they are an integral part of the audience. They will be seated close enough to the stage to see the performers, without too many other children in front of them obstructing their views. At or below 350, during the audience participation time, the children who volunteer to come up on stage will be chosen, or at least someone around them will be selected.

Above this number, less positive things begin to happen to an audience of children in most school settings. Children in larger audiences feel alienated. The ones far away from the stage and performers have trouble seeing. Some children usually are forced to sit too close to the stage and have to view the entire performance with a head painfully tilted back. Soon their shoulders start to scrunch under the load since children's heads occupy proportionately more of their body length than those of adults.

When our company first began touring, a veteran children's performer from Canada warned us about the difference an audience's size could make. Not surprisingly, we found it was true. Since we kept an ongoing assessment (in the form of an evaluation) going throughout the fifteen years of touring, we were astonished to see that there was a direct statistical correlation between audience size and rating of the performance. Even if an audience size were only 20 over the 350 limit, ratings would go down. It was uncanny to see this relationship — between numbers and experience — materialize out of the records we kept. It is real, and companies will do best to heed the warning that our performing compatriots gave us all those many years ago.

Certainly it is possible to dance for larger audiences — dance companies do it all the time. Our company has performed for audiences of 1,000 and more. However, the work that it takes to maintain an outward performance "projection" that will reach all the children in a large audience is exhausting. As mentioned in the previous chapter, you must have a great microphone and powerful amplification or speakers. A normal presentational performance in a theater, with lights, with a minimum of personal introductions, and dancers not breaking proscenium, are all better scenarios for larger audiences. If the viewers are a mixed-age, general-audience format, more than 350 is okay because more adults are present to balance out the kid energy and to supervise individual child behavior.

Know the exact timing of your show. Make sure you know the length of each individual dance. The length of each dance does not matter — it can vary from short to long. How it is choreographed and presented to children is what matters. Timing is vital, so that you can know, not just estimate, when the show needs to begin in order for it to end at a certain time.

Dancers need to remember to dance all the way past the stage wings, so that even on a small or unconventional stage, the illusion of the dance is maintained. Sometimes young dancers forget to do this. After the great leap on the upstage diagonal, they drop out of the movement and "schlep" offstage, thinking that they have completed the "important" movement. Experienced dancers realize that the dance is what happens in between the feats of athletic skills — necessary as they are for excitement. Dance is gestalt — the total expression. I remember seeing a performance at a famous venue in New York City, where one "angel" whispered out ribald jokes to his neighbor during an Easter show. It was disgusting because I knew that performer really had no respect for the show, much less any respect for the audience.

Remember, when on a new stage, dance into the light if you possibly can. Before the show, find out if there are hot spots of light on stage. Hopefully, they correspond to where you need to be; but if not, if necessary and/or if possible, nudge the choreography over to find the light. Great movement is always more powerful if it is visible. If there are miming or acting portions in the dance; you must move into the light. Nothing matters more than facial expression crucial to the story actually being seen.

Menagerie Dance Company in *Flute Song*, a Sioux folk tale of how woodpecker, a hollow tree branch, and wind created the first flute; dancer and choreographer Mark Magruder brings out the flute out to the youngest in the audience (credit Lee Luther, Jr.).

In the ebb and flow of performance, remember to never leave a blank stage. A vacant stage is a dead stage. Music or a moving prop or a lighting change can fill in for the absence of a human being — but not for long. A silent, empty stage invites a mind to break with the illusion. Mundane things — like becoming acquainted with the person who sits next to you — take over if there is no action on stage. Audiences of children can veer out of control unless the times between dances, between sections of choreography, and between entrances and exits, are as alive and electric as the dancing.

Audiences have their own individual energy, as all performers discover. This audience is reserved, that one is rowdy — this one low on volunteers, that one bursting with ideas and questions. It seems random, but it is predictable in some ways. Friday afternoon audiences are almost always "on the edge" — ready to lose control with the slightest provocation. Children and teachers are totally exhausted by Friday afternoon. Even the best teachers are close to the end of their rope. Avoid booking Friday afternoon if possible. If that is impossible, ratchet up your performance to the utmost to counteract the "chaos monster" lurking in the halls. All morning performances, especially the earliest ones, have more sedate responses from the children. It takes a while for the kids to wake up too.

Always make sure you allow enough time for a good warm-up — never, never skip warm-up unless you want a short performing career. Warm-ups prevent injuries. Have several different types of warm-up that you can do, depending on if the floor is dirty, if it is carpeted, cement, and so forth. Test the floor for turns while you're warming up. Our modern (barefoot) company has enough horror stories on floor textures to fill a book. Suffice it to say, remember to bring your first aid kit everywhere, and always include a disposable ice pack.

All your final rehearsals should be videotaped before you begin touring. Everyone involved must have a chance to see their own handiwork as the audience will see it. Video is the most important innovation of the past century for dance. It allows us to monitor our own dancing and see what the critics might criticize. Then we have a chance to correct it before we perform.

Unfortunately, now it's time to list the don'ts and negatives. While dance does not hold the patent on tastelessness and self-indulgence on stage, sometimes it seems that way. One crass, sloppy, pointless, or cheapening performance can taint an entire genre. Sadly, we have seen some dance performances that almost made us dissolve in tears and they weren't tears of empathy. It is awful to even have to make a list, but since we've actually seen all these things happen in performances for children, it is serves as a precaution. So here goes...

The List of Don'ts

1. Don't be self-indulgent. It's not about "you, you, and you." It's about the activity and the dance.
2. Don't strip (even to a sports bra and brief) onstage. It fuels the invectives against dance. No plunging necklines, revealing costumes, or padded jockstraps either.
3. Don't pretend to be a kid onstage just because you are performing for kids — unless it is a part of a clearly defined role in a story that you are performing. Pretending to be a child is inauthentic and disrespectful to your young audience. Likewise, don't pretend to play with toys — it's condescending.
4. Be sincere in performance; be real.
5. Don't use scatological (bathroom) humor. And be respectful of cultural mores. A dance about "kitty litter" is inappropriate in all circumstances in the U.S.
6. Don't be funny just to be funny — it isn't valid. The humor must make a point.
7. When you choose a volunteer to be on stage, don't put her/him on the spot unless you can handle all aspects of the situation and respectfully have the volunteer participate.
8. Don't pass off a shoddy show or concept and think it's OK because "they're just kids."

Chapter 15

Audience Participation

The most important thing to do when you want to use audience participation is to teach the children your procedure for calling the group back together again to be still and silent after participating. In other words, what will you use as a signal? We have found the most convenient signal is one that is used in many schools, to have the leader, speaker, or master of ceremony (emcee) simply raise a hand high in the air.

When audience participation is at the end of your show, then immediately take a bow, thank the children, and let them raise their hands and ask you questions about the program (this is optional for audiences under seven years of age). Then simply tell them that you will teach them a hand signal. Explain that when you lift your hand "like this" (demonstrate it) then that means it is time to be still and listen to what you are saying. With a signal procedure in place to call the group back to order, you can begin audience participation.

Begin by saying "I would like quiet volunteers to raise their hands. I always choose the quietest people who raise their hands." Next send someone into the audience (unless you are a solo performer) to choose some children from the back of the audience. The onstage emcee can choose a few in the front. Bring small groups onstage — and make sure beforehand that you have checked out and safety-tested the route onto the stage space. Any wires on the floor that might trip kids should be taped down ahead of time with duct tape. (See Chapter 9.) If the stage is high off the ground, you should let teachers know before the performance that you will need them to stand at the steps to make sure children come on and off the stage safely.

When you are finished with one group and plan on choosing another group you should direct the first group down in a clear manner. Ask the first group to return quietly to their seats and to help smaller ones down the steps (if necessary). As they begin to leave the stage space, stand between the children and the edge of the stage so you can encourage the older children to help the smaller children and you can also watch for pushing or shoving and immediately prevent it.

Never let children run and jump off the stage. It is a recipe for injuries and an invitation to chaos. The first run and jump leads to more, so be vigilant and prevent that first child from jumping. If you miss and one jumps, quickly and quietly bring that child back and have them go back up and walk down the steps. One example of correction and a verbal positive "I like how this person is walking carefully down the steps" and children will get the message that this is not a daredevil time.

To summon the second group of audience participants, bring the audience to order with your raised hand. At this time all dancers in the company who are onstage should stop and look at the dancer/emcee and raise their hands too. It takes a while for the first children to get back to their places (this is where aisles really expedite movement) so the emcee should wait until most are seated before raising a hand. The emcee and other dancers should use the forefinger to lips in a silent "shhh" sign if the audience is still talkative. The emcee should wait as long as it takes for silence (with only a few whispers). Then say (if it's true), "I like the way this group came to order, your teachers should be proud of you!"

Positive feedback in the beginning of audience participation sets the tone for respectful behavior on the part of students, teachers and performers. Teachers especially appreciate children being rewarded for following rules; in turn, your compliments reflect on the good job that the teachers are doing. This makes a winning situation for all concerned.

Then continuing, the emcee/dancer should say, "I would like *new* volunteers, who have never been up on the stage before, to raise their hands, and when I point to you please walk up the steps [or into the stage space]." Then begin the process once again.

Depending on your activities planned for the audience participation, the type of dance you do and the time you have remaining before the end of the performance, you may have time for two or three rotations of volunteers. Since our company's philosophy is to involve the children in the creative process through movement improvisation, we usually have two or three rotations of children in creative dance — perhaps points of balance, shape maker/shape filler, and then an energy pass.

Then, in accordance with the "golden rule" for performers for children in schools, to calm the children down, we always finish with a quiet activity — like mirroring — that all children can participate in from their seats. If you violate the "golden rule" in a school setting and end the performance by sending a wild group of children out of the auditorium, you pretty much have guaranteed that it will be years before another dance performance is hosted by that school during school hours. You owe it to your fellow companies to calm down the children, and when you take your final bow, tell the children that they need to remain in their seats and wait for the teachers (or principal) to tell them what to do.

Before you take your final bow, however, you might have time to answer a few questions. When taking questions, call only on children who seem to be at least in third grade (eight years) and up. If you select kids younger than that, you might get students' statements about random things, like what they had for breakfast that morning! Again, ask for raised hands; be sure to let them know that you especially welcome questions about the performance (this is to weed out questions like "Are you married?" and other precocious or irrelevant queries).

Usually you will get the best questions from children who have had more art-related assembly programs. These children are more advanced in the ability to see symbols as meaningful and also have a sense of what discipline is involved. Economic, racial, or environmental (urban or rural) factors do not change the quality of questions from children as much as previous exposure to arts programming does — at least in our dance company's experience. A group of children who have seen more artistic performances tend to ask questions that are thoughtful and pertinent to the performance — in contrast to the type of unsophisticated questions asked by a group that sees a live artistic performance for the first time.

When you call for volunteers in a performance setting, the sad fact is that some children will raise their hands, but not be chosen. Yet despite this drawback and because of the inherent value of giving children a chance to see their classmates active in movement, go ahead and select as many as you can, even if you never can bring everyone who volunteers onstage. Our company always addresses the inequity of this right away, by saying, " For those of you who don't get chosen, you have an important role. You are the living video recorders. Remember all the rules and how to play each improvisation and perhaps on a rainy day your teacher will let you do these movement games again!" That tends to mitigate the disappointment of not being chosen.

In addition, most schools have children who are in wheelchairs or otherwise disabled. Be sure to call on at least one such volunteer to help set an example for movement/dance possibilities for special circumstances. Students with disabilities almost always have an aide who will move the wheelchair to the front of the area below or beside the stage and set the brakes. Then the aide or one of the dancers can assist the student. The aide or dancer can gently encourage or even help move different body parts — or if the child is not capable of appendage use — rock or roll the wheelchair forward and back (always make sure the seat belt is securely fastened, and the wheelchair lock stabilized after.) Inclusion of this sort usually makes everyone involved feel great and encourages the ambulatory students to look at what their disabled or wheelchair-bound peers can accomplish, which often surprises everyone by being quite a lot. Teachers will notice and appreciate your efforts of inclusion.

It is a good idea to have one dancer circulate in the audience (or to announce from the stage) as you ask for the second round of volunteers that teachers may send a person from their classroom if no one from their class has been selected yet. That way you are sure to have included at least one audience volunteer from each grade level and room.

Once the children are onstage, it is important that they be cautioned to find a personal space where they can't touch anyone or anything. If everyone is too far upstage, then ask the entire group to take a giant step or two baby steps (or whatever it takes) — forward to spread them out. Be mindful of the stage drop-off or relative closeness to seated members of the audience.

If you have a set you think needs to be protected, then post a dancer next to it — to prevent damage to the set or to a child. One dancer can circulate during the participation activities to ensure that the children are not too close together or to be near mischief-makers. Most often, though, you will discover that discipline is practically no problem. Mostly the children are excited beyond belief to be onstage and put their whole attention and focus on the emcee and on the activity. Sometimes the excitement can prove to be too much. It always pays to have paper towels or something to clean up bathroom accidents from a really excited young one! (Yes, this actually happens — but for us, only twice in 20 years!)

Conversely, if you know that you have a mess onstage — of props, say — that you need to have moved off before your audience participation begins, then before the show, enlist some volunteers who, when given a signal from you, will come up onstage with you to help. If you use these types of volunteers, be sure to give them a memento of thanks. For instance, we presented our helpers with a shiny metallic star after our *Stars and Constellations* cleanup. They were thrilled and we had an easy solution to quickly clear a huge number of props offstage.

Menagerie Dance Company dancing the Navajo legend of how coyote throws stars into the night sky from *Stars & Constellations*. Choreography: Mark Magruder. Pictured in a mask, he shakes out the blanket of sparkling, floating metallic paper "stars" that eventually fall onto the stage (credit Andrewwildsphotography.com).

If you have room in front, below the stage, for more volunteers, you can bring children to this area as well, if you have an eager crowd. Just be careful always to make sure they are safe doing what you ask them to do in the participation. It has been our experience that in the younger grades (K–5), just as many boys as girls volunteer. Always try to choose a cross-section of children, boys, girls, younger, older, different ethnic backgrounds, a quiet one, a "bubbly" one, children who are different — someone with glasses, or someone with clothes that might reflect an impoverished background. Celebrate everyone. They will love it and those happy faces will cheer you up and make you glad you're a dancer on tour.

Full volunteer participation is best for K–5. For middle school, grades 6, 7, 8, and for high school performances, a better format for your show is to avoid audience participation and turn the entire performance into a lecture demonstration format (with microphone). The goal of middle school and high school students is to belong to the crowd and not to be different. Honor that need. Instead of asking for volunteers to come onto the stage, show these older audiences parts of your warm-up and relate it to sports conditioning, or to other parts of their lives. Talk about the ideas in your dances that you will perform and show a phrase or a lift from the dance — then explain the mechanics. This method trains these older students to be good observers and lets them know what to expect. Sneak in a little participation — perhaps mirroring, or lifting a heavy imaginary object and then a light one — they can do this from their seats in the audience and don't have to single themselves out!

Chapter 16

Don't Be a "Drop-In, Drop-Out" Company: Master Classes, Workshops and How to Handle Them

When you perform in a school setting, recognize that schools have an enormous task; they have to educate all the children who attend, no matter the diversity of children's backgrounds. To accomplish this they struggle to develop and fulfill goals — some mandated by state and national standards. For every school, it is the proverbial "united we stand, divided we fall" organizational matrix that gives results. The best schools are like unified planetary systems or complicated engines. Each part turns or revolves on its own, yet interfaces with all the other parts. In schools, good work is accomplished — education. Your dance company presence must be a part of that system. Where do you fit in with the educational goals of a school? The worst-case scenario is to be the loose bolt that throws the whole engine into dysfunction — disrupting normal schedules to the extent that the important work of teaching is interrupted. The best-case scenario is to avoid the drop-in, drop-out syndrome — where nobody is ready for your presence and nobody remembers to integrate your performance into the teaching matrix when you're gone.

Instead, seek to promote a full connection to the educational goals of a school. First, ask the school ahead of time what you can do to enhance specific educational topics and standards though the focus of your performance, master classes and workshops. Chances are you and the principal or arts presenter will already have discussed this as a part of the booking process. Probably your company's topics will accomplish part of this for you. When we performed Native American stories like *Flute Song*, the principals were quick to point out that this was what a particular grade level was studying. Push this connection further. Suggest specific topics in the teacher guide and in conversation with the principal or contact person. The school library could even feature books related to the topics that are presented in your dance performance and in the classroom.

Try always to expand your presence beyond the stage and performance. Offer master classes and workshops for particular grade levels or interest groups — such as all the children who are working with drama (or dance). Ask if the principal has special needs student, or any students who love performing, who might benefit from a more in-depth after per-

Child's drawing after seeing Menagerie Dance Company's *Fog Woman & Raven*, a dance based on a northwest coast Native American folk tale. Dances can bring topics in history, literature, or geography to life.

formance experience. Sometimes principals have the teachers choose students who they think will benefit from a kinesthetic and creative experience. Innovative principals will have children interview you for the school newspaper or on video or audio tape to be broadcast later for announcements or special television time. Travel from room to room and teach fifteen-minute mini-workshops. You can involve the children and teachers in creative problem solving through movement, using activities that the children could participate in from their seats or while standing beside their desks.

When teaching any workshop, always end with an activity that returns control to the teacher, such as having a teacher lead a final activity such as mirroring. This kind of ending both encourages the teacher to engage in an movement activity — something they might not be completely comfortable with or even know how to approach — and ensures that the teacher does not have to struggle to regain control of an excited and motivated group of children who have just had a lot of fun in a workshop.

The teachers who participate in these workshops learn how to use teaching tools that appeal to the kinesthetic intelligence of the children, such as when teaching adverbs: "Move your hand smoothly in front of you, now softly, forcefully." Harvard University educational psychologist Howard Gardner's research into multiple intelligences has transformed many attitudes in education. Many educators are more willing to add ways for children to use their kinetic intelligence and learn content kinetically as well as visually and musically.[1]

Mini Master Classes

A sample activity from a short mini master class *in a classroom* might include "shape maker/shape filler." This old chestnut has a lot of depth; it appeals to varying age groups, can be done in a classroom setting without moving desks, tables and chairs, and is so much fun that students don't even realize that they're learning prepositions, geometry and practicing skills of all sorts until you call their attention to the content that they have mastered!

To play shape maker/shape filler, first have the students find a partner. One person is the shape maker, making large, open shapes, and the other partner is the filler, who moves through the empty space. This is a wonderful chance to talk from a visual artist's perspective about positive and negative space — or from a scientific perspective. Is the space really empty or is it filled with air, oxygen and carbon dioxide? Or you can talk from a perspective of contrasts and opposites: the shape maker moves *slowly* and the filler moves *quickly*. Or you can approach the activity from a grammar perspective — the shape filler moves *over*, *under*, *around* and *through* the empty negative spaces. Or concentrate on the social interaction as the dance educator Anne Green Gilbert elaborates in her version of the activity. As the shape filler moves, that child must take care to respect the personal space of the shape maker and not bump or push. Then the shape maker has the responsibility to be strong and move with strength and balance so as not to bump the

A good (and calming) transition from your dance company's workshop back to the classroom: Ask a teacher to lead mirroring with students.

shape filler. If you examine them carefully, you will realize that movement activities in dance are filled with the most basic and crucial lessons.

Large Master Classes

Master classes and workshops are a wonderful chance for the dance company to deepen children's experience of dance and to touch the hearts and creative minds of children. However, disorder can ensue if conditions and expectations are wrong.

Location

The best place for a master class is usually the gym, if there is one (and that's a big if). If you use the gym, ask the principal or contact to make sure the physical education teacher knows that you will be teaching there so that there won't be other classes in the gym competing for the children's attention. If it rains and the gym has to be used for P.E., find out other places where the alternative teaching space will be — perhaps the class might be held in a multipurpose room or in the library. If you have the master class in the cafetorium, make sure you know ahead of time if meal preparation or serving is planned during the teaching time; if it is, perhaps a door to the kitchen can be closed, or you can invite the cafeteria workers to watch when they're done. That way at least they know that you plan to teach while they are working and they may make an effort to be quiet.

Sometimes the only space available is the stage; even if you stick to an optimum size of 40 children per workshop, if the stage is small the space will be inadequate for teaching. Under these circumstances, you can divide the group in half— alternating each as the half that moves and the half that watches. Then be sure to switch groups frequently and regularly. Sometimes these are the best classes because everyone learns by watching. This also gives you another shot at developing children's audience skills. Ask the half that watches, "What does a good audience do?" You can tell them that a good audience uses their eyes to watch, think inside their head (not out loud), and applaud at the end.

In all teaching situations and environments, you must briefly give rules and talk about these rules and procedures for stopping and starting an activity. Your rules might be:

> *Rule #1 Make sure you move in empty spaces — not close to anyone or anything.* (At this point you might want specifically to set boundaries, i.e. as far as the last table in the cafeteria, up to the basketball hoops — or an arm's length from the edge of the stage or stage curtain.)
>
> *Rule #2 Respect personal space.* (Specifics of this rule are "to silently put on your brakes" when you are moving too close to someone else and to "use your eyes" to see. This includes instructions like, "Turn your head and neck so you can see people around you.")
>
> *Rule #3 Listen and follow directions.* ("Keep it safe, keep it kind, and work as a team.")

Then, give procedures or ways that you will direct the children to help them follow your directions.

Use a drum accompaniment for signals in a master class.

Procedure #1— To signal a time to listen —"When I [beat the drum once] or [raise my hand] or [stop the music]" then "stop and freeze" or "listen and sit down."

Procedure# 2 — To find a partner —"Look to the right or left, and silently find a partner, then sit down." (Anyone left standing can be the classroom teacher's partner, join a group to become a trio, or be the workshop teacher's partner and help demonstrate.)

Always bring along a drum in addition to any other recorded music. Live accompaniment is always a vital way to establish a link between leader and participants and the drum is the greatest attention getter of all. When we first began to tour we purchased an elaborately carved African "talking" drum. It presents a wonderful way to begin a master class — students always have questions about the drum's origin, design, and the role it will play in class. A loud drumbeat means "freeze" and "listen" in many languages!

If you are teaching a technique-type master class that includes lines going across the floor as a part of the format, optimize moving time and avoid having times where children have to wait in lines. Also, if you do across-the-floor work, never tell a group to back up without first telling them to look behind and ask the person behind them to move back so that they can step back without bumping into one another.

A good strategy for teaching is not to use lines at all. Just ask students to move throughout the space. Yes, this works for leaping as well as running phrases if you practice setting up personal space boundaries ahead of time. For young children, the analogy of a "force field" around each person is a useful one. Another coping strategy is for the teacher to be in the middle of the space and have children circulate like planets around the sun. Then reverse and go counterclockwise. The advantage of all these methods for locomotor patterns is that all children are participating all the time.

If you must arrange children in rows, then appoint a lot of leaders and have lines with no more than five children. Then quickly say, "Everyone who is second in each row, raise your hand," then repeat for third in the rows, fourth, fifth. Next, set up counts, signals, and proceed — "Ready, now first people go across, second in each row go across," and so forth. Remember, as discussed earlier, after a workshop, master class, or even a performance, it is your duty as the workshop leader to calm the children down with a quiet activity like mirroring or breathing pattern *before* you send them back to the classroom teachers.

Discipline

In the best of circumstances, the classroom teacher will join in and/or watch the master class and be ready to intervene when students behave inappropriately. However, sometimes you may be the only adult present. It is important for you to be aware of normal motor skills and behaviors for each age so that you do not ask children to do things beyond their skills or abilities. Children who are pressed beyond their capacities sometimes behave inappropriately, a situation that you can avoid in teaching if you understand what children normally can be expected to achieve. For instance, many five-year-olds can't skip.

For the same reason it is also important to be aware of how children behave socially and developmentally at different ages. It is normal for eight-year-olds (third graders) to talk incessantly. A room of quiet but active third graders is only quiet relative to other third graders. Socially, middle and high school students want to blend in with their peers; for them, circle warm-ups are a good way to include everyone. (Everyone stands on the perimeter of a circle rather than spread out through the space.)

Never force a boy and girl to be partners if they don't want to be. Ignore developmental skills and social information at your own peril! You want children to enjoy your workshops; then they'll want to try it again.

Have zero tolerance for physical violence — hitting, bumping, tripping, and so on. This is the most basic form of respect, to not harm another person. Consequences of a repeated behavior after a warning should include time out until the student perpetrator regains control and decides to rejoin the group. A third infraction should result in removal from the class.

Never belittle a child — either verbally, with derogatory words, or nonverbally with negative gesture or facial expression. This is a basic rule of respect. The teacher must model appropriate behavior and control. It is amazing that a few classroom teachers and some dance teachers mistakenly think that motivational speech involves "put-downs," criticism and other forms of negative feedback.

Conversely, positive feedback is the most powerful tool a teacher has. However, make a three-layer-deep positive compliment part of your effective teaching strategy. First

When children dance together around the teacher in place and throughout the space, everyone moves more; this minimizes boredom of standing in lines and waiting.

layer — *"Great! Good!"* Second layer — *"Great leap!"* Third layer — *"Great leap! I like how you use your energy pushing away from the floor!"*

In this way, positive reinforcement includes praise, what the child is being praised for (a leap) and how she does it. The other children in the class benefit from this kind of compliment as much as the child who is being praised, because they hear how they can be better — they can push away from the floor, for instance. When we first began touring we inevitably had to walk past classes in session. It was fascinating to see how some teachers and principals obviously were much better than others at motivating children and at helping children develop appropriate behavior. We began to study these effective educators to try and figure out what they were doing differently from their less effective peers. Most of the tips and information in this section of the book originated from watching great teachers and principals in places where we have performed.

Chapter 17

Assessment and the Structure of Evaluation: Questions to Ask Yourself and Your Audience, and Why

A written evaluation form is a great tool to give you important quality control feedback and to let you know if you are accomplishing your mission in the eyes of others, such as the teachers who attend your performances. In addition, written evaluations give you unexpected insights into what you may be accomplishing without even knowing it. A written, anonymous form frees people to convey to you what they may be embarrassed or too shy to say to you after the show. It is extremely important to know your impact — positive or negative.

Sometimes little difficulties with costume or set may pop up in evaluations that you may not have recognized as being problems. Most presenters and teachers will gladly offer suggestions for improvement in presentation and so forth and most of the time they are right on target. Sometimes, though, you will receive criticisms that are not applicable. That's okay; you are always free to use or disregard a comment!

There are several other important reasons to have a tool to assess your show. One is to gather data that may help you when you write a grant. If you have written testimonials or glowing comments about your show — these are very useful to convince grantors that you are doing what you claim to be doing. If you tour in varied types of performing environments — urban, rural and in-between — your evaluations (hopefully) will reflect the broad appeal of your artistic work. In addition, you may be able to use comments or quotes from your assessment data in your publicity materials, such as your brochure or website. Since teachers, principals, and presenters will have just seen your show when they fill out an evaluation, their comments often are fervent and enthusiastic. These immediate reactions reflect the vitality of your performance in a way that comments written several days or longer after your performance do not.

Additionally, compiled data over time can reveal trends; in ratings that compare the success of one show over another, for instance. We first spotted the tendency of young audiences to prefer our abstract dances like *Cranes* or *Symbiosis* over our dances based on stories about human characters through the compilation of our long-term evaluation feedback. Normally, once a show is up and running, too much time and money have been spent to change it drastically; but if you're getting consistent comments about a particular set item, costume or presentation tool, then those aspects of the show can be modified to correct and improve the reactions of audiences. Also, data can show social trends, prejudices towards certain content areas, or other aspects that affect the reception your dances receive — such as the big attitude shift that we discovered in the early 1990s that made us decide to stop wearing unitards and start wearing "real people" costuming.

"Wait," you say. "Why should I care about social norms and mores when I'm expressing my artistic vision?" Well, often dance material or an entire show that might be criticized or even rejected outright — as too sexy, too ugly, or too whatever — can be changed just a little to make it acceptable for an audience of children and teachers — without compromising your message. Perhaps it's not the material, costume or theme that should be changed, but the way in which it's presented.

In a fifth grader's mind there is not much difference between a man wearing a Renaissance tunic and a man wearing a dress, until you explain the difference and add in a little history — perhaps when you circulate through the audience before the show begins and answer questions from children. That is why verbal explanations and communication with an audience — usually through formal explanations built into your show or through Q & A sessions — are crucial when you are working in an educational environment or in any area where people are not familiar with live artistic performances (which is to say, certainly most of the United States).

Take nothing to be common knowledge. Some children have never heard of any kind of music but "rock" or "country." They have no frame of reference to actually "hear" Western classical music, or music from any unfamiliar culture. Put any part of your dance that is being criticized by a child, teacher or principal into a suitable frame of reference — one that reflects a particular historical, stylistic, or content area — and you may solve the problem of misinterpretation as well as reception.

We learned our first hard lesson on this point early in our performing career. Deep in the heart of the Appalachian Mountains we were booked for a single performance at a rural high school. Thinking (wrongly, as it turned out) that high school age equaled "almost adult," we decided to dispense with the audience pre-performance discussion and just do our dances. We figured that the costumes, dance and music would pull the audience along as it had in our New York and Washington, D.C., performances for general audiences. We were so mistaken that it was as if we had arrived from another planet.

Complicating the situation (unbeknown to us) before we had arrived, the principal, unfamiliar with live performing arts assembly programs (and in an honest attempt to motivate his students and reward the teachers for their hard work), told the students that if they attended the assembly, they wouldn't have any more classes that day. Then, he told the teachers that they did not have to attend the assembly; they were free to go and relax.

When we arrived, we found no stage, only a cavernous gym space, surrounded by bleachers on two opposite sides. While we hastily set up we tried to figure out what to do about the fact that the audience would not be seated in front of us. (We were late arriving because we were unfamiliar with the region and we had been trapped behind a coal truck going two miles per hour up steep mountain slopes!) Suddenly, all the students in the high school began trickling, then rushing in — pushing, laughing and shouting — all one thousand of them. No teacher and unbelievably, no adults — *including the principal* — ever showed up to introduce us. We plunged in, dancing away to the audience that sat on either side of us but not in front. To most of these inexperienced and unsophisticated teen-agers we were freaks in strange clothes. A kimono to them was a bathrobe. Since we gave no frame of reference for them to latch onto, they were hopelessly lost, confused and, as a result — raucous. This was the only show in twenty years that we ever canceled in mid-dance. It was cultural misunderstanding at its least tolerant and most confrontational.

Shaken, we dismissed the group, trying to contain our anger. Amazingly, one boy came up to us and said, "Please forgive my school, they [the students] have just never seen anything like this and they don't know how to behave. I really loved your dancing." With that he thanked us again and went off, leaving us feeling like we had somehow "missed the boat" — and we had.

It was painful really, to examine the reasons for our performing failure. We only had this one boy's verbal evaluation and our own experience to review to try and assess what had gone wrong. That was when we realized the absolute imperative of the *verbal presentation* of the cultural frame of reference — especially for teen-agers. Six months later we returned to a nearby county high school. The arts presenter was nervous; she told us that the previous performing arts assembly by a different group had gone badly and she was worried that the same might happen to us. This time, though, we were prepared when a new audience of a thousand teenagers trudged into the auditorium. We engaged the audience right away, and we held them enthralled for an hour.

You could have heard a pin drop as we led them through a verbal frame of reference talk. Using a microphone and amplifier so that we could avoid shouting and talk with them more casually, using a tone of voice that implied that we knew they were adults and were interested in everything including dance, we showed them a dancer warm-up. We talked and showed stretches, feats of strength (Mark does a great handstand push-up), the mechanics of partner work with lifts, a phrase from one of the dances and talked about the meaning of that phrase.

Then we danced for them the same kimono dance from the six months previous disastrous performance. This time we had a standing ovation at the end of the show and I don't think we have ever felt as triumphant leaving the stage! Yes, you can bridge that cultural divide, but you need a "Rosetta stone" — something that will serve as a translation guide — a sports metaphor, for instance.

Another lesson here for you as a company to understand, is that whatever effort you make to assess and correct your failures will pay you back multifold in the future. Granted, there were some other differences in environment — auditorium seating rather than bleachers, adults present — but believe me, *any crowd can veer out of control if you blow the presentation*.

Below is a sample evaluation form. Notice that it has only a five-point scale — the maximum you should use. It also has a place for written comments, a crucial element. We hand one to each teacher and adult who watches our program. We ask that they return the form after the show to the principal, who can look them over and then return the forms to us. Teachers sometimes ask their students to help them rate the show. The principal always appreciates a chance to evaluate assembly programs and to read what the teachers thought also. After all, the principals usually are the first contact people who take the chance and bring you into the school. They need to know if their expenditure of time and money was fruitful.

Performance Evaluation

Please Help Us by Filling in the Following Evaluation:

Site: _____ Date: _____ Time: _____

Sponsor: _____ Grade Level: _____ Number present ____

1. Audience response:	not at all enthusiastic	1	2	3	4	5	very enthusiastic
2. Artistic ability of performers	very low	1	2	3	4	5	very high
3. Rapport with audience	very poor	1	2	3	4	5	very good
4. Pace of program	unsatisfactory	1	2	3	4	5	satisfactory
5. Appropriate for age levels:	inappropriate	1	2	3	4	5	appropriate
6. Children's participation	passive	1	2	3	4	5	active
7. Quality of content	very low	1	2	3	4	5	very high
8. Overall impression:	very bad	1	2	3	4	5	very good

Feel free to elaborate on your impressions. Do you have any additional ideas or suggestions for future performances?

Thank you for completing this form.

[Your Dance Company]

[Address, Telephone #, and email]

What if you have unexplainable results on the evaluation form? Dancers and choreographers are notoriously thin skinned and sensitive when it comes to their work. Unjustified (or even justified) criticism of the dance or dancing can ruin someone's day. This is unfortunate, but you just have to be brave and deal with the criticism. Try to discern whether the negative assessments are accurate and if they are, then work to improve that area.

Sometimes, however, it will be beyond your control to change a situation. What follows is a list of things that we have found can skew the results of written evaluations toward the negative. They are things that you may or may not be able to change, and you just have to recognize and understand their impact on the public perception of a performance:

1. Weather — If students have been cooped up indoors all day with no recess they will be more restless if they have to sit for any length of time. If you perform in a warm climate and it starts to snow, forget it! Snow is way too big an attention diverter to fight!

2. School Leadership Problems — Principals who leave the room during a performance or who obviously are dictatorial and unsupportive of teachers give a sour note to the entire school environment. Everyone tends to be grumpy. Your performance evaluations will reflect this.

3. Time of the Show — Shows held too close to the end of school, especially on Friday afternoon, tend to have more restless and/or inattentive audiences.
4. Temperature — If the air conditioning or heating/ventilation systems are inadequate, or the floors are freezing and children have to sit on them to watch the show, everyone suffers, including the audience and its perception of your show.
5. Seating Arrangements — If the principal insists on seating students at cafeteria tables, most of the audience will be uncomfortable and will be too far away from the stage or performing space to see well.
6. Too Large an Audience — There is a strong negative correlation between the size of the audience and the rating of the performance if there are more than 350 in a school audience of elementary age children.
7. Religious/Racial/Gender Stereotypes — In some areas of the country certain children are prevented from attending dance performances because their religious beliefs prohibit dancing. Evaluations from teachers who belong to certain religions that have strictures against dance can skew your data, as can prejudices of any type.

This list is meant to help you understand puzzling evaluation results. However, you need to pay attention to all feedback — positive or negative — that seems to be well founded. Your goal as a company is to pay attention to quality control and constantly to try to figure out how you can present a better performance and residency. Evaluations help you do this, and you will treasure some of the positive comments for years to come!

PART IV

Dancing Their Dreams:
Ten Successful National
and International Dance
Companies, and Interviews
with Their Artistic
Directors/Choreographers

This section highlights ten national and international dance companies that perform and work with youth. Most also dance for general audiences too. One of the common themes within these companies' philosophies is that many of the choreographers/artistic directors do not believe that it is necessary or financially wise to limit their audience ages. Rather, they create performances with broad appeal and choose to tailor these shows specifically in the ways that the material is presented for children.

As the descriptions of dance companies included in these chapters illustrate, companies that perform and/or choreograph for youth organize in a variety of different ways. Each company presented here has a distinctive institutional make-up and a unique mission, yet there are many similarities in the experiences that they relate, the advice and cautions they offer, and in the value they place on maintaining the aesthetic quality of the work they perform for or with youthful audiences and/or young dancers.

Each chapter begins with a summary of the company's purpose and history, and then concludes with interview questions and responses. Interview lengths vary according to responses given by the busy artistic directors. In all my representations of their work I have tried to be as faithful to the information they provided as I could. As I researched each of the ten companies, I can say that I fell in love ten times because of the wonderful and unique work they do!

The purpose of these next ten chapters is both to inspire my readers to think broadly about the potential goals of the dance company they may want to form in the future and to show the creative organizational possibilities already successfully at work in the field. Some of these organizational categories include: professional dance company with performances for children; young graduate professionals trained in a university dance program who join together;

college/university based company directed by a professor of dance; youth dancers directed by dance studio owner; solo performers/choreographers; community outreach dance companies; and large, professional companies with extensive outreach goals. I hope you have as much fun learning about each of these organizations as I did in researching them.

Chapter 18

Dr. Schaffer and Mr. Stern:
Two Guys Who Dance
About Math

Dr. Schaffer and Mr. Stern Dance Ensemble is based in Santa Cruz, California. In 1990, after dancing together for three years, Karl Schaffer and Erik Stern conceived, choreographed, wrote, and performed in an outstanding show, *Two Guys Dancing About Math*. This performance follows two characters as they reveal the connections between mathematics and dance. Karl and Erik are professionally trained dancers and also are professional educators — Schaffer teaches math at De Anza College in Cupertino, California, and Stern is a dance professor at Weber University in Ogden, Utah. Based on hundreds of performances throughout North America and their experience in classrooms, they created (along with puzzle master and mathematician Scott Kim) an excellent resource for math and dance teachers, their text *Math Dance with Dr. Schaffer and Mr. Stern: Wholebody Math and Movement Activities for the K–12 Classroom*. Their website www.math dance.org offers ideas for classroom teachers. Video clips are at http://www.youtube.com/watch?v=aVsZdx7cTjc.

Their performance approach is innovative and kinetic, using modern dance, tap dance, and highly engaging verbal explanations and interactions to connect audiences of all ages to the areas that math and dance share. *Two Guys Dancing About Math* is one of the first of many performances that they have choreographed together as co-directors of their modern dance company. Their company size varies anywhere from two to five dancers.

In 2010 the ensemble performed *The Secret Life of Squares* in the Bridges conference in Pécs, Hungary, and was part of the European Capital Cities of Culture Festival. In the United States Schaffer and Stern serve on the Kennedy Center for the Performing Arts roster of master arts educators. According to the website, for cross-disciplinary performance work linking dance and mathematics, they have received five National Endowment for the Arts Access to the Arts awards. They travel across the United States performing and teaching workshops to other educators, in schools, and for general audiences. Yet, when questioned, they stress that they choreograph "serious works, seldom just for children." "More," Karl Schaffer says, "like circus, which appeals to everybody."

In their explorations and in the final stage product Schaffer says they draw the two subjects of math and dance together "at the deepest level." According to Erik Stern, in

Dr. Schaffer and Mr. Stern Dance Company in *Signs*. Choreography: Karl Schaffer (above) and Erik Stern (below) (credit Hazen Imaging).

their choreography they spend time "really sensing things. It's not didactic thinking, but rather a different type of thinking." Karl adds that there are "lots of misconceptions about how a mathematician thinks. In mathematics we use intuition, emotions, and feeling. It takes a full range of feeling to do math." In 1990 when they premiered *Two Guys Dancing About Math* at the California Math Council for an audience of over 1,000, the show was an overwhelming success. They performed it over 500 times touring across America.

Yet Erik says, "The initial idea failed," although "the failures were more private [than public]. It is important to get feedback. We used people in Santa Cruz and vetted the work a lot. We showed it to people like my wife, Greg Lizenbery [a dancer and collaborator], and his wife, Marilyn. The feedback that we got from them was that our audience interactions were 'lame.' We looked at those interactions very hard and began to recreate

Dr. Schaffer and Mr. Stern Dance Company in *Private Fly.* Choreography: Karl Schaffer & Erik Stern (pictured) (credit John Bakalis).

them in order to have interactions that flowed with our dances. We moved away from trying only to entertain to asking substantive questions."

"[We formed questions] that connect to what we were doing onstage," Karl adds. Erik continues, "It was easy to find connections between dance and math, but it took a lot of time to make a show that revealed those questions smoothly. In the same way, it took a lot of trial and error to make the workshops accessible and clear." Karl reflects, "The work involved is enormous — the studio rehearsals, the conceptual aspect, and the script don't happen automatically or by just sticking things together. We spent as much time on the theatrical aspects and script as we did the choreography."

EHM: Erik Stern and Karl Schaffer, what works for youth audiences?

Erik: Looking at everyday things helps with youth audiences. We used a handshake sequence, a basketball duet, and tap sequences.

Karl: What people think succeeds for youth audiences is often what sells — like Disney. But, in reality what appeals is something else — clear physical ideas that connect to or reveal an abstract idea, such as patterns in space.

Erik: The progression needs to be clear, whether abstract or a literal story. If it is muddled, it takes too much effort to understand, and you've lost the audience. If it is clear then the form is understandable...

Dr. Schaffer and Mr. Stern Dance Company in a concert titled *The Bounds of Discovery*. Choreography: Karl Schaffer and Erik Stern (pictured) (credit Hazen Imaging).

EHM: Did you use a booking agent?
Erik: We did it all own our own, no agent.
Karl: We did negotiate, but agents never stuck.
Erik: With youth performances you can get on a performing arts roster in counties or in a state; you can represent yourself and you can do your own representation in university seasons and theaters too.

EHM: What about grants and arts councils?
Erik: When we first began we applied to a local cultural arts council, but we didn't communicate [our concept] well, so we didn't get the grant. Later, that arts council asked us to reapply and we got a grant.
[Dr. Schaffer and Mr. Stern Dance Company has received grants from the California Arts Council, The National Endowment for the Arts, The Cultural Council of Santa Cruz County, and the Djerassi Resident Arts Program, among others.]

EHM: What is a professional life in dance like?
Erik: It's a challenge and always uphill in the arts. There's no way to sugar coat it. But if it means pursuing what you feel like doing, and you are not doing it for the money or the prestige, it can be very satisfying. It's a tradeoff, and it depends on what is most important to you.
Karl: If you ask, "should you be a dancer?" you may have already answered the ques-

tion in the negative — since dance probably needs to be something you just have to do no matter what. Outreach work has been pegged as [just] for children, and that can be frustrating. It is part of what you do, but it doesn't [have to] define your work.

Dr. Schaffer and Mr. Stern Dance Ensemble
P.O. Box 8055
Santa Cruz, CA 95061
http://www.schafferstern.org

Chapter 19

Plankenkoorts: A "Dutch Treat" Trio from the Low Country

Plankenkoorts Youth Dance Theater[1] (Jeugddanstheater Plankenkoorts) is a company from the Netherlands that has toured for fifteen years. The Dutch company has three dancers, all of whom graduated together from Rotterdam Dance Academy (now Coarts), a professional, degree-granting institution for higher education in dance, music, and circus. As dance majors, they formed their company as a shared venture soon after graduating from college.

The company offers in-school performances and workshops for children as well as full theatrical performances. According to Katjoesja Siccama, spokesperson and choreographer/dancer in the company, Plankenkoorts brings "spectacular and poetic modern dance performances that make you want to jump up and join in. Plankenkoorts dancers by nature like to climb, fly, jump, and fall.... Acrobatic elements are thus always naturally incorporated in the performances. More than spectacular tricks, they [acrobatic movements] are part of the Plankenkoorts dance vocabulary and convey meaning as well as beauty and awe."

Plankenkoorts is unique in the Netherlands because it always performs for children age four and older. However, as with most of the companies featured in this case study, the performances have broad appeal. Their shows are widely inclusive in terms of age, and bring laughter, awe, and exclamations of delight from enthusiastic audiences of all ages. Their performance in the 2006 Dance and the Child conference in The Hague brought a standing ovation from dance educators from around the world.

EHM: Katjoesja Siccama, as a co-director of your company of three, what do you wish you three had known before you began your company; i.e., what information would have made your experience easier?

KS: Caroline Bon, Marja Wijnands and I started our company almost twelve years ago from the simple wish to create and perform dance performances for children. We specifically chose to aim for an audience age four and up, since we all had very positive experiences performing for this age group with other companies. There are many things that we learned along the way, but I'm glad that we did not know all of these things beforehand. The knowledge might have prevented us from just throwing ourselves into this venture.

As our company slowly grew, we have always had a lot of support from our

Plankenkoorts logo (courtesy of Jeugddanstheater Plankenkoorts).

families and friends. Apart from their emotional support, their enthusiasm for our performances and of course faith in us, they have helped us many times with volunteer work, with great advice and even with financial support. In fact, a loan from our parents made it possible to start our first performance, without the hassle of going to a bank or through the different channels of funding. After presenting our parents a very rough sketch of the costs and revenue of creating and touring this performance, they loaned us enough money to start and even to buy our own van, which we could tour in!

[*Running a business*] Having your own company means running a business. We did not fully comprehend this when we started. We have always approached the business aspects — the sales, finances, phone calls, arrangements, and contracts, etc. — as means to make our company and our performances possible. We try to handle our business the same way as our performances, with the same joy. Taking it seriously but at the same time with a sense of relativity. And we learned as we went along.

Performing in schools often comes with harsh circumstances: cold gyms, early-in-the-morning starting times, and inexperienced organizations. By standing up for our dancers, we are also standing up for the quality of our performances. If the circumstances are good, both the audience and the dancers have a better performance. Teachers and organizers seldom realize this. This task in arts education of making them aware, I was not prepared for. If I had realized sooner that I am the professional in dance who has to teach them [teachers and organizers] about quality, dance, price, respect, and circumstances, the first years could have been less harsh. If I want to perform in the educational sector I'm the one who has to show them the what, where and how.

[*Vision (mission) statement*] When we first started, we knew more or less the kind of performances we wanted to make; our vision on youth dance already existed but it was not as developed as it is now and also not that outspoken. I would have liked to have more guidance in developing this vision. A clearer vision makes the performances stronger and the creating process easier since you can "defend" or explain your artistic choices. On the other hand a vision is one of those things that need to grow, will keep on growing and transforming, changing with new experiences and new insight. But still, more guidance would have been helpful.

[*Funding*] When we were able to express our vision on youth dance more eloquently, it became easier to write applications for funding. In the Netherlands there are many different funds that you can apply to for creating a performance, but for many years we did not make use of these funds. That gave us independence but also made our work very hard. Since we had no money to pay others we did everything ourselves. Having access to these funds after seven years made a big difference in creating our performances. For the first time we were able to work with professional décor and costume designers; we had more time for paid rehearsals and got help from a production assistant. This has professionalized our company on- and off-stage. With hindsight I would have used these funds sooner. And again some guidance in expressing our vision and our creative ideas on paper would have been extremely useful.

[*Evaluations*] When Caroline, Marja and I first started I don't think many people expected us to last this long together. One of the things we learned pretty quickly was that we had to take the time to talk together; to make sure that everybody is still on the same path. Each year we took the time for a meeting to evaluate the creating process and the tour of the last performance and to set our goals for the next year. We tried to make sure that there was enough room for everybody's own personalities and our artistic growth. And we have always had a lot of fun together!

When we started to work with other people (dancers, costume designers, technicians, etc.) we realized that the same rules applied. We were working with professionals but they were of course still also people. So if there were things not going well, we had to address them — the sooner the better. The evaluations we always had with the three of us, we also had to have with others. And again if there is enough room for everybody's own artistic growth and goals, they'll make a happy and inspiring team and original performances. As I said before, it was after seven years that we, for the first time, started to work with other professional costume designers, stage designers, technicians, and more dancers. This has been very inspiring for me and enriching for the productions. I can highly recommend it!

[*An outside eye*] In general I can also highly recommend working with people for a longer time, having a commitment with them, developing your collaboration. Apart from the dancers we have worked from the beginning with a dramaturge in creating our performances. Her critical view and her excellent advice have been a great help and a deciding factor in our performances.

EHM: Considering the young age of the children for whom you perform, how abstract can your company go?

KS: We chose our audience, age 4 and up, very deliberately. I like this age when the children are still so open to use their imagination. The abstract language of dance is a perfect communication for this age group since they are not so capable with words and linguistics yet. They don't feel the need to explain everything in words, making it into a "logical story." Instead they receive the images of the dance freely, welcoming them, allowing us to touch them in their hearts. Over the years our performances became more and more abstract. To a point where the question, "How abstract can you go?" came up. But I have not seen that border yet. On the contrary, the more abstract our performances got, the more the children appreciated them.

Keep [age] in mind, but… Although the form we use is abstract, there is always a philosophical and emotional layer underneath our performances. Children like to ask questions about the world in which we live. Art is a way to address these questions. Don't underestimate your audience! Having said that, it is of course also necessary to keep your audience in mind. Children have a shorter time of attention. We keep our scenes shorter, use inspiring music and make sure there is a right balance of different spheres and tension. We found our own way of doing this over the years. Our shows never last longer than 45 minutes. It works perfectly!

EHM: What is the most practical advice you can give to someone who wants to tour and to dance for children?

Katjoesja Siccama replies:

1. Do not ruin the market for yourself and others by selling yourself cheap. Explaining about production costs might help. Buyers will always go for a reduction/bargain. Be prepared for that.

2. To keep your dancers fit try to perform in the afternoons instead of the mornings as much as possible. It is much better for your body! A couple of years ago we started to perform two shows in a row in the afternoon, instead of one in the morning and one in the afternoon. Our bodies are more awake when it's showtime; our days are shorter and we don't have to wake up at 6:00 A.M. any more. Results: fitter dancers, more quality and more fun.

3. Don't perform more than 2 shows a day if you want your company to last and keep your dancers fit.

Plankenkoorts in *Castles in the Air (Luchtkastelen)*. Choreography: Katjoesja Siccama. Dancers: Femke Luyckx, Caroline Bon (credit Mieke Kreunen).

4. During touring: Always ask for adult, strong and enthusiastic volunteers to help build up the set in the schools.

5. During preparation time/production time: Try to get assistance. We have worked with interns, both as production assistants as well as tour managers. What a luxury! Ask volunteers, friends and family to help with promotion videos, photos, loading and unloading the truck, etc. It's not only helpful but also more fun with more people.

6. Don't perform on a concrete floor.

7. Make a contract in which you stand up for yourself, the dancers and the quality of the performance, so you feel comfortable with it and your company can last.

8. Don't let the hassle come in the way of your joy of touring and dancing.

9. Keep it pure. Don't alter your artistic views because you think you have to make a performance more accessible for children. They can handle more than you think. You'll last longer if you don't stray too far from your own ideas.

10. The most important thing is to keep believing in yourself and to follow your passion.

11. Make your costumes comfortable (be nice to yourself) and durable (they have to last!).

Opposite: Plankenkoorts in *Castles in the Air (Luchtkastelen)*. Choreography: Katjoesja Siccama. Dancers: Caroline Bon, Laura van Hal (credit Mieke Kreunen).

Plankenkoorts in *Risk! (Risico)*. Choreography: Katjoesja Siccama. Dancer: Caroline Bon (credit Willem Schalekamp).

12. Make your décor [set] practical (be nice to yourself). Not too heavy, easy to build up and durable; you have to carry it and set it up so many times, it's worth the effort (and the price).

EHM: What has been the best part of your dance career, as a young professional dancer?
KS: Having my own company makes it possible for me to create my own performances, which is something I have always wanted. I can express myself this way and am very happy that I'm able to do this. In my dance career I have always been able to do many different things. In my own youth dance company, Plankenkoorts, I am able to combine both choreographing and dancing. I'm glad to do both; I love both and wouldn't want to give one up. Also doing both has made me both a better dancer and a better choreographer. I'm also very happy that I've been able to combine dancing with (aerial) acrobatics. It has enriched my modern dance vocabulary, it is spectacular, and it is so much fun to do!

Apart from Plankenkoorts, I have always continued to work for other companies as well, mostly as a dancer, but sometimes as choreographer. Plankenkoorts is a small company. We tour with one performance at a time and have one cast that rarely changes. Our performances are in schools and theaters throughout the Netherlands and sometimes Belgium. Our audiences are children and never more than a couple of hundred.

One of the other companies I work for is a street theater company called Close-Act Theatre that has over thirty people working for them. We play amidst the audience in the streets or on a square, sometimes for thousands of people at a time. Then I've worked as a freelance dancer for different choreographers creating modern dance performances for adults. I consider myself very lucky to be able to combine these different jobs. The different audiences, different stages, different creators, different disciplines, different performers and different experiences have influenced and enriched my work greatly.

Jeugddanstheater Plankenkoorts[2]
Katjoesja Siccama
Kattenburgerkruisstraat 26
1018 JR Amsterdam
The Netherlands
+31 20 42 10 659
www.plankenkoorts.org

Chapter 20

Frequent Flyers™ Productions: Soaring through the Air, Rocky Mountain Style

Frequent Flyers™ Productions, founded in 1988 by artistic director and choreographer Nancy Smith, is an aerial dance–theater company based in Boulder, Colorado. The twelve-member company incorporated as a nonprofit in 1990. The Frequent Flyers Productions company mission is "to create and promote the magic of aerial dance through performances and education."

The multitude of ways and places that the company serves this mission is truly astounding. In its twenty-three-year history Frequent Flyers Productions (FFP) has toured schools in Colorado and the Northwest with its lecture demonstration company performances, performed in Montreal for Cirque du Soleil and at national conferences and political conventions; and, according to the company website, FFP has hosted the largest aerial dance festival in the world for the past thirteen years.

Its venues have included performances in traditional theater spaces as well as in a drive-in theater, a church, galleries, a graveyard, a meat locker, a junkyard, and abandoned greenhouses! The company repertory history includes aerial dance performance collaborations with heavy equipment operators, snakes, composers, computer graphics, children, and visual artists. FFP repertory ranges widely from pieces about comic book heroes to swing dance, from vampires to a gorgeously inspirational and colorful dance to music from Orff's *Carmina Burana*.

FFP founder Nancy Smith first danced with Joan Skinner's company (a choreographer noted for development of "Skinner Releasing Technique") in Seattle, Washington. Then Smith fell in love with aerial work, and trained with Robert Davidson, who became her low-flying trapeze mentor in 1987. She has been producing her own work since 1986. Nancy Smith has won a number of awards, among them Women Who Light the Community 2007 and The Colorado Dance Alliance 2005 Cutting Edge Award. She has received grants from foundations and corporate, state, regional, and national agencies, including the National Endowment for the Arts.

Smith's vision for her company is "to help people to see the world from a new perspective through experiencing the upside-down realm of low-flying trapeze." She believes "this expanded consciousness helps people to maximize their creative potential." From this perspective she has developed truly extraordinary programs for youth and educational outreach.

In 2011 alone the company taught more than thirteen hundred students in workshops. Since opening its dedicated Aerial Dance Studio, FFP educational programming has grown nearly 400 percent. FFP's Kids Who Fly classes are offered free of charge to youth at risk. These classes inspire young people "to view their world through art and joy, not fear and drugs." Smith believes that "youth of our community need a positive environment in which to take risks safely, build self-esteem, and experience the arts positively in their lives." The company has seen from its work with children and with at-risk youth in particular the benefits that result: such as confidence building and positive group dynamics — as well as an understanding of calculated risks and a new appreciation of arts of action, as opposed to leisure time that is passive — such as watching television.

In addition, the company explores the nexus between the art of aerial dance and classroom studies of math and science — physics in particular. They offer classes "to high school physics and math students and their teachers for a hands-on experience with low-flying trapezes to explore the physics, geometry, and mathematical principles inherent in the activity." Over one hundred youth and teachers from the Boulder, Colorado, area have participated in these two-week sessions. The workshop participants develop skills on the trapeze, and "explore circular motion, pendulums, harmonics, and torsional oscillation as physical experiences and through cognitive processes." Another purpose of this

Frequent Flyers Productions in *Midnight Antics*. Choreography: Danielle Hendricks. Dancers: J. Darden Longenecker, Danielle Hendricks (credit Robert Goldhamer).

program, called Aerial Sci-Arts, is to reach out in a fun way to youth who might not otherwise have the knowledge or opportunity to try an arts-based activity such as dance. Foundation support monies was the initial funding for this project.

Frequent Flyers Productions has an eleven-person board of directors. The board meets once each month to plan upcoming activities. Smith asks that her board members not only have lots of energy to give to the organization but also have an appreciation for "eccentricity." This is because, she insists, her work is eccentric, and board members must be willing to support her artistic vision for the company, as well as volunteer for myriad duties including "volunteer coordination, fund raising, graphic design, light clerical, costuming, box office/ushering, and stage managing."

In a tone and message that is only partially tongue-in-cheek, Nancy Smith reiterates her own personal goals that also are a part of her artistic vision. She says that her "penultimate ambition is to make upside-down, spinning dances in zero gravity and/or to receive a prehensile tail through the miracles of modern science." For at least the first part of that personal artistic vision, it seems that her board plays an active part. For the rest — the prehensile tail part — science may be lagging a bit behind!

EHM: Nancy Smith, what do you wish you had known before you began your company, Frequent Flyers Productions?
NS: That I was starting a company! It was never my intention. The funding was more readily available for a nonprofit corporation and one thing led to another.

EHM: What information would have made your experience easier?
NS: Surround yourself with champions of your cause.

EHM: What is the most practical advice you can give to someone who wants to tour and to dance for audiences that are comprised of or include children?
NS: Make sure your work is tour-able and appropriate for children. Make excellent work. Don't underestimate the power of beauty and art to reach children (don't dumb it down!)

EHM: What has been the best part of your dance career?
NS: Surviving it!

EHM: What has kept you going in the field?
NS: The opportunities to make interesting work and do interesting projects, combined with the fabulous people who have been a part of our company for twenty-three years (and counting).

Nancy E. Smith
Founder & Artistic Director
Frequent Flyers™ Productions, Inc.
P.O. Box 1979
Boulder, CO 80306
303-245-8272
www.frequentflyers.org

Chapter 21

Flatfoot Dance Company in KwaZulu-Natal: Outreach in South Africa

Flatfoot Dance Company, created in 2003 by dancer and award-winning choreographer Lliane Loots, is a company located in Durban, South Africa. The company's home is at the University of KwaZulu-Natal, Howard Campus, in the Drama and Performance Studies Program. The university provides facilities but no monetary support for the dance company. Funding comes mainly from the National Arts Council of South Africa, and other granting organizations both national and international. The company organization has eight full time, two part time, and two volunteer members.

The goals of the company are threefold. The first is to be a company that, in the process of entertaining its audiences, addresses contemporary issues that reflect the reality of time and place. The company utilizes the vibrant dance within the province of KwaZulu-Natal to make choreography that raises social awareness. One priority for the company is to exchange, perform, and work within Africa. In 2008, Flatfoot Dance Company performed in a festival in Lagos, Nigeria.

The second goal is to offer quality training and professional development for young adult dancers. It does this through a program for thirty dancers sixteen years and older, called Flatfoot Training Company. The purpose of this training program is to address the racial policies of the past that have prevented young black dancers from becoming professional dancers, teachers, and choreographers within South Africa. Classes are held so that the young adults can continue to go to school and hold jobs while in the training program. The rising number of young black dancers and choreographers who have graduated illustrate the success of this training program.

The third goal (and one of the aspects that makes this company unique and of interest in the context of this book) is its focus on both teacher training and development and on extensive community outreach for urban and rural youth in KwaZulu-Natal. Flatfoot Dance Company conducts over one hundred dance workshops each year in schools throughout the province. Most notably, they create specific dance projects, such as the extraordinary "Rights of the Girl-Child" Project that came from the realization that girls were often silenced during group projects. Since 2004, when the company received start-up funding from the Royal Netherlands Embassy, Flatfoot Dance Company has reached over five hundred girls though this project, which uses dance to address life skills train-

Flatfoot Dance Company in ***Zakubuyiswa Ngubani Na?*** **(*Who Will Bring Them Back?*) Choreographed by Sifiso Khumalo for a season called "Six." Dancers: Sifiso Khumalo, Vusi Makanya, S'fiso Magesh Ngcobo, Jabu Siphika, Shayna de Kock and Nobuhle Khawula (credit Val Adamson).**

ing — on topics of identity, sexuality, and HIV/AIDS education. Other projects with youth include Dance for Justice, Rights of the Boy-Child, and disability dance, among others, taking place throughout the province of KwaZulu-Natal.

According to the Flatfoot Dance Company website, Lliane Loots, artistic director, has taught dance and choreography throughout the globe, "Nigeria, Sweden, Denmark, Holland, India, Cameroon and Mali" among the countries where she has worked. Her dance "*Bloodlines*," opened the 2011 Dance Umbrella in Johannesburg and was performed in the Harare International Festival of the Arts in Zimbabwe that same year.

EHM: Lliane Loots, founder and director of Flatfoot Dance Company, what would you liked to have known before you started your company?

LL: Often, as young dancers and choreographers, the idea of starting a company is full of the euphoric ideals of days spent in rehearsal rooms creating and dancing and eventually showing dance theater to the public, of getting good reviews and of managing to live by the craft that we love so much. The reality is a little different! So while we do all the things above, the things that I would have really valued knowing about before I set out on this journey to create Flatfoot Dance Company was a much more keen sense, firstly, of the funding landscape of my own country. It is very rare, in South Africa, for dance companies to be financially viable without serious knowledge of how to go about accessing support funding from our National

Arts Council and various other funding bodies (both local and foreign). In a developing country like South Africa, accessing funds for what is often perceived as [a] "soft" priority (against a landscape of people needing water and housing and food) is a tricky terrain to negotiate for someone wanting to create dance and dance theater.

Secondly, I would have benefited, as a young dancer/choreographer setting out on starting a company, to have had more business knowledge simply around things like how to register your company, how to apply for tax exemption where it is applicable, how to write employment contracts for the dancers I work with.... Often, in our dance study and training, we do not give over enough attention to learning about the arts administration that will be required of us over and above the making of dance and the rehearsing in a studio. I feel that one of the things that might have made my journey easier, would have been an "arts mentor," someone to call up and meet with every now and again to talk through mostly the business side of running a dance company.... I would have valued a guiding intellect and some knowledge of the arts administration and business side of setting out to create a dance company.

EHM: What is the most practical advice you can give to someone who wants to tour and to dance for audiences that include children?

LL: Creating and dancing for children is perhaps the most difficult choice you can make because youth dance work is about MORE not less! It means you need to do your research really well. [Find out] who your audience is and, perhaps, how performance/dance literate they are. Children have the incredible ability to suspend belief and journey with you to all sorts of magical and theatrical spaces and places — this should be encouraged in whatever work you create and perform.

EHM: What has been the best part of your dance career?

LL: Once I got over the many administrative and business hurdles of starting a company, one of the great delights (almost seven years on) is to see the company flourishing and growing. I work with seven incredible dancers who are also exceptional teachers and, over and above the creating of dance and choreography, [the best part] is also to see the people I work with fulfill their enormous potential as both dancers and human beings. I think this is something to remember as you begin a dance company; that you will be part of working alongside some pretty amazing people who, like you, need to find their voices. [Isn't this,] after all, the great politics of our art form?

Lliane Loots, Artistic Director
Flatfoot Dance Company
c/o Drama and performance Studies Programme
University of KwaZulu-Natal
Howard College Campus
Durban 4041 South Africa
Fax: +27 (031) 2601410
http://flatfootdancecompany.webs.com
http://www.ukzn.ac.za/department/extra.asp?id=5&dept=dramperfund

Chapter 22

Peanut Butter and Jelly Dance Company: A Sticky Boston Quartet Named for Food

Peanut Butter and Jelly Dance Company is a Boston, Massachusetts–area company created by Jeanne Traxler, who is the artistic director and administrator. Jeanne co-founded PB&J in 1976 in Cincinnati, Ohio. The four company members are professional dancers who perform and do workshops in schools, libraries, and at festivals. In addition to other membership positions she holds in the dance world, Traxler is a board member of a dance and the Child international U.S. Chapter (daCi USA). DaCi is an organization under the auspices of UNESCO. The motto of daCi is that all children have a right to dance, and the goal of PB&J is to offer children a chance to experience dance by viewing performances, participating in workshops, and dancing in classes.

The focus of the PB&J Dance Classes for Kids is teaching creative dance for ages three through ten. Additionally, Peanut Butter and Jelly Dance Company sponsors a small youth performing company, made up of young people from these classes, called Small Feets Dance Company. Besides Traxler's extensive teaching experience, she has received grants from the Massachusetts Cultural Council and the Brookline Arts Council for choreographic projects; has choreographed school musicals; and has created site-specific pieces for Brookline's 1st Light Festival. She served as a co-chair of the daCi-USA: Massachusetts Day of Dance Conference in Worcester. Jeanne is the current treasurer of the Massachusetts Dance Education Organization and a founding member of the Children's Dance Festival, which for the past nineteen years has been presenting a day of dance with workshops and performance for youth.

According to its website, Peanut Butter and Jelly Dance Company is a group "whose performance approach is energetic and direct, combining colorful dances, movement concepts, and lots of audience participation. Their fifty-minute performances allow the young audiences to become involved with the dancers as they explain and explore the elements of dance movement and show finished dance works. The material presented corresponds to the dance standards in basic movement content in the various arts standards listings. The company members present workshops for teachers or students — integrating dance with curriculum, creating dances, or basic principles of dance."

EHM: Jeanne Traxler, founder and director of Peanut Butter and Jelly Dance Company, what are some of the issues that you have observed or encountered with school performances?

Peanut Butter and Jelly Dance Company, Shape Section. Dancers: Danielle Houk-Nino, Jim Banta, Paul Kafka-Gibbons and Lynn Frederiksen (credit Delia Marshall).

JT: There are different kinds of groups who go into schools.... There are the people who go in with basic "intros" for concert works and maybe [just] one little participation. But I think it is a wasted opportunity if that's all you're going to do.

    The children should have participation that teaches them something. Every teacher should say to you, "I learned something from watching this." Dance is not like music. There is so little of it [dance] everywhere that when you're in a "lec/dem" [lecture/demonstration] company, increasing dance literacy has got to be a subtext of everything you do. Nobody knows much about dance [here in the U.S.]; our famous dancers don't get themselves in the newspapers very much!

    I think that although it is OK to tour with young dancers as performers, you just can't go in with your recital dances to commercial music; you have to have something more.

EHM: What specific advice would you give to a company about performing for youth?
JT: It's really important to have a focused script.... If you want to start to work with kids you need solid, scripted ideas to work around, because they [the youth] need participation and a fair amount of it. And you need to know how to talk to your audience.

    The trick is to find that balance between the artwork you show (because even in a lecture/demonstration company you want to show full dances or longish completed sections) and what are you doing when you are not showing the pieces [the script and participation activities]. I believe that's really, really crucial.

EHM: What else would you like to tell someone who wants to create a dance company?
JT: Be prepared to spend a lot of time and energy. I was reading an arts management book that said that small arts organizations need to have their names in the media once a month. That's a lot of work!

Jeanne Traxler, Artistic Director
Peanut Butter and Jelly Dance Company
86 Greenough Street
Brookline, MA
(617) 738-7688
http://www.pbjdanceco.org

Chapter 23

Jasmine Pasch and Phew!!! Arts: London's Visionary and Her Company of Art Collaborators

Phew!!! Arts Company London choreographer Jasmine Pasch founded Phew!!! in 1997. Her company comprises three artists from different disciplines. It includes Jasmine, the choreographer and dance specialist, composer/musician Ian Stewart, and sculptor Jane Jobling. When working together, the three artists offer intensive, site-specific arts residencies in schools.

Within each school where they conduct residencies and projects the trio of artists, led by Jasmine Pasch, bring the members of the school communities — many of them special needs students — together to create, to learn, and to make art. Each project is carefully planned and developed to fit the atmosphere and actual experience of the children and staff participating in the residency rather than being imposed from outside. The experiences, often culminating with a performance and/or exhibition, reveal something new both to the artists themselves and to the children. The Phew!!! Arts Company mission in these projects is "to celebrate their [the students'] achievements through dance, music and visual art." Funding for residencies comes from various sources including the national dance trusts and arts councils, lottery funds that sponsor health and social service initiatives, private trusts from industry, and local arts organizations.

The artists in Phew!!! have separate careers, but they work together on a project-by-project basis. In addition to Jasmine Pasch's choreography for companies, festivals, and the many school and community dance/arts projects in the U.K. that she has created over the past twenty-five years, she creates innovative and challenging dance choreography with young people outside England. In 1998 she created a dance performance called *African Eagles* with street children in Durban, South Africa, and in 2001 she worked with children who were orphaned from, abandoned because of, or themselves suffering from HIV/AIDS.

Jasmine creates and dances with people of all ages and abilities, from deaf, physically and/or emotionally disabled children to mothers with their children and the elderly. She describes her abiding belief in the power of art to transform experience for those who participate in it as well as for those who see it: "I believe that dance is movement with meaning; that in dance we literally embody thoughts and feelings. My role as an artist and teacher is to create with the group that sense of shared meaning."

Early in her career after she trained as a professional dancer at the London School of Contemporary Dance, Jasmine studied pedagogy for adults and then received postgraduate education in counseling with emphasis on early child development. Between 1987 and 1995 she worked on more than fifty projects — pioneering innovative combinations of dance, sculpture, large-scale drawing, painting, sound installation, instrument making, singing and songwriting, and the use of electronic and acoustic music. The work laid the foundations for Phew!!! Arts Company.

Jasmine has published a number of articles on movement and child development, arts collaborations, and her work with special needs children. She is an excellent writer, and one of her most profoundly moving articles is about the *African Eagles* choreographic project with the young street children in South Africa. The sensitivity with which Jasmine delves into these types of complex social issues through dance collaboration and choreography is amazing. Both her writing and her artistic work explore the nexus between philosophical questions of human existence and social realities.

Jasmine frequently works with populations that offer significant challenges to society. For example, she has worked extensively both with elderly persons who suffer from dementia and with autistic children. Her writing for a journal called *The Autism File* includes an article called "Gentle Giants" about rough-and-tumble play with children on the autism spectrum, and another, published previously by the Foundation for Community Dance, begins with the following quote from the playwright George Bernard Shaw: "We don't stop playing because we grow old, we grow old because we stop playing."

Jasmine Pasch believes that the arts make a difference on both an individual and a

Phew!!! Arts Company's Jasmine Pasch (credit Chris Kelly).

community level, and that the arts "can make us healthy and happy." She seeks "to find out what factors enhance psychological and physical well-being, and foster resilience, and what destroys these." It is a testimony to her powerful artistic ability and sensitivity that Jasmine is able to integrate the fragmented diverse personal experiences of the participants of her projects, residencies, and choreography through her unique combination of dance, her philosophy of inclusion, and the deeply intensive and therapeutic creative investigations she uses in her choreographic residencies.

EHM: Jasmine Pasch, what can you tell us about your solo career as a choreographer?
JP: I do not run a conventional dance company as such. I work freelance.... Sometimes I work with other artists on collaborative projects in schools, which are called "residencies" here.

With the introduction of our [British] National Curriculum some years ago, many of these arts projects were simply squeezed out of the timetable as pressure mounted to teach the three R's. Now [in 2009] the notion of "creativity" is finding favor once more, and a government initiative called Creative Partnerships is bringing together artists and teachers again. Reinventing the wheel, or what?

EHM: What types of dance do you do in your residencies?

JP: I have just worked on a couple of such projects, one encouraging teachers to use dance and movement across the curriculum, and the other looking at the way children problem-solve in their bodies when they find using words difficult, or have English as a second language. There are many such children here.

Sometimes I simply go into schools to work with teachers and children on a specific project, story, or topic.... Sometimes I am hired in as a choreographer to work towards a performance.... Most recently, I worked as an artist-in-residence at a school for youngsters on the autistic spectrum. We spent a year "playing" and dancing. Much of the work happened outdoors as the children thrived in an informal environment rather than a classroom. Rough-and-tumble play became a firm favorite too, and I wrote an article on this for publication.

I am now working as a consultant and trainer for some of the London boroughs.... My interest is in the way that moving, dancing and playing help the brain and body to grow the capacities needed to be able to do things.

EHM: What is the most practical advice you can give to someone who wants to tour and to dance for children?

JP: It seems to me that choreography is choreography and no matter whom it is for/with, there are the same joys and headaches. It all hinges on the relationships with the dancers, and the curiosity around exploring the chosen theme together, whatever that may be.

EHM: You collaborate with a musician and a sculptor. How did you begin these collaborations?

JP: I have always used live music for my dance classes, and worked with many musicians over the years. One musician in particular suited the way I worked as he improvised so well, and could play anything in any style and was also a composer. He was also interested in visual art, drawing, and painting so relished the opportunity to work with a sculptor. The art forms just connected as I guess we three connected, and out of our conversations and friendship came the inspiration for our projects together.* Well, that's how it all began.

EHM: How have these artistic relationships affected your perspective on dance?

JP: I can't honestly say how it affected my perspective on dance. The art forms remained distinctive, but triggered connections and ideas between artists as a result of their relationship in a cyclical way. It would be hard to predict the outcome of a project at the start, and there would be many surprises and delights along the way, as well as nail-biting moments when things appeared to be going awry. Out of some of these dark moments would come a flash of inspiration, a bit of dark humor, and

*One project is on Haring's website: http://www.haringkids.com/lessons/envs/live/htdocs/lesson128.htm.

off we would go again trying something out that would lead to the next challenge or surprise. I was the leader of these crazy projects, and I never doubted that we would get there in the end. I think this helped a lot. I had total confidence in my team.

When Einstein was asked how he worked, he replied, "I grope." I think I do too. I describe my role as that of a "tracker," looking for clues, sniffing the air, noticing something small, a detail, a change in the wind.

Jasmine Pasch, Artistic Director
Phew!!! Arts Company
London, England
United Kingdom
http://www.phewartscompany.co.uk

Chapter 24

Kinnect Dance Company:
A University Troupe in Utah

Marilyn Berrett founded Kinnect Dance Company in 2002. She is the company's artistic director, a professor of dance, and head of the dance department at Brigham Young University (BYU) in Utah. Kinnect is a dance-education university-student performing group. The members of the group change each year according to the enrollment of the university course. Two days a week the company presents classes and tours an energy packed lecture/performance in schools, museums, and theaters in urban and rural areas throughout Utah and at national and international conferences.

The mission of Kinnect is to improve the teaching, creative, and performing skills of its members, and to serve as a dance performance outreach of the university. One semester each year a new group of dancers enrolls in the course. They then prepare to present dance as a creative process in elementary and middle schools. Their lecture/performances follow both the state and the national dance standards.

In 1997–98, after fifteen years as a full-time faculty member in the dance department at BYU, Marilyn Berrett took professional leave to pursue an elementary education certification and to teach in the public schools. She did this as a way of immersing herself in the curriculum requirements so she could train her university dancers to be better dance teachers, and also to examine how dance could serve the needs of elementary and middle school educators. After teaching in a public school she returned to her full-time university position. This experience prompted her to develop a program for "side-by-side" dance specialists and elementary teachers, to explore dance topics in children's literature, and to create Kinnect, a performing and teaching company.

Since that time Marilyn has won a number of awards and has traveled widely as both an artistic director and master teacher — traveling to (among other places) Turkey, Greece, Israel, South Africa, and Zhuhai University in China. At Shaunti Bahvan School in Bangalore, India, Marilyn received the honored title of "Teachers' Teacher." She has served as the U.S. representative of dance and the Child International and has presented many workshops for that organization all over the world, and in 2008 hosted the U.S. national daCi conference at BYU.

EHM: Marilyn Berrett, you worked closely with Virginia Tanner, the great children's creative dance teacher from Salt Lake City. Can you tell us how that influenced you?
MB: Virginia Tanner gave me a dance scholarship as a young child. She allowed me to

Kinnect Dance Company. Dancer: Shelley Vrooman Fitzgerald (credit Mark Philbrick/BYU Photograph).

dance. I couldn't have done it otherwise because of my family's financial situation. I also danced in her company. There is really no way to describe Virginia's magic. Her gift was to teach her students the wonder and the moving potential in everything. Her magic was so tangible. It was the transformative power of dance in the life of a child. That was the legacy that she gave to me. She believed that children's innocence needed to be guarded, that a child's approach to dance should be an engaging, wondrous activity — not pseudo-adult.

EHM: How is it to direct and work with a company of university-aged (18- to 21-year-old) dancers?

MB: For them it is authentic. All jobs are essential on tour. The performing and teaching experiences have high stakes, and they rise to them. There is research out there [in education] about how important actual problem solving is, [using] teaching skills in real classes, not just hearing about it in a lecture. The Kinnect company dancers' motivation is so strong. Authentic, is the word.

I think we really can't underestimate the potential of students who are these ages. What a great time of life — young adulthood! And for me to have some opportunity to influence their lives ... as they are creating who they want to be and what

Kinnect Dance Company. Dancers: Joshua Eaton, Chase Thomas (credit Mark Philbrick/BYU Photograph).

they want to do — is a great privilege. To be the one to introduce them to a new paradigm, to have the chance to show them things that they have never thought of— is an honor. They come [to the university] with simplified beliefs —"I'm a dancer, I want to perform, I love the applause." To help them understand that it is not about "you," it's about the *child* you teach. To help them mature and shift from an inward view of themselves to an outward view — to others, that is the great privilege and honor.

EHM: What have you learned about children (as audiences) who watch dance performances?
MB: When Kinnect performs, the child engagement factor is so high. We hear over and over again that "These kids have never been still for this long," or "Our kids are still dancing two weeks later!" or "Your students really know how to teach." Children are so in need of something meaningful in their lives.

EHM: What advice would you offer to someone thinking of creating a company?
MB: It takes incredible energy; it never stops being demanding. The rewards are powerful and amazing. But the demands are always high. This year, for instance, we created a show in six weeks — beginning in our university winter semester. We were commissioned by the art museum at BYU to create dances based on the work of the artist Walter Wick, who created ... the *I Spy* series [of children's books]. Our first performance was for an audience of over two thousand people!

[Maybe it's harder because] I bought into the idea that each new group [of university dancers who tour with Kinnect] needs to be actually creating what they are going to perform, each lec/dem — each performance. We don't tour repertory. Each winter semester the new set of dancers in the course creates its own responses to a new idea, with new sets, and new music. I don't redo the old pieces. I think every group deserves the chance to have their own identity. [Then] they are invested in the creative process — they are invested in their own creativity, and that is for them, magnifies the value of the experience.

However, I do admit that a pattern that I see in myself— is that I do things the hard way ... but I think you learn a lot and build character!

Marilyn Berrett, Artistic Director
Kinnect Dance Company
Professor of Dance and Department Chair
College of Fine Arts and Communications
Brigham Young University
Provo, UT 84602
http://www.byukinnect.org
http://dance.byu.edu
http://danceisbest.com

Chapter 25

CoMotion Dance Project: In Motion in Montana

CoMotion Dance Project is founded and directed by Karen A. Kaufmann, a professor of dance at the University of Montana in Missoula. Her company performs in schools throughout the state and region. CoMotion is a university-affiliated professional company directed by a professor of dance. Kaufmann has published many articles about making dance and working with people who have disabilities, and her lecture for the 2011 National Dance Association's Scholar/Artist Award was included in *JOPHERD*, the *Journal for Physical Health Education, Recreation and Dance,* a publication of the American Alliance of Health, Physical Education, Recreation, and Dance (AAPHERD). Her 2006 keynote address for The National Dance Association Conference "Dance Pedagogy for the 21st Century" was published in *Focus on Dance Pedagogy: The Evolving Art of Teaching Excellence* (2010).

Kaufmann is the author of *Inclusive Creative Movement and Dance,* a text for educators that presents tools for teachers to use dance in inclusive classrooms, "to celebrate and value differences, and to help all students discover the uniquely personal art form of dance" according to Kaufmann.

Karen Kaufmann teaches dance education on the University of Montana's College of Visual and Performing Arts faculty and directs the University of Montana's summer graduate program in arts education called The Creative Pulse. In 2008 Kaufmann introduced MoDE (Montana's Model Dance Education Program) which, according to its website, "brings professional dance educators into K–12 schools to get students and teachers moving."

Karen Kaufmann has taught dance to people of all ages and abilities for more than thirty years. Before founding CoMotion, she served for thirteen years as Education Director for Mo-Trans, another University of Montana–affiliated dance company. A choreographer, Karen has toured the Pacific Northwest both as a solo performer and artist-in-residence.

She was awarded a Montana Individual Artist fellowship for her lifelong work in dance education. Karen's dance work with adults with disabilities was the focus of a television program produced by Montana Public Television. She has presented at numerous conferences nationally and internationally and has a long affiliation with VSA (formerly known as Very Special Arts) Montana. She creates her CoMotion Project master classes and performances so that they are inclusive and accessible to people of all ages and abilities as well.

CoMotion Dance Project in the Whitebark Pine dance from *Fire Speaks the Land*. Choreography: Karen Kaufmann. Dancers: Allison Herther and Michael Becker (credit William Munoz).

EHM: Karen Kaufmann, artistic director of CoMotion, what advice do you have for anyone who wants to create a touring company?

KAK: Give ongoing feedback to the performers so they feel noticed and appreciated. Be sure to choose dancers who are flexible. Performing for children means cold gymnasiums, concrete floors in lunchrooms with squashed peas and dancing in mashed potatoes. Often there isn't time for an adequate warm-up. Dancers have to think that is fun — not have it be something they are putting up with. With the right group it makes for fun stories later on.

If someone isn't working out — deal with it soon. Don't let things fester. Be sure to keep the *business* side of your company organized but also pay attention to the *people* side of your company. Consider the group dynamics since being on tour requires that everyone be in very close quarters — living and dancing together. A company of individuals who get along well is essential.

Karen A. Kaufmann
Professor of Dance
Artistic Director, CoMotion Dance Project
College of Visual and Performing Arts
University of Montana
Missoula, MT 59812
comotiondanceproject.com

Chapter 26

Kaleidoscope: Seattle's
Rainbow of Dancing Children

Kaleidoscope Dance Company was founded in 1981 by Anne Green Gilbert, who is also the founder and director of the Creative Dance Center in Seattle, Washington. The company is housed in the Creative Dance Center, a large nonprofit studio that offers creative dance, modern, jazz, and ballet classes for infants through adults. Kaleidoscope is a modern dance company of youth dancers age eight through sixteen that performs throughout Washington State and tours internationally.

Kaleidoscope performs a wide variety of dances, choreographed by well-known choreographers such as Bill Evans, Anna Mansbridge, Shirley Jenkins, and Christian Swenson, as well as by emerging choreographers and young Kaleidoscope dancers themselves. The repertory varies from the playful *A to Zap*, about children's games, to a dance titled *Oh Be Gentle*, which is a piece that uses American Sign Language in a movement choir form to deliver a message about the environment. Gilbert's philosophy is that young people are able to achieve a professional level of artistic expression. The choreographic sophistication of the topics has, on occasion, caused controversy. Anne defends the subject material that her young dancers create, saying that young people think deeply about all kinds of important subjects. *Tribute to Stephen Biko*, choreographed by two of her young dancers, is a moving dance drama with a powerful message for peace and freedom.

In addition to her work as director/choreographer for Kaleidoscope, Anne Green Gilbert is also a noted lecturer, pedagogue, and active member of National Dance Association, and dance and the Child international, for which she was the past U.S. representative. In 2011 the National Dance Education Organization (NDEO) presented Anne with its Lifetime Achievement Award. She is recognized as one of the leading dance educators in the United States and abroad. Anne conducts teacher training though her Summer Dance Institute and has conducted hundreds of workshops for children and adults across the United States and in Japan, Australia, New Zealand, Canada, Finland, Russia, Denmark, France, Germany, the Netherlands, Brazil, and Portugal.

Anne is the author of *Teaching the Three R's Through Movement, Creative Dance for All Ages, Brain-Compatible Dance Education, Teaching Creative Dance* (DVD) and *Brain-Dance* (DVD). She is founder and past president of the Dance Educators Association of Washington, an organization promoting quality dance education in all Washington State K–12 schools. As a member of the Arts Education Standards project, she helped write the Washington State Dance Standards and Learning Goals. Anne has received numerous

Kaleidoscope Dance Company in *Retro Boogie*. Choreography: Deborah Birrane (credit Bronwen Gilbert Houck).

awards, including the 2005 NDA Scholar/Artist Award, and was featured in *Dance Teacher* magazine May 2006.

EHM: Anne Green Gilbert, when did your dance company with young dancers get its start?
AGG: I started my company 27 years ago when I was young and adventurous. The company grew from twelve boys and girls (ages eight to twelve) to thirty-eight boys and girls (ages seven to sixteen) [in 2008]. In the 90s, for a few years I had another company for teens that was an offshoot of Kaleidoscope because so many young people wanted to stay in Kaleidoscope. Then a Kaleidoscope graduate, Danielle Payton, at age 19, started Enertia Dance Company for high school and college dancers. She directed Enertia for ten years, from 1999 to 2009.

EHM: What motivated you to start the company?
AGG: I have always loved giving young people the tools to create their own dances and the space and support to do so. This energizes me every year. I love every part of my career — teaching all ages, training teachers, directing a school, and dance companies, choreographing, watching my dancers create and perform....

EHM: What special situations arise in a company made up of youngsters, other than scheduling around their school time, and being careful to not tire them out from over-rehearsing?
AGG: Tiring out children has not been a problem for me — they have endless energy. Plus we only have one two-hour rehearsal a week. Getting them out of school for school concerts is becoming a bigger problem. They constantly grow so costuming is

Kaleidoscope Dance Company in *From the Other Side.* Choreography: Mackenzie Dallas (Kaleidoscope graduate) (credit Debora Petschek).

a problem. Working with thirty-nine children of different ages and genders and abilities can be a challenge. Parents always are challenging. Many of the dancers come from broken homes and we deal with one to four parents [per child] and all of their complex schedules. Communicating rehearsal schedules, concert information, carpools, et cetera, to everyone can sometimes be overwhelming. I feel like a general plotting a campaign much of the time.

EHM: Does your company perform locally year round and tour just in summers?
AGG: We perform about once a month in schools. A major concert in December, a series of four concerts in May, a summer concert in July and then at national conference once every three years and an international conference every three years. Occasionally we have an extra community concert.

EHM: Do any other issues arise when working with young dancers as performers?
AGG: Once in awhile a parent will be a bit overbearing but I have learned to handle that part.

EHM: What do you wish you'd known when you started your company?
AGG: How much costume laundry and sorting I would have to do!

EHM: What is the farthest you have toured your company of children?
AGG: Australia, Japan, Brazil, Netherlands, Finland, and Russia.

EHM: How many chaperones?
AGG: We usually have one chaperone for every five to six dancers.

EHM: What is your advice to anyone who wants to create a company and work with young people?
AGG: You have to be flexible. You also have to be good at business, an artist, a nurturer, a PR person, and a little crazy. Or hire people who can fill some of these roles — not the crazy one! I think you also have to have a strong sense of self.

Anne Green Gilbert, Artistic Director
Kaleidoscope Dance Company
Creative Dance Center
12577 Densmore Avenue North
Seattle, WA 98133
(206) 363-7281
http://www.creativedance.org/kaleidoscope

Chapter 27

Dance Imagination:
Creative Kids in Canada

In 1990 Chris LePage and Dawn Howey founded their nonprofit youth dance company, Dance Imagination, in Burnaby, British Columbia. In a tribute to international inspiration and cooperation, they credit as crucial the advice given them by an American dance educator, the director and founder of Kaleidoscope Dance Company, Anne Green Gilbert. Like Kaleidoscope, Dance Imagination has dancers that span a wide age range — in Dance Imagination the performers are ages six to eighteen.

The young performers study dance at the Creative Dance Association, Chris LePage and Dawn Howey's nonprofit studio. Their studio places an emphasis — as its name suggests — on creativity. The classroom students in each of the courses create their own dances for the year-end production rather than learning a dance choreographed by someone else. Dance Imagination, the children's touring company, echoes this creative note and performs dances that mainly are choreographed by the dancers themselves, although it also performs work by guest choreographers, and traditional folk dances. Dance Imagination performs throughout the year at local elementary schools, in local, national, and international festivals, and at venues like Vancouver's Children's Hospital. They also appear in parades, at Canada Day, and other special events such as the Pacific National Exhibition. Each year they produce their own show to premiere their new dances. In addition, Dance Imagination has a well-deserved reputation in the international daCi (dance and the Child international) festivals for its dancers' friendliness and generosity of spirit.

Co-director Chris LePage is a longtime dance educator who taught dance for two decades in the local schools. He is also a movement teacher in the Orff music program (Carl Orff composed *Carmina Burana* and created a widely used system for teaching music to young people, using instruments like wooden xylophones and hand-held percussion instruments). Chris has worked with the Canadian Ministry of Education on dance resources. Co-director Dawn Howey has taught dance for fourteen years. Before she co-founded the studio and company with Chris, she danced with Arts Umbrella, Terpsichore, and Pacific Ballet Theatre. Together they have directed the local Burnaby Festival of Dance.

EMH: Chris LePage, as co-artistic director of Dance Imagination (along with Dawn Howey), what do you wish you had known before you began your company of young dancers?
CLP: Luckily when we were starting our company we had the help and advice of a

very special person, Anne Green Gilbert. We were in the process of setting up our company when we met her and she was kind enough to let us visit and observe her group in action and offer suggestions of what to do and what not to do. Having someone to talk to that has gone through this process before was extremely helpful! What made the process harder were the differences in regulations between our two countries [U.S. and Canada] and the expectations of our [Canadian] government. The legal process of setting up a company is not really designed for what we thought would be a small nonprofit group. The rules and hoops that one must go through are quite specific. I wish I had a better knowledge of working through the government circles. We are still learning — they change the rules and expectations from time to time.

EHM: What information would have made your experience easier?
CLP: As above, complete knowledge of the process — a lot of paperwork! — before beginning. It was easier for us because Anne helped us [avoid] a lot of pitfalls.

EHM: What is the most practical advice you can give to someone who wants to tour and to dance for audiences that include children?
CLP: Have a strong, supportive group of people around you. As the directors we are trying to focus on the children and make sure they are ready to perform. Having someone else in charge of dealing with parents, answering questions and looking after the many details that pop up is essential.

At one conference we had a problem with transportation. We were housed off site and the conference committee had arranged for buses to pick up the off-site groups first thing in the morning and return them after the late evening performances — but had not thought that the dancers may need to return to change, rest, get supplies, et cetera. [Our solution] was to have our parent in charge look after and arrange the details; that allowed Dawn and me to focus on the dancers and their needs during the day. Traveling and performing with children is fun, but there are always things that pop up and having people around who know what your goal is and can handle problems or changes quickly and efficiently is essential. It is impossible to do it by yourself, no matter how much you have planned in advance or think that you are prepared.

EHM: What has been the best part of your dance career?
CLP: Working with the young dancers, performing and traveling around the world and meeting other dancers. When we started we were dancing and performing in our community (lots of fun!) but as we grew and became involved with daCi we had the opportunity to travel to different countries and meet and learn about people from different cultures. This has definitely been an experience that most people never have the opportunity to do. You can travel anywhere in the world, but in the dance community [as a part of an international conference] you actually meet and interact with others at a level that is not always possible when on a family vacation. Our dancers get to meet, work, and dance with people from around the world, and thanks to the Internet and email are able to keep in touch with friends they have met on their travels. We have dancers who still email with friends from Jamaica, Germany, Regina [Canada], Brazil, the Netherlands, and the U.S.

Dance Imagination in *Angels*. Choreography by Dawn Howey (credit Wanda Mulholland).

The dancers in our company are like a family — the older ones are always help-ing, teaching and supporting the younger dancers who, as they grow up, take over the leadership role. Our company started out with dancers between eight and twelve years of age, but the dancers never wanted to leave and our company now goes from six to eighteen (and the dancers still come back and teach or choreograph dances even after they graduate). The friends we have made and the experiences we have gained are by far the best part.

EMH: What particular issues come up touring with a dance company of young performers?
CLP: There are different issues depending on whether you are traveling locally or longer distances. Our company regularly travels around our district performing at local schools.

- Know where the dancers will be performing and that the space is safe — checking ahead of time so that you can practice different entrances, exits or formations that may be site specific.
- Maps are good! Make sure that the drivers picking up the dancers know where they are going.
- Dancers have to learn to be flexible — when working with young children there are lots of times when the dancer will be sick, or may have a test at school and be unable to miss school that day to perform and you need to adjust on the fly (a skill our dancers have gotten very good at — we have had five school shows so far this year and none of them have been the same!).
- Dancers will also try and perform when they are not feeling well or are hurt and you have to make sure the dancer is safe at all times!

[When traveling long distances from home:]

- Be prepared for changes in behavior. Children [who are] not with parents react dif-ferently.
- Make sure that all dancers and parents know and understand the rules you have set out for the trip (we have behavior expectations that are explained to the parents and dancers ahead of time and have both [parents and children] sign a contract agreeing to follow the rules. For example, when at daCi the dancers are there to participate in the dance program. Parents may not take their child away for the day to do some sightseeing or shopping. While at the conference the artistic directors are in charge and have the final say: the parents know that all decisions are made in the best interests of the child and the performing group. For safety reasons a parent is in charge of looking after all money and passports — not a problem with younger dancers, but teenagers want to look after their own money and be able to buy things on their own.
- Make sure you have backups of all media and make sure that it will work where you are going. Also make sure that the back-up copies are not kept with the originals.

EHM: Are there any other issues you have encountered along the way?
CLP: One issue that we face that does not come from touring with young performers but from preparing is that we often have trouble finding [financial] support. Com-panies (and sometimes our own governments) are often reluctant to fund or support "children's groups." They are willing to give money to "professional" adult compa-

nies, but not to us. This makes it hard to raise funds. Plan ahead and start saving money early! For example: one way [one child in our company found to fund her international performance travel] was to ask grandparents, aunts, uncles [and] cousins to make a donation to a savings account instead of birthday presents. Over the course of two years she had saved enough to pay for her trips to Brazil and The Hague.

Chris LePage and Dawn Howey
Artistic Directors
Dance Imagination
Burnaby, B.C.
Canada
http://www.danceimagination.ca

PART V

Epilogue

Chapter 28

"Dancing with the Lettuce Leaf": Things That Can Happen While Touring, with Suggestions and Advice

Travel

In the course of many years of choreographing, booking and touring a dance company, many things have happened to us — some heartwarming, some awful, some sad, and a lot of funny situations! Touring a dance company is a lot like living the rest of your dance life. Just when you think you've worked out all the problems, trained yourself to be strong and flexible, some circumstance comes along that makes your turn at life go off center or your faithful leap into the future land off balance.

Most of the common bad car stuff has happened to us. A tire went flat the one day we had booked two performances at two different schools with not much time to go the ten miles between the two, and this was before the days of cell phones. Another time car trouble happened again at the worst moment: Two hours away from a university where we were supposed to meet the technical crew and stage manager in three hours for rehearsal, the engine blew in our van, right in a deserted stretch of the interstate highway. Providentially, the next exit had a car dealer who lent us a car to go rent a van. That extra hour we had allotted "just in case" we had problems really came in handy. Moral: Always allow extra time for the unexpected.

Fortunately when I rear-ended a car at a stoplight, I was just rolling and no one was hurt. I was tired and inattentive because of an early morning start and the length of the drive. After that incident we never traveled more than two hours to get to a morning performance. If it was farther, we went the day before and spent the night at a motel. Performers need to do everything they can to stay alert on the day of performance. Make sure you have a good night's sleep and don't drive in a sleep-deprived condition.

When traveling between schools or performance venues when you must perform at both in the same day, make sure you have a set of written directions. Never rely on verbal instructions given over the telephone. Get the directions ahead of time so you can trace them out on your detailed road map. The best scenario is when an arts council has a person who will serve as your guide from school to school. Additionally, the advantage

Drawing of Child with "The Lettuce Leaf." Portrait of child dancing: Claudia Van Koba. Digital leaf collage: Conan Magruder.

of arriving early on the night before a morning performance, or earlier than is scheduled, is that you can get a test run in to the site of the performance — to find the school or theater and relax knowing that you exactly where you have to go.

One of the worst moments in the early years of touring was with a set of verbal instructions didn't jibe with reality. This became clear ten minutes before show time because the previous performance at another school, on the other side of town, started a half hour late (delayed because the children that had been bused in from surrounding schools hadn't arrived on time.) Frantically we scanned the highway for the road we were supposed to see on the right; it was on the left. We were screaming hysterically in unison by the time we arrived. Luckily we had our windows rolled up and the police couldn't hear us. After that, we swore (literally) *never* to allow ourselves to perform at two different schools or at different sites in one afternoon. Our usual travel plan is two back-to-back shows in the morning, then travel to another site — or one show in the morning, the other at a different site in the afternoon to give ourselves school search time (also to have a map with written directions!).

Motel adventures have been, as they say, "interesting." Probably the night we'd like to forget first was in the only hotel in thirty-mile radius in a run-down little burg. The walls were paper-thin, and that night my husband and I heard from next door an explicitly graphic acoustic bedroom experience — and unfortunately it wasn't just a movie that we were hearing in the next room. We couldn't change the channel. We had to sleep with two pillows over our heads. Touring has made us connoisseurs of the chain motels, the ones with thicker walls between the rooms. Some serve breakfast — they're the ones dancers need.

Dressing Rooms

On arriving at schools and theaters, expect the unusual. Our worst moment in this regard was going to our "dressing room" at one school and finding it so cold that water was frozen on the floor! Not too agreeable for barefoot modern dancers. After that we always stipulated in our contracts that the changing room (teacher's lounge, usually) be clean, well ventilated or heated appropriately — with the same requirement for the performing space.

Onstage

Of course we have had many adventures in "creative" performing. They include an instance of having to cope with a platform stage that came apart in ever widening chasms as we danced about. Finally, when the gaps were eight inches apart, we stopped the show, informed the audience (who were seated cross-legged on the cafetorium floor) that we would be moving the next dance closer to them. After directing the audience of 300 in a massive 25-foot back-up, we moved the set forward off the dangerous platform stage, turned on the music and continued with the next dance. Nobody seemed to mind.

Once while we were changing before a show, we returned to find the janitors slopping water and bleach over the floor area where the audience was supposed to sit. Hastily one of us helped to mop it up, while the other went back to take allergy medication! Always carry an inhaler, emergency allergy pack supplies, and other medical supplies whether anyone in the company is allergic or not, because allergic reactions can happen unexpectedly at any time.

Another fun moment was during an after-lunch performance, when one of us looked down while holding a shape for several counts — and stared straight at a lettuce leaf on the floor of the performing space. Those moments give you pause and make you respect the vital role that janitors play in any school or theater.

Double-stitch those costume gussets under armpits and in the crotch. Not to be indelicate, but remember to wear an undergarment or athletic supporter that is the same color as your costume, if you can manage it. You can feel very exposed when you realize that (as you're leaping in front of 350 people) suddenly there is a draft happening in a place on your anatomy where drafts don't normally occur. To avoid indecent exposure, it's amazing how fast you can sew (or change choreography) when you have to!

Sometimes it is really hard to pretend that every unexpected onstage catastrophe is a part of the show. Especially when the end of a spool of thread from the backstage sewing kit has gotten twisted up onto your costume and suddenly you become aware that you unknowingly have danced it all over — leaving an intricate web of thread everywhere on the stage. It gets worse when you realize that soon your partner is going to enter and is in danger of getting tangled up in it. And worse, you can't warn him without disrupting the show! Yes, this happened — it was a thin pink thread, as I recall. No, thankfully it didn't cause an accident; but some of the footsteps in that part of the show evidenced a peculiar shuffling as both of us attempted to get that thread off our ankles and toes as inconspicuously as possible! This type of thing will make you neaten up your messy backstage habits in a hurry! What's the lesson here? All inessential contents of the costume box need to go back in place *before* the show.

Once in a production of *Camelot,* I saw the actor who played Sir Lancelot stick his (sharp) sword straight through the cloth of his trousers, instead of into his scabbard. (He was a brave man.) Even if there was no way to ignore it from an audience's perspective, the actor kept in character — which, at least, was more fair to the actress playing Guinevere. (The actor portraying King Arthur could have gotten some laughs off from it too, but he wisely resisted the temptation!) I also did my best to stay in character when I accidentally gave Mark a bloody nose on stage with an over-exuberant arm fling. Fortunately he was able to turn his head away from the audience and end the dance without it showing. This is yet another reason for taking a well-equipped and readily available first aid kit on tour.

On stage, all sorts of creatures can make guest appearances as unexpected parts of your show. Moths are attracted to stage lights, spiders suddenly dangle from overhead, centipedes make a direct locomotor pathway, and even the occasional roach and water bug premiere. Usually it's best to just dance a little lighter and hope that if you step on the thing that it's a clean kill (of the bug, not of you!). It's just not professional to scream (out of character) or to make a big production out of squashing or swatting insects and rodents.

We have danced through two fire drills; one was at an outside stage that was next to a fire station. We paused the steps and music, and waited until it was over. The other drill was in a school where we were performing in a gymnasium. The children in the audience were seated in bleachers that stretched twenty feet high. All of them had to be evacuated. The arts presenter was filled with frustration and angry with the principal for not having been mindful that there was an assembly going on. However, once in progress there was nothing to do but to wait until the drill was over, the children back in place, and then to begin where we had left off. Fortunately, it was the last show of the residency and was scheduled to end with enough time for us to finish before the children had to go home. It does sort of damage that "willing suspension of disbelief" that you ask an audience to have when you suddenly need to evacuate an audience.

Occasionally the stage itself is a challenge from the beginning — slippery, sticky, with bad acoustics, or lighted by only one overhead fluorescent light (even though your technical sheet stated clearly what lights you needed). A stage may not be level; it may be beveled, have holes, or have drop-offs that fall four or five inches below the remainder of the stage. A stage may not even be a stage! At one first night celebration, the New Year's Eve performance tradition that many cities in the United States host, we performed in a courtroom devoted to juvenile and domestic cases. We danced around the defendant's chair, which was fixed and immobile right in the middle of the space. It was one of those "Should we or should we not dance?" decisions when we arrived and saw what was awaiting us, stage-wise. That night we decided to live with it, and when the audience began arriving, we even seated some audience members *in* and around that chair. They had the equivalent of a "surround sound" experience — in movement — as we leaped and tumbled around them. Immersed in dancing — that was a performance we are sure that those people never forgot! We were exhilarated afterwards. It was a close encounter situation and it took all of our coordination just to not leap into the courtroom furniture! It was actually a fun challenge.

We have arrived to find a "plenty big stage" — in the words of a presenter — in actuality be *anything* but. We have danced on stages that were only six feet deep, stages that were only twelve feet wide, and stages that had hidden towers of junk piled behind the back curtains. Once, one of those piles came tumbling down and hit our set while we were involved in an onstage Q & A session. Speaking with our backs turned to the set, we suddenly saw expressions of shock and horror on the faces of the children in the audience in front of us. They pointed, and we turned around — just in time — to catch our (fortunately fairly lightweight) set in our arms! No one was hurt, thank goodness. The set was only minimally damaged. But just try to get your audience control back after something like that happens. You'll find out just how good you *really* are at crowd control! After that near miss, we instituted regular backstage safety checks before the performances.

Remember to articulate your words well when speaking onstage and run sound checks for your speaking voice too. Performing-space acoustics may be worse than you realize and the room shape may distort your words without you knowing it. In one performance of *Stars and Constellations*, we couldn't figure out why the group of children drew back in fear when we talked about meteors. Surely, we thought, astronomy was not *that* scary a subject. Then one child asked us after the show if we had seen any of those big "meat-eaters." Finally understanding what confusion the room acoustics had wrought, we thought, "Now that's something to worry about when you're six years old. Grown-ups telling you about big 'meat-eaters' in the sky!" Before your show, clap your hands and speak a few times onstage before an audience enters and have someone planted in the empty audience to judge if what you say is what they hear! If you don't check acoustics, the "meat-eaters" may get you!

The Human Element

Sometimes the dancers themselves have a condition or an injury that might make you have to change the steps or even the concept. Mark broke his ankle in an accident at home, but we had a series of performances scheduled and no one available to take his place. He changed the choreography and entered on a skateboard and then danced while standing on one leg with a well-decorated crutch to help him keep his balance! His phenomenal strength and quick choreographic inspiration transformed this dance. The children in the audience loved it. We got a lot of pictures that they drew where his leg was prominently featured.

Menagerie Dance Company in "Praying Mantis" from *Metamorphosis*. Choreography: Mark Magruder (pictured) (credit Lee Luther, Jr.).

Another time I was six months pregnant, with just one more show to do for the season before beginning my maternity leave. We had been redesigning the costume to camouflage my "condition" as it progressed; but at that last show, when I went into an upside-down balance, the elastic slipped and the voluminous shirt "gave it up" to gravity. I was balanced *and* exposed to the audience with the curve of the leotard foretelling the future blessed event! In hindsight, we probably should have canceled that last performance, but my daughter still loves the music that I performed to that season and she's a normal kid! And although it was not too professional a look, I imagine the children in the audience turned out fine, too, despite it all!

Sometimes it's local, national, or even world events that intervene. One of our most memorable residencies happened many years ago (before we formed Menagerie Dance Company) when Title IX in Education was first enacted. No one told us that we were going to be the ones who get to teach girls and boys together in gym class for the very first time. It was *not* an easy task, especially with no warning. Girls lined up and plastered themselves to one side of the wall. The boys knotted in tight clumps of adolescent energy at the far end of the gym. On the scale of difficult dance master classes, it was a ten.

Complications arise offstage too. Once when touring during a presidential election year, we made a severe faux pas. We allowed ourselves, during a dinner with an art presenter and her family, to be drawn into a heated political discussion with the presenter's husband. Whatever the strengths of your beliefs, it's probably not a great idea anytime to let yourself become involved in a political argument pitted against your employer's spouse. As the British say, it needs to be sorted in a different venue, especially if you are spending the night as guests in their home. It is also a great argument in favor of using motels where you do not have to share such close quarters with your hosts!

Drawing of Menagerie Dance Company in *Flute Song*. Choreography: Mark Magruder (pictured).

Other Factors

Events can happen in communities that affect the mood of an audience. Once we had to perform in a school where, sadly, several children recently had lost their fathers in a coal mining accident. It was difficult to perform then, especially our happy dances.

An excruciatingly hard moment for us as performers happened when we found ourselves performing at an elementary school in Newport News, Virginia, home of a huge U.S. naval base, on the day the first Gulf War broke out. A number of the children in the school had just bid goodbye to their fathers or mothers who were shipped out to the Middle East; one child had both parents called to active duty. When we arrived the principal was in tears. We offered to cancel the performance, but the principal insisted that we perform. She said that the children needed our performance on that day more than any other. It was only by pulling from somewhere deep inside that we danced convincingly through the gamut of emotions and moods. The principal was right; everyone in the audience was grateful for the diversion from harsh reality.

Another day we found ourselves wondering why there were so many state police on the highway, not realizing that the state governor had ordered hundreds of police to the county where we were to perform. The police were there as a show of force in a labor dispute that threatened to become violent. You live a full life when you tour. You can't be in an isolated bubble — all the forces that shape a state, province, region, or nation affect you, the performer, in some way.

Be open to the people that you meet when booking and touring. One of the school administrators we met, when we first came to Virginia, brainstormed an entire summer arts program with us. That relationship and the arts program expanded and we have grown with it from its inception more than twenty years ago. Some of our most valuable arts collaborations and most valued friendships have come through being open to the wonderful people we meet in the arts business.

While touring has its shocks, it also can be the best high for a performer. When you walk into a grocery store and a wide-eyed little girl, who has just seen you perform that day, tugs on her mother's shirt and says breathlessly "There they ARE, the dancers!" Or when a starry-eyed little boy in ragged clothes comes up to you after a performance and says fervently, "I'm going to be a dancer when I grow up!" Or you walk down a street in a town or city and a car pulls up and someone yells out, "HEY! I LOVED YOUR SHOW!" Then, by all that is dear to you about dance, you know you have made a difference; you have touched hearts and minds through dance. You are at once a convert and a missionary for the great art we love. Sisters and brothers, dance on, dance on, dance on!!!

Appendices

A: More Successful Companies

Australia

Kurruru Indigenous Youth Performing Arts Company. Emma Webb manages this southern Australia organization located in Port Adelaide. Kurruru is Australia's only indigenous-youth performing arts company. Its mission is to provide quality performing arts opportunities for indigenous children, young people and their communities. According to their website, the larger Kurruru organization conducts "an extensive performing arts workshop program, produces award-winning performances, engages in regional arts and health partnerships, operates the Kurruru dance ensemble, undertakes their innovative Kulcha Moves projects — focusing on cultural maintenance — and maintain a presence across South Australia at festivals and community events." Supported by philanthropic giving, the organization has since 2006 been participating in Artsupport, which is an indigenous philanthropy-mentoring program. Kurruru received support from such funding sources as the National Foundation for Australian Women, the Foundation for Young Australians, and other private foundations. http://www.kurruru.org.au

Brazil

Balangandança Cia (São Paulo). This broadly acclaimed company was founded in 1997 by Geórgia Lengos with the goal of making a "contemporary dance language directed at children, respecting them as creators and participants, based on their interests and realities" (daCi Brazil 2003 Programme). Balangandança Cia, a company of adult professionally trained dancers, presents consistently innovative, imaginative, and infectiously charming work to audiences of both young and old. Its repertory varies from year to year. One memorable dance has characters emerge from a broken television and take a group of bored young viewers on a wildly imaginative journey — a kinetic romp through the world of props and improbable dance motion (including audience participation.) The company has received local, state, and national recognition in Brazil, in 2000 earning an award from the Ministry of Culture of the Brazilian Federal Government.

Canada

Canadian Children's Dance Theatre (Toronto, Ontario). Deborah Lundmark and Michael de Coninck Smith created this company for gifted young dancers age thirteen to nineteen in 1980. In 1983 they established the School of the Canadian Children's Dance Theater; both are located in a historic renovated theater. This professional modern dance company, with its movement core of Limón dance technique, has performed over a thousand performances from the farthest outposts of Canada to Beijing. The company's repertory includes choreography by Lundmark, the director, and such well-known Canadian choreographers as Margie Gillis and Danny Grossman. Auditions are held yearly. The company receives funding from the Canada Council for the Arts, the Ontario

Trillium Foundation (a part of the Ministry of Tourism, Culture and Recreation) and support from the Canadian Department of Foreign Affairs and International Trade. During the eleven-month company season, the Canadian Children's Dance Theatre performs in Toronto and on tour for more than fifty performances as well as offering master classes, lecture-demonstrations and professional development for dance teachers. http://www.ccdt.org

Denmark

Ragnarock (Humlebaek). Ragnarock is a theater group, that strongly emphasizes on music and movement. Joachim Clausen, now director, created the organization — which comprises both the performance company Ragnarock and a school, Dramaskolen — in 1975. With more than one hundred participants ages seven to twenty-four, Ragnarock has no auditions. Anyone who wishes may become a part of the next theater project and performance. The company collaborates with theaters through carefully planned student exchange trips, performing collaborative theater productions. Ragnarock has performed and worked with student exchange theater projects in Brazil, South Africa, Australia, England, Iceland, Italy, Greenland, Norway, Sweden, and Finland, among others. http://www.ragna.dk/english.php

Finland

Vantaa Dance Institute (Vantaa). The twenty-six year old Vantaa Dance Institute believes that the challenge of dance is to learn how to teach today's child. The institute provides classes and a home for several performing groups. The school participates in cultural exchanges in Namibia and in Cuba, and sends its performing groups out to international festivals. Isto Turpeinen founded Vantaa Dance Institute and created The Dancing Boys of Vantaa. This group of boys performs its own choreography, combining different styles of dance, theatrics, and acrobatics into their own dance language. The group channels the dynamics of "guy power" into a "controlled expression of adventure" and energy. In one choreographic piece, the boys begin the dance behind a ten-foot wall of cardboard boxes, breaking this divide down in a dance that is a combination of martial arts and break-dance movement — and in the process destroys the stereotype that boys don't dance. Tiina Jalkanen, current director of the institute, created the Vantaa performance group Girl Power. Choreographic ideas for their performances arise from the imagination and contemporary lives of girls, using both improvisation in dance and theater — movement, text, and words. http://www.vantaantanssiopisto.fi

Jamaica

Khulcha Theatre School of Dance (Mandeville). Carolyn Russell-Smith founded this group in 1988. The school for young dancers presents performances with choreography firmly grounded in traditional Jamaican dance. The group regularly appears in international daCi festivals to great acclaim for its high energy and verve. Russell-Smith has received a number of local and national awards including a special plaque from the Jamaican High Commission in London. (44 Manchester Rd. Mandeville, Jamaica 9620023); tel.: +1 876–962–0023.

The School of Dance, Edna Malley College of Visual and Performing Arts (Kingston). Nicholeen Degrasse-Johnson directs this school of dance. She has been a teacher and choreographer since 1992. Degrasse-Johnson's troupe of young performers regularly performs lecture demonstrations and performances of indigenous dance of Jamaica both nationally and internationally. The company presentations are energetic and are wildly popular with audiences. The Edna Manley College of Visual and Performing Arts provides careful training in dance as well as giving its young performers permission for personal, joyful expression through age-appropriate choreography, performed to a high level of dance technique and skill. Also, choreographers Barbara Requa, Kevin Moore, and others create modern pieces for the young company. http://www.emc.edu.jm

The Netherlands

Introdans (Arnhem). In 1971 Hans Focking and Tom Wiggers formed Introdans, a ballet company that is now one of the three largest dance companies in the Netherlands. It performs internationally, in such venues as Aruba, Belgium, Curaçao, Germany, Indonesia and Switzerland. The company mission was to introduce ballet to the public at large. From the company's beginning, in addition to its theater shows Introdans offered performances, workshops and residencies in schools. In 1980 the directors created Introdans Ensemble for Youth, appointing Roel Voorintholt as director. According to writer and dance researcher Juliette Hofman's presentation on the subject from the daCi Proceedings (2006 at The Hague), at first Voorintholt choreographed the school performances and the company continued to dance in gymnasiums. However, he was dissatisfied with the results, and in short order Voorintholt decided not only to bring in noted choreographers like Kylián and Parsons to create works for children, he also made the decision to no longer perform in gyms, because he believed that children should be given the same theatrical dance experience as adults. Lights, sound, and theatrical effects are essential to a highly refined aesthetic experience, which translates to a better artistic experience for the youth audiences. This attitude is echoed in many arts outreach programs in the United States and around the world, which bring children to theaters rather than take dance into the schools. Introdans Ensemble for Youth does conduct workshops, classes, and projects in schools. http://www.introdans.nl

South Africa

Moving into Dance Mophatong (Johannesburg). In 1978 when this company was formed in South Africa by the exceptionally gifted dance education leader Sylvia "Magogo" Glasser, her entire concept was at once politically defiant, socially revolutionary, and personally risky. The world of South African dance was very different then (over thirty years ago) because of the ugly policy of racial separation known as apartheid. As in all cases of extremist ideology, policies of "separate but equal" led not to so-called ethnic purity, but instead to deprivation in almost every way for its poorer citizens — economically, socially, and racially. At this critical point in history Glasser courageously, and with no small element of personal danger, formed an integrated (non-racially segregated) dance company called Dance Mophatong (MIDM) Performance Company. From this venture came a new form of dance that blended African and Western dance genres, called Afrofusion. This dynamic new form created its own dance aesthetic and ultimately helped forge a new generation of dancers and dance that was a blend of cultures — in the most positive and affirming sense. As Glasser expanded her vision, Dance Mophatong (MIDM) Performance Company performed around the world to much critical acclaim. Out of this came successful educational training programs: the 1980's Edudance used dance to teach school subjects such as science and math. It was followed in 1997 by the Edudance In-Service Training Programme (INSET), which trains teachers in the Edudance methodology; and the Community Dance Teachers Training Course (CDTTC) was set up in 1992. In 2000 INSET was extended into rural areas throughout various provinces of South Africa. This initiative is known as the Rural Edudance Advisory Project (REAP). http://www.midance.co.za

United Kingdom

Sutton Young Dancemakers (Sutton). This is a group of dancers age five to twenty-one years old. The goal of this group is both training in technique and education in choreography, but just as importantly to boast the participants' self-confidence, positive body image, and to encourage the ability to co-operate within a group. Janis Coley is co-director of the group. She is a high school teacher and co-author (with Anne Allen) of a series of outstanding books called *Dance for All*. The books offer an extraordinary set of ways to approach content and meaning in creative dance and in life, for students in classrooms and dance schools.

United States

AXIS Dance Company (Oakland, California). In 1987 Thais Mazur taught a movement class for women who use wheelchairs. The award winning AXIS Dance Company grew out of this experience as the dancers explored movement possibilities available to them. In 1997, one of the founding members of the company, Judith Smith, became co-director (along with Nicole Richter). They began to address the future development of the company's integrated dance, which includes dancers on wheels as well as dancers who are not. Under their leadership the company began commissioning choreography from well-known chorographers. AXIS tours and performs regularly nationally and internationally, mostly on proscenium stages in addition presenting their programs in K–12 schools for nearly forty performances each year. The AXIS repertory includes the work of Bill T. Jones, Meredith Monk, Joe Goode, and Victoria Marks, among others. The aesthetic quality of the dance that the company performs is exceptional, and its national reviews note that its dances transcend the topic of disability. In fact, the company's focus is to prove that dance is inclusive. Its challenge to audiences is to transcend expectations for bodily perfection and see different movement possibilities as capable of carrying the metaphoric imagery necessary for dance as an art to move hearts and minds. The company, which receives grants from the National Endowment for the Arts and from many national, state and philanthropic agencies, offers workshops on dance and disability, and maintains ongoing efforts to make theaters, dance spaces, and dance accessible and inclusive. AXIS conducts workshops for children on a regular basis and maintains a strong commitment to outreach for youth with its program *DanceAccess/Kids!* It provides after-school classes both for children who are disabled and others who are not The AXIS website has an extensive and current listing of publications and links on dance and disability. http://axisdance.org

Arpana Dance Company (Oakland, California). In 1985 Ramya Harishankar formed her Bharata Natyam company with skilled members who had graduated as accomplished dancers (in the vocabulary of that technique) from her school of Indian dance. Over the more than twenty-five years of its existence, Arpana Dance Company has performed nationally and internationally in Europe and India, and has raised over $60,000 for charities such as the American Cancer Society, the Make-A-Wish Foundation, and the Pediatric AIDS Foundation. In 2005 Arpana Company dancers placed first in their category for dancing at the International Danz Grand Prix in Barcelona, Spain. The company received a grant from the National Endowment for the Arts for a special project entitled *Ganga, Life as a River*, as well as awards and grants from the California Arts Council, Alliance for California Traditional Arts, and the Fund for Folk Culture. In 2007, Harishankar received a Cultural Legacy Award from Arts OC and her company received the Los Angeles Treasures award from the Los Angeles County Board of Supervisors and the California Traditional Music Society. As director of Arpana and as a solo performer, Ramya Harishankar has a commitment to education and dance for young audiences through performances at festivals where audiences of all ages can view dance, workshops and lecture demonstrations in the schools. In 2002 she served as one of Disney Company's featured artists for schools; and she continues to work on other children's projects, such as the Children's Creative Project in Central California and San Diego's Center for World Music. http://www.danceramya.com

The Kids from Beasley Performing Ensemble (Chicago). Eddie L. Boulton-Howard, founder, is a teacher/educator and the choreographer at Beasley Academic Center Elementary School. Boulton-Howard is the artistic director of the young troupe, which is composed of her dance students. These young dancers, many who come from economically and socially challenged backgrounds, are enthusiastic and energetic performers. Dance has offered the "Beasley Kids" a chance to tour and perform locally and internationally. Boulton-Howard has served as a fine arts and dance advisor on the Illinois State Board of Education.

FLY Dance Company (Houston, Texas, 1999–2006). Kathy Wood founded this company with the goal of "utilizing street dancers to develop a nationally recognized dance company with unequaled community outreach," according to their website. In addition the goals initially were "to organize [hip hop street dancers] to perform locally in outreach shows with positive social messages for schools." Although the company stopped touring in 2006 and reformed its mission to local (Houston) outreach efforts, Fly Dance Company, during the seven years of its existence, performed for nearly 30,000 school students each year as well as at the Kennedy Center, Lincoln Center, and Jacob's Pillow. It toured in over thirty states and five countries. This exhausting schedule led to the reformulation of the company as Fly Works, and then FlyKiDs was formed with fifteen to twenty young local school-aged dancers. FlyKiDs performed live at public schools, produced dance-training videos, conducted teacher workshops, provided youth dance camps, and hosted youth dance festivals for Houston-area youth.

The Tennessee Children's Dance Ensemble (Knoxville). Dr. Dorothy Floyd founded the company of talented young teen dancers in 1981. Using her background in Graham and Wigman dance techniques, Floyd's vision was to create a company of young professional dancers who through hard work, diligence, and persistence would come to know and understand excellence in dance and be recognized for it. Since the passing of Dr. Floyd in 2002, Irena Linn, a graduate of the Mary Wigman School of Dance in Berlin, Germany, has served as the company's artistic director, and Dr. Lenette Perra, a medical doctor and former principal dancer with the National Theater in Munich, is the ballet master and resident choreographer. The Tennessee Children's Dance Ensemble is the only member of Dance/USA with youth performers. They have performed throughout the world, from Taipei to London, and dance the works of noted choreographers such as Eleo Pomare and Michael Mao. http://www.dev.tcdedance.org

The University of Utah Children's Dance Theatre (Salt Lake City). Master educator Mary Ann Lee is the artistic director of the Children's Dance Theater. Virginia Tanner, famed children's creative dance teacher, founded the company in 1949. Tanner first coined the phrase "roots and wings" in reference to what an ideal children's dance experience should provide. Her philosophy established the framework for subsequent development, not only of her company of young dancers, but the many organizations that promote dance for children and for children's audiences. Tanner said of her company, "*The motivating force behind my work is not only developing excellent dancers, but more importantly, developing young people who are useful, imaginative, worthwhile human beings.*" The children who perform in the company participate in the dance-making process, and perform locally as well as internationally. Their performances are renowned for a profound sense of heartfelt joy and performed with fine aesthetic quality under the sensitive direction of Mary Ann Lee and her associates. According to their website, the young dancers — ages eight to eighteen — perform their dances for over 45,000 people throughout Utah annually under the sponsorship of the Utah Arts Council and the Utah Zoo, Arts, and Parks Fund. http://www.tannerdance.utah.edu/cdt/cdt.html

---

B: More Dance Performing Groups — Children, Professionals and Schools

Argentina

Expresión Corporal Uno, Tiki Marchesini, Zullay Acuña Humenny
Mitanz, Judith Wiskitski

Aruba

Aruba International Dance Foundation, Wilma Kuiperi-Jansen

Australia

Buzz Dance Theatre, Cadi McCarthy (Perth) www.buzzdance.com.au

Dance groups with young performers

Extensions Youth Dance Company, Townsville, Queensland: www.xtnsions.org.au
Fresh Bred, www.ausdance SA youth dance ensemble
QL2 Centre for Youth Dance (Sydney) Ruth Osbourne
Restless Dance Theatre, Adelaide (integrated company for disabled and non-disabled dancers): www.restlessdance.org
Steps Youth Dance, Perth: http://www.steps youthdance.com.au
Stompin: http://stompin.net
youMove youth dance company, Western Sydney, New South Wales www.youmove dance.com.au

Belgium

Dance groups with adult performers

Nat Gras, Goele van Dijck

Brazil

Dance groups with adult performers

Dança Pra Crianca
Gicá Cia Jovem de Dança — Projeto Axé
Ziuiziras & Pitis, Katia Figueiredo
Grupo de Dança João (Pernambuco) Marcia
   Virginia
Escola de Dança da Fundação Cultural do
   Estado da Bahia
Grupo Cultural Quimtaci (Bahia) Joaquim Lino
Núcleo de Dança Votorantim (São Paulo)
Cia Opaxorô Apae Salvador (Bahia) special needs

Dance groups with young performers

Afunxé— Bagunçaço (Bahia)
Escola Municipal Maestro Fernando Borges
   (Pernambuco) Celia Meira
Grupo de Dança Ilê Aiyê (Bahia)
Ballet Rosana Abubakir (Bahia)
Ebateca Itaigara (Bahia) Camila Vianna
Tempestade de Passos do Colegio Militar de
   Juiz de Gora (Bahia) Lilian Gil
Jazz Karla Landim (Bahia)
Grupo Infantil da Escola de Dança da Fun-
   dação Cultural do Estado (Bahia)
Projeto Mocan — Opô Afonjá (Bahia)
Escola Contemporânea Ballet (Bahia) Daniela
   Stasy
Ebateca Graça (Bahia)
Escola Contemporary Ballet (Bahia) Sheyla
   Barbosa
Bankoma Comunidadae Negra (Bahia)
Grupo Cultural Male de Balê (Bahia)
Grupo de Dança do Liceu (Bahia)
Ebateça Coste Verde (Bahia)
Academia Bahiana de Dança de Salão, (Bahia)

Canada

Dance groups with young performers

Alberta Dance Theater for Young People,
   Emily Forrest

Canadian Children's Dance Theatre,
   Deborah Lundmark, Michael de Coninck
   Smith www.ccdt.org
Carousel Dance Group, Ontario
Canada Can Dance Project, Heather
   Tsachuk, Chris LaPage
Children and Youth Dance Theatre, Andrea
   Douglas
Conservatory of Music and Dance
DansEncorps, (Moncton, New Brunswick)
   Chantal Cadieux
Dance Saskatchewan, Jill Reid
Do It with Class Young People's Theater
Extremely Moving (Yukon) Andrea Simpson
   Fowler
FadaDance, Misty Wensel, http://www.fada-
   dance.ca
Groundwork Sessions Whitehorse Yukon
   Performance Crew, R. L. Merkel
impuDance (Montreal) Susi Lovell
Northern Lights School of Dance, Yukon,
   Rebecca Reynolds, Deborah Lemaire
Youth Ballet Company of Saskatchewan
Youth in Motion
York University, Dance Department

Choreographers

Judith Marcuse Dance Projects, Producer of
   Kiss Festival (Youth focused ICE, FIRE)
Sarina Codello, *Thank You Tanzania*,
   documentary recounts her work with
   AIDS orphans

Croatia

Dance groups with young performers

Zagreb Youth Theater, Branka Petricevic,
   Mijana Preis, Desanka Virant
Ana Maletic School of Contemporary Dance,
   Ira Bicanic, Katarina Djurdjevic, Andreja
   Radan.

Denmark

Young Dance Stage, Anita Bødker

Estonia

Estonia Dance Agency, Elo Unt
Viljandi Culture Academy of Tartu University, Äli Leijen

Finland

Dance groups with young performers

Capella Dance Group, Salla Pakarinen-Rasanen
Dance Institute of Lahti
Dance Institute Tamara Rasmussen, Vivianne Budsko-Lommi
East Helsinki Music Institute
Kajaani Dance Theater, Minna Palokangas-Sirviö
Kuopion Tansitudio, Sannamaria Kärkkäinen
Northern Connection, Nuppu Niemi
Nurmijärvi Dance and Music Institute, Ritva Norkia
Oolu Dance
South-Savo Dance Institute, (Mikkeli) Fanny Gurevitch
Theater Academy, Eeva Antilla
Young Dance on the Riverside, Marketta Viitala
Warkauden Tanssikellari, Hanna Pohjola

Germany

Dance groups with young performers

Buckow Children Dance Group/Boys of Buckow, Marold Langer-Philippsen
Die Zersausten 8, Andrea Marton
Electric Fact /TanzlandRostock, Peter Mann
Jazz-Tanz-Theatre (Berlin) Robert Solomon www.placement-berlin.de
Rainbow Dancers (Frankfurt) Helga Chernenilov
Samsen Dance Theater, Tanz Tangente (Berlin) Leonore Ickstadt
Tanzteam Step-By-Step, (Berlin) Evelyn Richter
Tanztheater Sieben Morgen, Dagmar Pilsner
Tanztheater (Jugengkunstschule Dresden)

Grenada

Spices Dance Company, Susan-Jones-Benjamin

Hungary

Adult performers for youth audiences

National Dance Theater (Budapest) specializes in production of and also invites in performances for children http://www.nemzetitancszinhaz.hu
Bartók Dance Theater (Dunaújváros)— branch of Bartók Chamber Theater and House of Arts that regularly presents dance performances for children http://www.bartokszinhaz.hu
Budapest Dance Theater (Budapest)—an independent contemporary dance company that performs extensively for children http://www.budapestdancetheater.hu

Jamaica

Dance groups with young performers

Anjali School of Indian Classical Dance, Gropa Ramani
Buff Bay High School, Erika McKenzie Bingham
Calvary Preparatory School, Verman Thomas
Drews Avenue Primary School, Lileth Nembhard
Lannaman's Preparatory, Robertha Daley
Liberty Preparatory School, Sharon Lue-Welsh
Norwich Primary School, Samantha Hardy
Praise Academy of Dance, Patricia Noble
Rollington Town Primary
St. Theresa Preparatory, Antoinette Harris
Smurfs Preparatory, Robertha Daley
Stella Maris Junior Dancers of Jamaica (Kingston) Monika Lawrence
Tivoli Dance Troupe, Robertha Daley, Jennifer Garwood
Vaz Preparatory School, Charmaine Blake
Wolmer's Dance Troupe, Barbara McDaniel

Dance groups with adult performers

National Dance Theatre Company Movements
L'Acadco, L'Antoinette Stines

Japan

Dance groups with young performers

SRD, Studio of Rhythm and Dance, Mikami Kumiko
Magic Time Kids, Kathleen Kampa Vilina

Dance company with adult performers

Strange Kinoko Dance Company (Tokyo) Chie Ito, http://www.stangekinoko.com/english
Author: Yoshie Kaku. *Tanda Batta—100 Years of Japanese Children's Dance*
Kathleen Kampa Vilina, *English as a Second Language*, magictimekids@gmail.co

Mexico

Dance groups with adult performers

Ixbalanque Folklore Group
Ollin Group
Dance Theater Huijanl

The Netherlands

Dance groups with adult performers

2 DA Point
David Middendorp Korzo Productions
De Stilte, Jack Timmermans
Dox (Utrecht) Sassan Saghar Yaghmai
Holland Express, Gus Van Kan
Jongerentheater 020, Maxi Hill
Meekers Uitgesproken Dans, Arthur Rosenfeld
Motive for Motion, Maria Speth (Maastricht) www.dansspeters.nl
Merkx & Dancers, Wies Merk
Penguin Dance, Carolin Boether
Sloot, Catarina Campinas Furtada, Marlou Stolk
WISH, Marco Gerris
Trash, Marrrij Voets
Theaterhavo/VWO, Catarina Campinas Furtado

Dance groups with young performers

Albeda College
Amsterdam School for the Arts Preparatory School of Dance
Artez School of Dance (Vooropleiding Arnhem)
Codarts/ Rotterdam Dance Academy, David Middendorp, chor.
Ex Nunc: Ex Nunc (The Hague) Joan Van Der Mast
Floor Burnin' (Weert Holland)
Fontys Dance Academy Preparatory Dance Training Tilburg

International Dance Center for Youth
Kunstfactor & Floral Dance Art, Moniek Koopmans, Henriette Wachelder
Jazz Danschool Bertha Huls
Jts Rabarber
Kadanst, Rodney Kasandikromo
Koorenhuis, Centrum Voor Kunst
Lucia Marthas Dance Academy
Risk
Stichting Walvis Dans Productions
Valkenburg Guel Ballet School, Joke de Backer

New Zealand

Modern contemporary dance with adult performers

Footnote Dance Company, contemporary dance
Java Dance, contemporary dance

Contemporary and traditional Maori or Pacifica dance with adult performers

Kahurangi
Black Grace
Atamira

Hip-hop with adult performers

Legacy

Others including groups with young performers:

DESIRE City Beats (students from Wanganui City College)
Modern Dance SRD
WAKATU Dance Theatre, Peta Spooner

Norway

Norwegian School of Sport Science

Slovakia

Dance groups with young performers

The Dance Theatre Laska (Bratislava) Miriam Tancerova

South Africa

Dance Groups with adult performers

Agulhas Dance Theater, Gladys Agulhas
    http://www.youtube.com/watch?v=plBN2s
    iBgAl
Siwela Sonke Dance Theatre, Jay Pather

Dance groups with young performers

Silver Leaf Youth Dance Company, Western
    Cape
Canto Vibe

Sweden

Dance groups with young performers

Danderyd
LEK Studio, Kristina Leren
Sodra Latins Gymnasium, Petra Frank

Choreographer

Anna Kallbald, University College of Dance
    Stockholm

Switzerland

Dance Groups with young performers

Kijuballet, Christina Schilling

Tanzania

Kihumbe Dance and Circus Troupe

United Kingdom

Dance groups with young performers

ADvANCE Youth Dance (Leeds, England)
    Pam Johnson
The Place/RCMJ Junior Department, Leah
    Callender Crowe, Mathew McAtamney

Dance group with adult performers

Green Candle Dance Company, Fergus Early,
    Rachel Elliott

Research and dance partnerships

University of Exeter, Linda Rolfe

United States

Dance groups with young performers

Las Vegas Children's Dance Theater,
    Kathleen Kingsley (Nevada)
Children's Dance Theater of San Diego
    (California)
Dance & Paper Theater & Junior Company,
    Kathy Kroll (Pennsylvania)
Riverstreet Dance Theater, Pamela Erikson
    (Montana)
pameladance@yahoo.com
Enertia Dance Company, Danielle Payton
    (Washington)

Performance programs for young audiences

National Dance Institute, Jacques D'Amboise
    (New Mexico)

Dance groups with adult performers

Canyon Mountain Company Sarah Roberts
    Cooke, Gina Darlington (Arizona)
Headwaters Dance Company, Amy Ragsdale
NOVA Dance Company, SaraKim Vennard
    (Delaware)
The Richmond Ballet, Stoner Winslett
    (Virginia)
Padmarani Rasiah-Cantu, Baharata Natyam
    soloist (Virginia)
Sparkplug Learning, Rachael Carnes (dance
    & disability) (Oregon)

Collaborations Across Borders

Australia and South Africa together

KINETIC THEATER GROUPS WITH
ADULT PERFORMERS

Ellis & Bheki of Durban, South Africa col-
laborated with the Tom Lycos and Stefo
Nantsou of Zeals Theater in Australia in
February 2007, premiered in 2008 "AUS-
TRALIA vs SOUTH AFRICA" about
nationalism, sport, media panic & racism.
They performed this together at the
ASSITEJ World Congress in Adelaide in
May 2008.

C: Websites, Resources and Publications for Dance Companies, Dancers and Dance Educators

Economic, Educational and Statistical Data Related to Dance and the Arts

Americans for the Arts — Arts and Economic Prosperity III Summary Report/Full Report, are good advocacy tools for board members, government officials, and other stakeholders. For example, according to the report in 2005 *"America's nonprofit arts and culture industry generates $166.2 billion in economic activity every year—$63.1 billion in spending by organizations and an additional $103.1 billion in event-related spending by audiences."*
http://www.artsusa.org/information_services/research/services/economics_impact/default.asp.

Additional data on student successes in relation to arts participation, compiled by Americans for the Arts in collaboration with the National School Boards Association, can be found at http://www.americansforthearts.org/information services/arts education community/default.asp.

Higher Education Arts Data Services compiles data from NASD (National Dance Accreditation in Schools)
11250 Roger Bacon Drive, Suite 21
Reston, VA 20190–5248
Telephone: (703) 437–0700, ext. 22
Fax: (703) 437–6312
http://www.art-accredit.org

Montgomery, A.S., and M.D. Robinson. "What Becomes of Dance Majors?" Journal of Cultural Economics, Volume 27, Number 1, February 2003, pp. 57–71(15), http://www.ingentaconnect.com/content/klu/jcec/2003/00000027/00000001

National Center for Educational Statistics
Digest of Educational Statistics
http://nces.ed.gov/programs/digest/d07/tables/dt07 265.asp

Office of Research and Analysis
National Endowment for the Arts
1100 Pennsylvania Ave. NW

Washington, DC 20506
Telephone: 202–682–5775
Fax: 202–682–5677
http://www.arts.endow.gov

Ostrower, Francie. "The Diversity of Cultural Participations: Findings from a National Survey; Building Arts Participation — New Findings from the Field." The Urban Institute. This substantial research document from 2005, sponsored by the Wallace Foundation, reveals ways in which local audiences participate in dance performances and offers suggestions to enhance arts involvement in communities. http://www.wallacefoundation.org.

Texas Education Agency — Better academic performance, lower dropout rates, and higher attendance rates in Texas public schools are correlated to fine arts course enrollment. Research on t he Texas Education Agency website shows that campuses with a higher percentage of student enrollments in fine arts courses achieved higher academic ratings.
http://www.tea.state.tx.us.

Arts Education Standards Websites

Americans for the Arts

Education World
http://www.education-world.com/standards/national/arts/dance9 12.shtml

Kennedy Center for the Performing Arts
http://artsedge.kennedy-center.org/teach/standards.cfm

National Dance Association (NDA)
http://www.aahperd.org/nda

National Dance Education Organization
http://www.ndeo.org/standards.asp

Other Arts Education Sites of Interest

AMS Planning and Research Corporation
Research on attendance at arts events in

regard to politics, current events
(203) 256–1616
http://www.ams-online.com

Articles to Support Arts Education and Arts
for Education
http://www.newhorizons.org/strategies/
arts/front arts.htm

Arts Education Partnership (Research
and Policy)
One Massachusetts Avenue NW, Suite 700
Washington, DC 20001–1431
(202) 312–6865
http://www.aep-arts.org

Dance/Performing Art Support Organizations

American Presenters and Performers (APAP)
A national organization of presenters and
performers with an annual booking conference in New York City each year.
http://www.artspresenters.org
http://www.apap365.org

Association Internationale du Théâtre pour
l'Enfance et la Jeunesse (ASSITEJ)
With centers in eighty countries, the members of ASSITEJ perform to millions of
children and young people each year in
Europe, Asia, Africa, the Americas and
Australia. ASSITEJ sponsors a world congress showcasing theater and dance performances.
http://www.assitej-international.org

Cultural Development Arts Management
Network
http://www.artsmanagement.net

dance and the Child international (daCi)
An international organization that hosts
dance conferences designed "to promote
opportunities throughout the world for
children and young people to experience
dance as creators, performers and specta-
tors." Triannual meeting usually involves
dancers from thirty or more countries. Use
this link to find out about the next international conference.
http://daciusa.org

Dance Magazine Dance Annual Directory
Has a dance teacher dance directory sub-
mission form. List your company and
update your information. Contact: Jared
Smallridge at jsmallridge@dancemedia.com

It is read by 60,000 teachers who influence
more than 15 million students.

Dance/USA
Support for professional companies,
dancers, and presenters of dance — offers
multiple services from funding and audience research to membership in the actors'
credit union and discounts in hotel rates.
You can download the Dance/USA
National Dance Company List, a spreadsheet detailing over 200 dance companies
in the United States.
http://www.danceusa.org

International Performers Arts for Youth
(IPAY)
An association of performers and presenters, opportunities for festivals, showcases,
networking, and regional and national
booking conferences.
http://www.ipayweb.org

National Endowment for the Arts
1100 Pennsylvania Avenue NW
Washington, DC 20506
Telephone: (202) 682–5400
Voice/TTY: (202) 682–5496
Email: webmgr@arts.endow.gov
http://www.arts.endow.gov

Young Audiences (YA)
Founded in 1952, it is the oldest arts-in-
education network, reaching seven million
children annually, It presents nearly
100,000 arts-in-education programs in
music, theater, visual and design arts,
dance, and the literary arts. These programs include performance, demonstrations, workshops, residencies, and
professional development services for
teachers. YA works with 4,600 professional
teaching artists.
http://www.youngaudiences.org

Additional Dance Resources

Gaynor Minden Dance Links
http://www.dancer.com/dance-links/misc.
php

Marketing for the Arts
This site has practical tips, creative ideas,
and best practices to save time, reduce
costs, and improve your marketing results.
http://www.artsmarketing.org

Voice of Dance
Online dance forum with reviews, blogs, publicity and announcements. Email your comments to info@voiceofdance.com or call at (415) 460–5150
http://www.VoiceofDance.com

Volunteer Lawyers for the Arts (VLA)
Offers services to nonprofits
http://www.vlany.org

Dance Publications

Dance Magazine,

Dance Spirit

Dance Teacher

Dance/USA e-Journal: From the Green Room
Features articles on issues of importance to the dance community; news stories relating to arts and dance; essays from leaders in the dance field; notes on changes, transitions and opportunities in the field; calendar of upcoming events; and highlights of Dance — USA sponsored events. Annual subscription rate: members, free; non-members, $40 (US), $50 (Canada), $70 (overseas).

Helflich, David. *How to Make Money Performing in Schools: The Definitive Guide to Developing, Marketing, and Presenting School Assembly Program"* Orient, WA: Silcox Productions, 1997. 190 pp.
http://www.schoolgigs.com
http://www.schoolshows.com/

Dance/USA publishes other resources, listed below:

Classical Ballet Training Study by Kathleen Bannon. 1995. 71 pp. (Ltd. availability.) ISBN 1-931683-03-4

Dance in the San Francisco Bay Area: A Needs Assessment. By John Munger and Libby Smigel. 2002. 84 pp. ISBN 1-931683-08-5

Developing the Whole Dancer: Issues and Challenges for Ballet Training Institutions By Mindy N. Levine. 2003. 26 pp.

Domestic Dance Presenting: Challenges and Change. 1994. 73 pp. + appendices. (Ltd. availability.) ISBN 1-931683-05-0

Domestic Dance Touring: A Study with Recom-

mendations for Private-Sector Support. 1992. 53 pp. + appendices. (Ltd. availability.) ISBN 1-931683-07-7

Frames of Reference: A Resource Guide from the National Initiative to Preserve America's Dance Edited by Janice Deputy. 2001. 80 pp. ISBN 1-931683-00-X

Invitation to the Dance: Audience Development for the Next Century By Mindy N. Levine. 1997. 107 pp. ISBN 1-931683-01-8

The National College Choreography Initiative: Supporting the Past, Present and Future of American Dance. By Suzanne Callahan. 2003. 32 pp. ISBN 1-931683-09-3

The NCCI's Artist–College Collaboration: Issues, Trends and Future Vision By Suzanne Callahan. 2003. 22 pp.

Seven Statements of Survival: Conversations with Dance Professionals Edited with an introduction by Renata Celichowska. 2008. 192 pp.

Widening the Circle: Towards a New Vision for Dance Education. By Mindy N. Levine. 1994. 109 pp. (Ltd. availability.) ISBN 1-931683-04-2

Related Topics in Regional Theater

Green, Jesse. "The New Suzanne Roberts Theater in Philadelphia," *New York Times*, March 9, 2008. Article details financial development of new theater and discusses connection between urban renewal, politics and responsibilities of regional performing arts to their communities and vice versa.

Career Information and Support for Dancers and College Dance Majors

America's Career InfoNet
http://www.acinet.org
Ball State University Career Center
Well-researched, accessible career information for dancers
http://www.bsu.edu/careers/students/links

Careers in the Arts
http://www.cln.org/themes/careers art.html

Dance Jobs and Employment
http://www.artslynx.org/dance/jobs.htm

Chapter Notes

Introduction

1. Elizabeth Hayes, author and former dance professor from the University of Utah in Salt Lake City, delivered an address at the founding convention of the National Dance Education Organization (NDEO), outside Cincinnati, Ohio in 1998. Her inspirational address outlined the need for dance educators to be advocates for dance on every level.

Chapter 2

1. Mihaly Csikszentmihalyi, *Flow: The Psychology of Optimal Experience* (New York: Harper and Row, 1990). He is a noted researcher on how human beings can lead happier and more fulfilling lives. In a lecture he gave to my choreography class at Sweet Briar College in November of 2002 as a visiting Phi Beta Kappa scholar, Csikszentmihalyi spoke about how deep involvement in a given field leads to a "flow" state and how that has positive effects on creativity and brings happiness into people's lives. Interestingly, Csikszentmihalyi also said that Guy Laliberté, the former street performer, told him that Laliberté founded Cirque du Soleil after reading about Csikszentmihalyi's concepts of flow and creativity. Cirque du Soleil is the famous and highly successful circus that does not use animals, and is noted for its original music, dance, and storyline.

2. Samuel Taylor Coleridge, *Biographia Literaria* (1817), Chapter 14. The poet Coleridge wrote about the difference between his poetic vision (he wrote the "Rime of the Ancient Mariner") and that of his co-author and friend the poet William Wordsworth. (Earlier, in 1798, they had published *Lyrical Ballads*, a collection of poetry, together.) In *Biographia Literaria* Coleridge introduces his often quoted and famous phrase: "That *willing suspension of disbelief* for the moment, which constitutes poetic faith." With these few words Coleridge explains the means by which art can be powerful and deeply moving despite its artificially constructed nature.

3. Doris Humphrey, *The Art of Making Dances* (Hightstown: Princeton Books, 1958), 159.

4. Camille Hardy, "Reaching Out to Young Audiences" *Dance Magazine* (June 1991), 54.

Chapter 3

1. For in-depth discussions on the topic of Ice Age art, see Paul G. Bahn, *Journey through the Ice Age* (Berkeley and Los Angeles: University of California Press, 1997), pp. 58–76, in the chapter "How Old Is Ice Age Art?" Another author with much to offer on this subject is John E. Pfeiffer, *The Creative Explosion* (New York: Harper and Row, 1982) whose foreword diagram places the age of drawing of human masks at 17,000 B.C.E.

Chapter 4

1. Jo Carson, Letter on the op-ed pages of *Johnson City Press Chronicle*, Sunday, July 22, 1990. Jo Carson was a writer and a founding member of Alternate ROOTS, a regional organization of theaters/arts in the American South (http://www.alternateroots.org).

2. June Panagakos Podagrosi, director of the children's theater company Child's Play, from Chicago, gave us this advice when we first began attending booking conferences and it stood us in good stead.

Chapter 7

1. Kenneth Laws, *Physics and the Art of Dance: Understanding Movement* (New York: Oxford University Press, 2002).

2. William H. McNeill, *Keeping Together in Time: Dance and Drill in Human History* (Cambridge, MA: Harvard University Press, 1995), 4. McNeill's small book is weighty in social application about the unifying power of intentional rhythmic movement.

3. Sylvia Glasser, keynote address for dance and the Child international conference July 28–August 3, 1997, in Kuopio, Finland. Also published in part in the *Proceedings from the 7th International daCi Conference: The Call of Forests and Lakes.* (Kuopio: daCi), 1–4. Glasser makes the argument that cultural fusion of dance forms is a positive result of assimilation, rather that a dilution of ethnic traditional dance. Certainly the argument is a persuasive one in the face of rigid cultural divisions, which seem constantly to foster turmoil and conflict worldwide.

4. Chet Raymo, *365 Starry Nights: An Introduction to Astronomy for Every Night of the Year* (New York: Prentice Hall, 1982) has clear illustrations and is a great all-around astronomy text for all ages.

5. Anne Green Gilbert, *Creative Dance for All Ages: A Conceptual Approach* (Reston, VA: AAPHERD, 1990). I have used Gilbert's book as a text for many years in my university pedagogy classes. Each year my college students tell me that this book is the most helpful of all the texts I require for my course in teaching methods of dance. This book relies soundly on Laban's principles of movement for the theoretical base, but goes far beyond that in its practical application of space, time, and force.

6. Susan McGreevy-Nichols and Helene Schriff, *Building Dances: A Guide to Putting Movements Together* (Champaign, IL: Human Kinetics, 1995). This is an excellent text for teachers who have never worked with creative dance, and it provides a solid base for introducing concepts of choreography to children.

7. Sue Stinson, *Dance for Young Children: Finding the Magic in Movement* (Reston, VA: AAPHERD, 1995) There are wonderful techniques for working with very young children in this book, and the chapters on discipline and solutions to common behavior problems for teaching are exceptionally useful.

Chapter 13

1. F.M. Alexander was an Australian actor who lost his voice and subsequently discovered that his head and neck posture was to blame. His work has been developed and widely adapted for many professions, especially by performing artists. An excellent introduction is Barbara Conable and William Conable, *How to Learn the Alexander Technique: A Manual for Students* (Columbus, OH: Andover Road Press, 1992).

Chapter 16

1. Howard Gardner, *Creating Minds: An Anatomy of Creativity Seen Through the Lives of Freud, Einstein, Picasso, Stravinsky, Eliot, Graham and Gandhi* (New York: Basic Books, 1993) p. 363. Gardner has a number of fascinating books on other topics pertinent to genius, and on educational exploration about the way we think.

Chapter 19

1. Since the interview printed here, and after touring for fifteen years with their reputation for excellence well established, Plankenkoorts founders and dancers Katjoesja Siccama and Caroline Bon have retired their trio company. Because both women became new mothers at about the same time, according to Katjoesja, they decided to stop while still at the peak of their performance careers. They ended Plankenkoorts after successfully touring the company for over a decade and a half.

2. The literal translation of Plankenkoorts is "stage fright."

Bibliography

Bahn, Paul, and Jean Vertut. *Journey Through the Ice Age*. Berkeley: University of California Press, 1997.

Carson, Jo. Letter on the op-ed pages of *Johnson City Press Chronicle*, Sunday, July 22, 1990.

Coleridge, Samuel Taylor. *Biographia Literaria*, 1817.

Conable, Barbara, and William Conable. *How to Learn Alexander Technique, a Manual for Students*. Columbus, OH: Andover Road Press, 1992.

Csikszentmihalyi, Mihaly. *Flow: The Psychology of Optimal Experience*. New York: Harper and Row, 1990.

Gardner, Howard. *Creating Minds: An Anatomy of Creativity Seen Through the Lives of Freud, Einstein, Picasso, Stravinsky, Eliot, Graham and Gandhi*. New York: Basic Books, 1993.

Gilbert, Anne Green. *Creative Dance for All Ages: A Conceptual Approach*. Reston, VA: American Alliance for Physical Health, Education, Recreation and Dance, 1990.

Glasser, Sylvia. Keynote Address for triannual meeting of Dance and the Child International July 28–August 3, 1997, in Kuopio, Finland.

Hardy, Camille. "Reaching Out to Young Audiences." *Dance Magazine,* June 1991.

Humphrey, Doris. *The Art of Making Dances*. Hightstown, N.J.: Princeton Books, 1958.

Laws, Kenneth. *Physics and the Art of Dance: Understanding Movement*. New York: Oxford University Press, 2002.

McGreevy-Nichols, Susan, and Helene Schriff, *Building Dances: A Guide to Putting Movements Together*. Champaign, IL: Human Kinetics, 1995.

McNeill, William H. *Keeping Together in Time, Dance and Drill in Human History* Cambridge, MA: Harvard University Press. 1995.

Pfeiffer, John E. *The Creative Explosion*. New York: Harper and Row, 1982.

Raymo, Chet. *365 Starry Nights: An Introduction to Astronomy for Every Night of the Year*. New York: Prentice-Hall, 1982.

Stinson, Sue. *Dance for Young Children: Finding the Magic in Movement*. Reston, VA: American Alliance for Physical Health, Education, Recreation and Dance, 1995.

Index

Numbers in **bold italics** indicate pages with illustrations.